MONOGRAPH.
SOCIETY FOR RESE
CHILD DEVELO

ATYPICAL ATTACHMENT IN INFANCY AND EARLY CHILDHOOD AMONG CHILDREN AT DEVELOPMENTAL RISK

Edited by Joan I. Vondra and Douglas Barnett

IN COLLABORATION WITH

Sandra Pipp-Siegel
Clifford H. Siegel
Janet Dean
Leslie Atkinson
Vivienne C. Chisholm
Brian Scott
Susan Goldberg
Brian E. Vaughn
Janis Blackwell
Susan Dickens
Frances Tam
Karlen Lyons-Ruth
Elisa Bronfman
Elizabeth Parsons
Jody Ganiban
Dante Cicchetti
Katherine Dowdell Hommerding
Daniel Shaw
Patricia McKinsey
Christine M. Butler

WITH COMMENTARY BY

Everett Waters and Judith A. Crowell

SERIES EDITOR

Rachel K. Clifton

© 1999 Society for Research in Child Development

Blackwell Publishers, Inc.
350 Main Street
Malden, MA 02148 USA

Blackwell Publishers, Ltd.
108 Cowley Road
Oxford OX4 1JF
United Kingdom

0-631-21592-1
A CIP catalog record for this book is available
from the Library of Congress

CONTENTS

ABSTRACT

VONDRA, JOAN I., and BARNETT, DOUGLAS. Atypical Attachment in Infancy and Early Childhood Among Children at Developmental Risk. *Monographs of the Society for Research in Child Development*, 1999, **64**(3, Serial No. 258).

This monograph brings together current theory and research on atypical patterns of attachment in infancy and early childhood to illustrate and help in understanding some of the key issues in cases that do not "fit" the traditional attachment coding system developed by Ainsworth and her colleagues (Ainsworth, Blehar, Waters, & Wall, 1978). Researchers in this area have taken different perspectives in exploring mother-child relationships that are believed to be at special risk for abnormality and/or pathology, including variants of the disorganized classification and alternative forms of organized classifications. Their findings, however, are consistent in suggesting that as caregiving, the caregiving context, and/or infant functioning becomes more extreme, constraints on behavioral and relationship patterns implicit in the traditional categories of attachment may not operate. The extent to which discrete behaviors versus behavioral patterns, versus broader behavioral systems are useful for understanding normal and abnormal development also must come into question. These issues are addressed in conjunction with empirical findings in order to open up discussion on the topic and shed light on fruitful directions for future research.

The volume opens with an introduction (Chapter 1) to attachment classification and the issues arising from identification of various forms of "atypical" attachments. Potential confounds between behaviors taken to be reflective of atypical relationships and symptoms of neurological impairments arising from congenital disorders (e.g., Down syndrome, cerebral palsy, autism) are discussed in Chapter 2. These two chapters set the context for a series of empirical studies that examine child cognitive functioning in a Down syndrome sample (Chapter 3), mother-child interaction (Chapter 4), infant emotional reactivity (Chapter 5), and maternal perceptions of child, self, and family as correlates of change in patterns across infancy (Chapter 6). Chapter 7 offers a developmental perspective on attachment organization in the context of developmental risk, and the final chapter summarizes and integrates the work presented in this *Monograph*.

Together, these chapters indicate the current status of theory and research about attachments that do not fit the traditional patterns among infants and young children at developmental risk. They also illuminate a variety of conceptual issues that warrant focused empirical attention in the next generation of research on parent-child attachment. Perhaps most important, they help strengthen the bridge attachment theory has forged, through its focus on pathways toward competence and pathology, between the fields of developmental and clinical psychology.

I. ATYPICAL PATTERNS OF EARLY ATTACHMENT: THEORY, RESEARCH, AND CURRENT DIRECTIONS

Douglas Barnett and Joan I. Vondra

John Bowlby developed attachment theory, in part, to help explain the mechanisms whereby social experiences beginning in early infancy influence the development of healthy and problematic variants of human personality development. Beginning in the 1940s, attachment theory was applied to understanding toddlers' immediate and long-term responses to extended (e.g., 10- to 30-day) separations from caregivers and to anomalous conditions such as abandonment and being raised in institutional settings (Bowlby, 1988). From a functional perspective, attachment theory guided changes in policies for minimizing the stresses of young children's separations from parents during necessary hospital stays, and helped establish guidelines for designing alternate care arrangements for young children who experienced loss of their primary caregiver (Bowlby, 1988). Bowlby (1969/1982, 1973, 1980) anchored attachment theory in diverse perspectives from psychology, including psychoanalysis and ethology, as well as cognitive and developmental science.

Attachment theory is rich in descriptions and explanations of human behavior and mental processes, both normative and pathological. Mary Ainsworth expanded the principles and perspectives of attachment theory and contributed a procedure and theory for describing and explaining individual differences in infant attachments to caregivers (Ainsworth, Blehar, Waters, & Wall, 1978). From Ainsworth's perspective, individual differences are categorical—differences in kind rather than amount. Ainsworth and her associates (1978) identified three patterns or styles believed to reflect infants'

1

coping responses to their caregivers' interactive styles. One type of attachment was viewed to be "secure," or Type B. Two categories were viewed to reflect insecure attachments: avoidant, Type A, and resistant or ambivalent, Type C, attachment patterns. Ainsworth's and Bowlby's perspectives have spawned more than 3 decades of productive research on individual differences in attachment patterns. The central tenets of the individual differences theory of human attachment are: (a) infants are predisposed to develop patterns of attachment though the process of relating to their primary caregivers, (b) these patterns reflect information (in the form of mental representations) that infants have internalized about how significant others behave in close relationships and about themselves as elicitors of nurturance from others, and (c) the mental representations of attachment that infants develop generalize to guide and influence their emotional well-being and social interactions beyond the relationship with their primary caregiver. Based on an ethological perspective, Ainsworth and Bowlby believed these processes (i.e., whereby mental representations or schema are derived from experience and guide future interactions) evolved because they improved the likelihood of eliciting care—and therefore survival—through interpersonal adaptation. Mental models of attachment relations are thought to improve the efficiency of social adaptation by streamlining the monitoring and processing of social information as well as the selection of response strategies.

The analysis of infant patterns of attachment based on Ainsworth and colleagues, system (1978) has alerted researchers to behavioral differences in infancy that appear to capture aspects of individual and interpersonal functioning with significance for subsequent development (Belsky & Cassidy, 1994; Oppenheim, Sagi, & Lamb, 1988; Sroufe, 1983). These analyses provide insights about the relative contributions normative environmental and constitutional factors may make to infant social and emotional development (Belsky & Rovine, 1987; Carlson & Sroufe, 1995; Fox, Kimmerly, & Schafer, 1991; Goldsmith & Alansky, 1987; Sroufe, 1985).

Exploring the Exceptions

Once a category system exists, there is a tendency to observe all cases to be within that scheme even when, in actuality, some cases only "fit" approximately and other cases are ignored exceptions. Yet it is precisely examination of exceptions to the classification system and to the principles on which that system is based that permits scientists to modify models, schema, and theory to reflect more accurately the full range of observations comprising a phenomenon and the functional significance of observed variations in expression. Important contributions have been made by attending to attachment patterns inconsistent with Ainsworth's original categorizations.

Since the late 1970s, researchers have identified infants thought to have insecure attachments, but whose patterns of attachment did not fit within Ainsworth's tripartite classification system (Crittenden, 1985; Egeland & Sroufe, 1981b; Lyons-Ruth, Connell, Zoll, & Stahl, 1987; Main & Solomon, 1986; Main & Weston, 1981; Sroufe & Waters, 1977). Uncertainty persists, however, about how many different varieties of attachment patterns there are and which reflect meaningful variation in functioning and development. Ainsworth argued that although there can be only one form of secure attachment, innumerable patterns of insecure attachment exist (Ainsworth & Marvin, 1995). Understanding the full variety of attachment patterns and linking each to experiential precursors, hypothesized mental representations, and developmental sequelae is the very foundation of attachment theory. Such information has implications for personality development in general, because research on infant-parent attachment styles continues to inspire the study of human personality. For instance, investigators have identified attachment classifications among older age groups that are believed to be analogous to Ainsworth's system for classifying infant attachment (Armsden & Greenberg, 1987; Bartholomew & Horowitz, 1991; Crittenden, 1992a; Hazan & Shaver, 1987; Lynch & Cicchetti, 1991; Main, Kaplan, & Cassidy, 1985). Thus, models of attachment and personality functioning in other developmental periods have borrowed extensively from the body of infancy research.

Examination of the behavior and development of infants and young children whose attachment relationships did *not* fit the traditional Ainsworth system have been conducted primarily with children who fall at the extremes of reproductive risk and/or caregiving casualty (Sameroff & Chandler, 1975). Research on these exceptional cases has extended understanding of the possible influence both contextual conditions and child factors have on individual development and emergent relationship patterns, but also the developmental significance of behavioral differences in patterns of relating to important others (Cicchetti & Greenberg, 1991; Crittenden, this volume; Jones, 1996; Jones, Main, & del Carmen, 1996).

This monograph brings together data and theory from several differing conceptualizations of "atypical" patterns of attachment, ranging from variations on subgroups of "disorganized" attachments (Lyons-Ruth, Bronfman, & Parsons, this volume; Vondra, Hommerding, & Shaw, this volume) to conceptual and methodological issues related to a disorganized category (Crittenden, this volume; Pipp-Siegel, Siegel, & Dean, this volume), to alternative conceptualizations of atypical attachments in infancy and early childhood (Atkinson et al., this volume; Crittenden, this volume). Atypical patterns of attachment are defined as sets of behaviors identified among

3

infants and young children judged *not* to meet criteria for the traditionally established Secure (Type B), Insecure Avoidant (Type A), or Insecure Ambivalent/Resistant (Type C) patterns, as they have been defined in the infancy and the preschool classification systems. Most of the work in infancy (up to 24 months) included in the monograph relates to the Disorganized (Type D) classification (Main & Solomon, 1990) and various distinctions among children grouped within this broad category. Attention also is given to children whose attachment is rated as "unclassifiable" (Atkinson et al., this volume) and to toddlers and/or preschool-age children whose attachment represents more extreme variants of the traditional patterns or combinations of insecure patterns (Crittenden, this volume).

Atypical patterns of infant or preschool attachments increasingly have been linked with (a) parental problems (Teti, Gelfand, Messinger, & Isabella, 1995; van IJzendoorn, Goldberg, Kroonenberg, & Frenkel, 1992), and (b) subsequent problems in social and emotional adjustment (Carlson, 1998; Greenberg, Speltz, DeKlyen, & Endriga, 1991; Lyons-Ruth, 1996; Lyons-Ruth, Easterbrooks, & Cibelli, 1997; Solomon, George, & DeJong, 1995; Vondra et al., in press). In light of these promising findings, many issues require attention; for instance, whether atypical attachments are simply another marker for risk or can help explain the processes that transform risk into psychopathology is unclear. In addition, there are compelling conceptual and methodological discrepancies in views held by investigators about what constitutes atypical attachment patterns. Several different patterns of atypical attachment have been identified—both in infancy and in the preschool period—and the meaning of various atypical patterns or subpatterns has been debated. Also controversial has been the relatively large proportion of atypical attachments identified among infants with pre-existing, organically based conditions such as autism and Down syndrome (Atkinson et al., this volume; Barnett, Hunt, et al., in press; Capps, Sigman, & Mundy, 1994; Pipp-Siegel et al., this volume; Vaughn et al., 1994). Through theoretical and empirical investigation, the chapters in this monograph grapple with these concerns.

A goal in preparing this monograph was to respect the diversity of perspectives and approaches being taken in the study of atypical patterns of infant attachment and to preserve the richness, but also the complexity, of the questions being asked and hypotheses being proposed. The Type D attachment appears to be the best known example of an atypical attachment pattern and is being incorporated into increasing numbers of attachment studies. It would be a mistake, however, to equate the study of atypical patterns of attachment with the Type D pattern. As illustrated in this introductory chapter and in several of the other chapters in this monograph, there are many unanswered questions and perspectives on atypical patterns. Consequently, investigators representing a variety of perspectives and somewhat different empirical approaches to studying atypicality were encouraged to present their current work in this collection. In every case, the focus of inquiry is attachment in the first 3 years of life among children at risk for developmental problems, whether due to neurological abnormalities, child maltreatment, or family ecological risk. The empirical questions range from identifying ecological, behavioral, and developmental correlates of attachment to the meaning of different patterns and behaviors used to classify atypical attachments. The varied approaches included here help consolidate the nomological net of atypical patterns of attachment, and examine principles and assumptions of attachment theory as they relate to children at developmental risk. Areas of current ambiguity or controversy, when brought into focus, can help guide the next generation of studies. The contrasting perspectives, data, and arguments presented here bring needed attention to ambiguities and controversies in the field that warrant further attention. They also offer a summary of current thinking about the status of atypical attachment in early childhood.

This introductory chapter provides a conceptual common ground for examining divergent perspectives and data on atypical patterns of early attachments. To do so, we review (a) basic theoretical terms and constructs of attachment theory, (b) the nature and function of the original classification system, (c) what is meant by "exceptional cases" or "atypical patterns," and (d) the implications of atypicality both for a classification system of attachment behavior and for a theoretical model of the significance of early attachment for socioemotional development. In this way, this chapter sets the stage for the empirical and theoretical work that follows.

Distinguishing Features of Attachment Relationships

Not all relationships are attachment relationships. Not all relationship functions serve attachment needs. Ainsworth (1989) articulated several characteristics of an attachment relationship. Foremost, attachment relationships provide a sense of security and self-efficacy, facilitating confident and competent engagement with the social environment. The attachment figure's role, referred to as a "secure base," is that of protection, but also that of a natural buffer against distress and anxiety (van der Kolk, 1987). The roles of play partner and teacher, for example, are not considered central to the attachment function of a relationship, although an attachment figure can certainly incorporate these roles in his or her broader relationship with a child. Rather, it is the psychological availability of a caregiver as a source of safety and comfort in times of child distress that distinguishes the attachment function within a relationship, and the attachment figure from other social partners.

Attachment relationships are long lasting. One attachment relationship cannot be replaced by another. A person may form multiple, distinct attachment relationships (e.g., to mother and to father), but none substitute for existing attachments. Stress results from sudden and unexplained separations from an attachment figure. Grief and mourning are the result of permanent loss.

Attachments develop in the context of relationships, but become internalized so that beyond infancy they increasingly become characteristics of the individual, referring to the affectional bond that is maintained as part of a person's mental schema. These mental schemata are based on the history of interactions with one's attachment figure.

Attachments are "organizational constructs" (Sroufe & Waters, 1977). That is, multiple developing systems (e.g., motor/behavioral, psychophysiological, emotional, cognitive, and communicative) are thought to become functionally coordinated around meeting attachment goals and needs (Barnett & Ratner, 1997; Bretherton, 1985; Cicchetti, Ganiban, & Barnett, 1991; Spangler & Grossmann, 1993). Bowlby theorized that response patterns within attachment relationships are organized into an attachment "behavioral system" (Bowlby, 1969/1982), a construct from ethological theory. It refers to underlying mechanisms that are thought to organize and coordinate behavior through a "control systems" model of motivation. Bowlby (1969/1982) described four behavioral systems—attachment, affiliation, fear-wariness, and exploration—that guide infant and toddler behavior. These behavioral systems are hypothesized to operate in a dynamic fashion, whereby the levels of activation within these systems are interconnected and influence each other.

In his view, attachment is thought of as a type of motivation in the sense that it energizes, guides, selects, and directs behavior (McClelland, 1987). Like other aspects of human motivation, there are biological, emotional, and cognitive underpinnings in the anticipation of attachment needs and strategies for satisfying attachment goals (or coping with their being thwarted). Unlike many other theories of motivation, however, individual differences in motivational "strength" are absent from attachment theory (Bowlby, 1969/1982). In this regard, the attachment system is no more motivated than systems underlying temperature regulation. Presumably there is a set-point and the system coordinates adjustments to maintain the comfort zone.

From this perspective there are not individual differences in strength of attachment needs. Instead, Bowlby proposed that salient individual differences develop in how affective, cognitive, and behavioral processes become organized to meet the goals of this motivational, or in his words, "behavioral" system. These differences stem, in part, from experiences with attachment figures' availability for and sensitivity in meeting the child's attachment needs for proximity, contact, and interaction. Attachment needs are activated during times of perceived stress (e.g., discomfort, environmental danger, fatigue, illness). Under these conditions the child must either have his or her attachment needs met (e.g., through contingent responding, availability, and contact comfort) or find other ways to cope with unmet attachment needs (i.e., suppress them, distract one's focus away from attachment needs, exaggerate distress signals to gain more responsiveness from caregivers).

Individual differences in strategies for regulating attachment needs (including the management of information that arouses or reduces the arousal of the attachment system) form the theoretical basis for the different patterns of attachment (i.e., Types A, B, & C) identified and validated by Ainsworth and her colleagues. For example, it is hypothesized that children whose attachment relationships are classified as anxious avoidant (Type A) have learned to reduce the activation of their attachment needs through distraction and dissociation, whereas those classified as anxious resistant (Type C) have learned to seek some minimum of caregiving responsiveness through chronic activation of the attachment system. In summary, individual differences in attachment are not due to the strength of an attachment drive or trait of dependency or security. Instead, Bowlby and Ainsworth's frameworks construe individual differences in terms of the qualitative styles in which people manage themselves in attachment relationships.

Attachment as an Internal Model

A central mechanism proposed by attachment theorists to explain how individuals coordinate physiological, affective, and behavioral strategies in the service of attachment needs are "internal representational models." Internal models are unconscious mental representations of the availability of the attachment figure and of the efficacy and worthiness of the self in getting and having attachment needs met (Bowlby, 1980; Bretherton, 1985; Crittenden, 1994). Representational models include, for example, infant anticipations about caregiver reactions to bids for comfort. These anticipations, in turn, guide infant strategies for modulating attachment stress.

Through these processes, internal models of attachment are thought to be an important aspect of the development of self-regulation of attachment needs (Cassidy, 1994; Cicchetti et al., 1991). It appears, for instance, that the anticipation (conscious or otherwise) that one will be soothed and comforted plays an important role in gaining (and, ultimately, realizing) the ability to self-soothe. In the case of secure attachments, the natural frustration and anger that is aroused by separation (Shiller, Izard, & Hembree, 1986) is reduced by the expectation that comforting is on the way (Donovan & Leavitt, 1985; Hertsgaard, Gunnar, Erickson, & Nachmias, 1995; Spangler & Grossmann, 1993).

The Organization of Attachment

Attachment patterns are said to be "organized" in that they reflect a consistent style of managing a variety of developing systems (e.g., physiological, emotional, and behavioral) in response to prior knowledge about the attachment figure's typical responses. They also are described as organized because they are believed to reflect a theoretically coherent strategy for behaving in relation to caregiver response styles. As Crittenden (this volume) points out, however, attachment patterns are often organized by interactions with a caregiver whose behavior is insensitive. When an attachment figure is either intermittently or chronically ineffective at modulating a child's stress, however, by being rejecting or unresponsive, the child's attachment system becomes organized over time to cope with repeated experiences of frustration. In response, infants' attachment organizations historically have been understood to assume one of two universally acknowledged varieties: the defensive self-distraction from perceptual information that activates the attachment system, as in the case of the avoidant (Type A) attachment (Main, 1981), or an inefficiency in reducing the arousal of the attachment system, as in the ambivalent or resistant (Type C) attachment (Cassidy & Berlin, 1994).

"TRADITIONAL" PATTERNS OF ATTACHMENT IN THE STRANGE SITUATION

Because the majority of research on infant, toddler, and preschool-age attachment relies on data from the Strange Situation (Ainsworth & Wittig, 1969), the procedure is briefly summarized here. The Strange Situation, a 22-min laboratory assessment that is videotaped from behind a one-way mirror, is divided into eight brief episodes, as noted in Table 1. It was designed to be a somewhat naturalistic experience, such as a visit to a doctor's office. It also was meant to be increasingly stressful and to elicit both curiosity and wariness in the infant. Beginning with a visit to an unfamiliar building and room, the child is introduced to new toys, new people, and two separations from his or her caregiver, including a period of up to 3 min of being left alone. The stress induced by the situation, especially the separations, is believed to activate most children's attachment behavioral system.

Although classification is based on the child's behavior across the entire assessment, great emphasis is placed on the child's responses during the two reunions with the caregiver. Reactions to separation, in and of themselves, do *not* distinguish securely from insecurely attached children (Sroufe, 1985; Thompson & Lamb, 1984). Seven-point ratings are made by trained coders for each of five interactive behaviors exhibited by the child during each reunion: proximity-seeking, contact maintenance, resistance, avoidance, and distance interaction (Ainsworth et al., 1978). Based on the pattern of

TABLE 1

SUMMARY OF AINSWORTH'S STRANGE SITUATION PROCEDURE

Episode/Duration	Participants	Description
1. 30 s	infant, caregiver, experimenter	introduction to room
2. 3 min	infant, caregiver	infant initiates
3. 3 min	infant, caregiver, stranger	stranger introduced
4. 3 min	infant, stranger	first separation
5. 3 min	infant, caregiver	first reunion
6. 3 min	infant	second separation
7. 3 min	infant, stranger	separation continues
8. 3 min	infant, caregiver	second reunion

interactive behaviors across the assessment and, particularly, responses to reunion with the caregiver, each child is assigned a major classification (Type A, B, or C) and a subclassification (Subtypes 1 through 4 for Bs; Subtypes 1 or 2 for As and Cs).

The Secure (Type B) Pattern

Approximately 60% to 75% of low-risk, 12- to 18-month-olds demonstrate the secure pattern when assessed in the Strange Situation with their primary caregivers (van IJzendoorn & Kroonenberg, 1988). Securely attached infants are typified by successful use of their caregiver as a secure base from which they can explore and interact with the animate and inanimate environment. Upon reunion, secure infants comfortably share positive affect with their caregivers and typically initiate some form of interaction with them. If overtly distressed by separation, secure infants will seek physical contact with their caregiver and be comforted by that contact quickly enough to return to some degree of independent play within 3 min of the caregiver's return. Demonstrations of negative affect, ambivalence, resistance, passivity toward, or avoidance of the caregiver are not common. When evident, they are relatively brief and of low intensity, rapidly dissipate, and are replaced by positive interaction.

The representational model of securely attached children is believed to be that their attachment figure will be available and responsive to needs. Evidence for this comes from research indicating that securely attached children tend to have a history of sensitive, contingent, and psychologically available parenting from their mother (Belsky, Rovine, & Taylor, 1984; De Wolff & van IJzendoorn, 1997; Grossmann, Grossmann, Spangler, Suess, & Unzer, 1985; Isabella, Belsky, & von Eye, 1989; Smith & Pederson, 1988; Vondra, Shaw, & Kevenides, 1995). Research on the constitutionally based characteristics of securely attached children indicates that they come from a wide range of temperamental dispositions, ranging from low emotionally reactive to high reactive neonatal temperaments (Sroufe, 1985). Indeed, within the Strange Situation, securely attached children demonstrate a wide range of reactions to separation from their caregivers, from overt and intense distress to low stress and an absence of crying during the separation (Thompson & Lamb, 1984).

The Insecure-Avoidant (Type A) Pattern

Infants with an insecure-avoidant attachment make up approximately 15% to 25% of low-risk, North American samples. During the Strange Situation, these infants are characterized by a paucity of positive, affectively engaged interaction with and interest in their attachment figures. If they exhibit positive affect, it is likely to be directed toward toys, experimenter, or stranger. During separation, they tend to demonstrate lower levels of overt distress than many securely attached and most ambivalently attached infants. Upon reunion, infants with avoidant attachments tend to divert their attention away from their attachment figure; they are less likely to approach their caregiver, or to seek or maintain contact following the stress of separation.

The representational model of avoidantly attached children is thought to be that the caregiver will subtly or overtly reject child attachment needs during times of stress, that bids for contact-comfort or reassuring interaction will be redirected and/or rebuffed. Thus, children with avoidant attachments attempt to keep their attention directed away from their attachment figures and attachment eliciting cues in an effort not to arouse feelings of anxiety and frustration.

Research indicates that maternal care of infants who develop avoidant attachments tends to be very active, intrusive, controlling and, at times, overtly rejecting (Belsky et al., 1984; Grossmann et al., 1985; Isabella et al., 1989; Smith & Pederson, 1988; Vondra et al., 1995). Mothers of infants with avoidant attachments also have been found to be less comfortable with close physical contact with their infants (Tracy & Ainsworth, 1981). Infants who develop Type A attachments have been described as less cuddly and more object-oriented, and less sociable than infants who develop Type B or C attachments (Blehar, Lieberman, & Ainsworth, 1977; Lewis & Feiring, 1989). Infants who develop avoidant attachments with their caregiver also tend to exhibit low levels of overt negative emotional reactivity during attachment assessments (Belsky & Rovine, 1987; Fox et al., 1991). Micro-analyses of facial expression, cortisol levels, and cardiac functioning suggest, however, that infants with Type A attachments experience significantly greater reactivity than would be estimated based solely on their overt affective expressions (Belsky & Braungart, 1991; Gunner, Mangelsdorf, Larson, & Hertsgaard, 1989; Izard et al., 1991; Spangler & Grossmann, 1993).

The Insecure-Ambivalent or Resistant (Type C) Pattern

Approximately 10% to 15% of North American infants are classified as having ambivalent (resistant) attachments in the Strange Situation. These infants demonstrate overt signs of preoccupation with their caregiver's whereabouts: During times of relatively low stress (the early episodes of the Strange Situation), they spend a larger percentage of their time in close proximity to or contact with their caregiver, and exhibit a relative paucity of exploration and play. During separations, they tend to show high levels of separation distress, and, upon reunion, remain overtly distressed for longer periods of time, often not becoming completely soothed by the end of the 3-min reunion episode. They demonstrate clear behavioral indices of anger and/or ambivalence toward their caregiver, as indicated by direct resistance to contact with their caregiver following bids for proximity and contact (e.g., pushing, squirming, rejecting toys). Ambivalence also may take the form of crying, distress, and need for comfort in the context of infant passivity, such as not making any overt efforts to approach or make contact with the caregiver.

The representational model of children with ambivalent attachments is thought to be that the caregiver will be inadequate at meeting child attachment needs as indicated by a combination of passive, unresponsive, and ineffective behavior on the part of the caregiver. The child's strategy is believed to be amplification of attachment needs and signals in an effort to arouse a response from the caregiver. Child and caregiver, it is believed, have negotiated a relationship in which the dependence and frailty of each are emphasized (Cassidy & Berlin, 1994). Research indicates that the mothers of ambivalently attached children are understimulating, unresponsive, and inconsistently available for meeting their child's bids for comfort (Belsky et al., 1984; Isabella et al., 1989; Smith & Pederson, 1988; Vondra et al., 1995). In terms of temperamental differences, children who develop ambivalent attachments have been found, on occasion, to exhibit more irritable temperaments in the neonatal period (Goldsmith & Alansky, 1987).

ATYPICAL PATTERNS OF ATTACHMENT

The Type A, B, and C patterns of attachment permit reliable classification of some 85% to 90% of children from low-risk populations (Main & Solomon, 1986; Main & Weston, 1981; Sroufe & Waters, 1977). The remaining children exhibit behaviors, express affect, or display patterns of behavior and affect that represent anomalies at the level of the classification system, making reliable classification problematic. In these instances, the criteria for classification either do not capture the full range of behaviors exhibited or are not met consistently enough to permit unambiguous classification into a single category.

Atypicality of attachment can be described at multiple levels: the level of behavioral *systems* (i.e., the coordination of attachment, exploration, affiliation, and fear-wariness systems), the level of social and emotional interactive behavior *patterns* (e.g., mixing avoidance with resistance, distress with avoidance, etc.), and the level of specific behavioral *indices* (e.g., lying prone during reunion, covering mouth or ears when caregiver approaches, dazed facial expression). Although signs of attachment atypicality are identified at each of these three levels, these levels are not mutually exclusive. That is, indices of atypicality may cut across these levels. Nonetheless, it is conceptually useful to attend to these levels of analysis in identifying atypical attachments. Consequently, markers of atypicality at each of these levels are discussed below along with questions they raise about attachment classification.

Coordination of Behavioral Systems

The broadest level at which atypical attachment patterns have been identified is in terms of the coordination of behavioral systems. Behavioral systems, as introduced in the opening sections of this chapter, refer to underlying hypothetical mechanisms that organize and coordinate behavior. Four behavioral systems—attachment, affiliation, fear-wariness, and exploration—are believed to operate to guide infant and toddler behavior (Bowlby, 1969/1982). Based on a "control systems" model of motivation, these behavioral systems operate in a dynamic fashion, whereby responses within one system influence the activation level of other systems. For example, increased arousal of fear-wariness typically activates attachment behavior, and decreases exploratory behavior. Behaviors that serve a behavioral system diminish when some "set goal" of the control system is reached. Thus, when attachment behavior results in some level of "felt security," say for instance by achieving nurturing contact with a caregiver, diminished activation of attachment gives way to increased activation of affiliation or exploration.

With knowledge about the relatedness of behavioral systems, sequences of infant behavior become relatively predictable over time (Bischof, 1975; Bretherton & Ainsworth, 1974; Cicchetti & Serafica, 1981). The balanced coordination of attachment and exploration systems, reflected in predictable sequences of approach and contact with the caregiver followed by autonomous exploration ("secure base" behavior) is an underpinning of attachment security (Ainsworth et al., 1978). Children whose behavior is thought to be representative of a secure attachment are observed to move smoothly between attachment and exploratory behavior. In contrast, children classified as insecure, Type C, tend to be comparatively slow in being able to deactivate their attachment system in the Strange Situation, whereas children classified as insecure, Type A, appear precipitous in diverting attention away from the attachment figure toward objects. Children classified as having an atypical pattern of attachment may demonstrate neither exploration nor attachment behavior in the presence of their caregiver. Instead, they may display fear-wariness or combinations of fear-wariness and attachment toward the caregiver, disqualifying them for placement in a Type A, B, or C pattern (Main & Solomon, 1990). Children classified with atypical attachments also have been observed to demonstrate heightened activation of their exploratory behavioral system in the absence (instead of the presence) of their attachment figure. Atypical patterns of attachment also include cases where attachment behavior is, at times, directed toward the "stranger" rather than the caregiver during the Strange Situation.

Interactive Patterns of Behavior and Emotion

The five interactive behaviors noted previously are the scoring basis of Ainsworth and her colleagues' (1978) original classification system, and have been used to develop a formula for automated category placement (Lyons-Ruth et al., this volume; Richters, Waters, & Vaughn, 1988). When demonstrated in an intense or persistent manner toward attachment figures, avoidance and resistance have been the cornerstone for identifying insecure attachments. Predictable combinations of avoidance versus resistance, in conjunction with patterns of proximity-seeking, contact maintenance, distance interaction, and emotional expression constitute a major part of the criteria for assessing traditional patterns of insecure attachment (Ainsworth et al., 1978; Sroufe & Waters, 1977).

Avoidance and resistance tend to be inversely related to one another (Thompson & Lamb, 1984). High levels of avoidance typically occur in combination with low to moderate levels of resistance, and vice versa. Avoidance implies a cutting off of attachment-focused signaling and related emotional reactions. Resistance, in contrast, implies a heightening of attachment-focused signaling and emotional reactions. Unusual combinations of moderate to high avoidance with moderate to high resistance can, therefore, be viewed as atypical (Crittenden, 1985).

Violations of expected patterns of association between emotional expression, mother-directed behaviors, and indices of insecurity also are criteria for considering classification of a child in an atypical category. Research on children from low-risk populations (e.g., healthy, full-term, middle-class infants) indicates a strong positive association between the intensity and duration of separation distress and the intensity of proximity-seeking and contact maintenance (and, to a lesser extent, resistance; Thompson & Lamb,

1984). Children who demonstrate minimal levels of overt separation distress tend to demonstrate low to moderate levels of proximity-seeking and contact maintenance. Children who demonstrate intense and persistent levels of separation distress tend to demonstrate moderate to high levels of proximity-seeking and contact maintenance. The incongruous combination of high separation distress with low proximity-seeking and contact maintenance upon reunion can, therefore, be viewed as atypical. Moreover, low levels of insecure behaviors (avoidance and resistance), typical of children who are classified as securely attached, normally are accompanied by displays of positive affect (e.g., smiling and positive vocalizations) directed toward the attachment figure (Waters, Wippman, & Sroufe, 1979). Children who demonstrate low levels of avoidance and resistance but a marked absence of positive affect may also be considered candidates for classification in a nontraditional category (Crittenden, 1988).

Discrete Behaviors

Infant attachment has traditionally been classified by the overall pattern of infant interactive behavior in the Strange Situation. Consequently, no single behavior has been considered to be uniquely indicative of one of the traditional patterns (Sroufe & Waters, 1977). Criteria for some atypical patterns, however, have been identified at the level of discrete Strange Situation behaviors. For instance, freezing or stilling, and expressions of fear or depression directed toward the caregiver are considered sufficient by some researchers for classifying attachments as atypical (Main & Solomon, 1986, 1990). Indices of severe stress, such as "head cocking or huddling on the floor" (Crittenden, 1985, p. 89), also are singular behaviors that have been used to characterize children with atypical attachments. Such behaviors have been considered sufficient to disqualify infants from assignment to a traditional Type A, B, or C classification, regardless of their overall interactive behavioral pattern, or sequencing of behavioral systems (Main & Solomon, 1990).

Such behaviors, however, must be characteristic of the *relationship* between caregiver and child, not simply a reflection of general functioning. For example, many children with neurological impairments, such as are found in disorders like Down syndrome and autism, demonstrate stress-related symptoms, including repetitious, self-stimulating behavior or behavioral stilling. To be considered indices of attachment functioning, these behaviors must occur with increased frequency around, or be directed exclusively toward, caregivers (Atkinson et al., this volume; Ganiban, Barnett, & Cicchetti, in press; Pipp-Siegel et al., this volume). A question raised by a discrete behaviors approach is whether atypical behaviors are indicative of an inherently different attachment pattern or are independent of attachment organization (i.e., they are not in and of themselves inconsistent with Type A, B, or C attachments). Vondra and her colleagues (this volume) consider this issue.

In summary, children's Strange Situation behavior is thought to reflect atypical patterns when (a) it fails to reflect the normative interplay between different behavioral systems, (b) its affective and behavioral organization violates expected established combinations used for classifying behavior into one of the traditional patterns, and/or (c) it includes one or more specific anomalies identified by researchers as indicative of atypical attachment patterns. Further research is needed to establish parameters between attachment patterns and to establish the full range of behaviors consistent *within* each attachment category. The chapters in this *Monograph* examine these issues from a variety of angles. Systematic attention with large samples of children is needed, however, to further resolve the different perspectives represented across the chapters. In the final chapter, criteria are proposed on how to evaluate the variety of categories that have been presented.

ATYPICAL ATTACHMENT CLASSIFICATION CATEGORIES

In this section, three atypical patterns of infant attachment that have been identified by researchers are reviewed: the Disorganized/Disoriented, Type D; the Ambivalent/Avoidant, Type A/C; and the Unstable-Avoidant, Type U-A. Criteria for their designation appear in Table 2. These categories are not necessarily mutually exclusive or independent of one another. The amount of overlap and/or redundancy across these patterns of atypical attachments is unknown, but likely to be substantial. Indeed, patterns considered unclassifiable in the Atkinson et al. sample may otherwise have been classified as disorganized by coders working with maltreatment samples (Barnett, Ganiban, & Cicchetti, this volume) or as coercive (Type C) by coders trained in the Preschool Attachment Assessment (Crittenden, 1990–1995). Similarly, attachments considered secure in the Lyons-Ruth et al. (this volume) sample had previously been classified as Unstable-Avoidant, and may otherwise have been classified as disorganized by coders trained in early use of the disorganized classification (Vondra et al., this volume). There is evidence that interrater reliability using the D category is lower than that using the A, B, and C categories exclusively and can be problematic (Belsky, Campbell, Cohn, & Moore, 1996; Lyons-Ruth et al., this volume). A problem that should be addressed is whether different research groups are coding the same behavior in different ways, assigning children to different atypical categories. Perhaps rater reliability will be improved by addressing the degree of overlap across the variety of approaches taken to classifying atypical patterns of attachment. At the time this monograph was written, the field was not ready to pursue questions about the overlap across laboratories studying atypical attachments. The hope of the authors of this *Monograph* is that juxtaposing the different approaches to classifying atypical patterns of attachment will stimulate the field to resolve some of the existing theoretical and methodological differences.

On the other hand, each of these patterns has received systematic theoretical and empirical attention. They are reviewed in their apparent order of inclusiveness, with Main and Solomon's (1990) Type D category having the broadest criteria for inclusion, and Lyons-Ruth and her colleagues' (1987) Type U-A having the narrowest inclusion criteria. Many children, perhaps all, who are described by Crittenden's (1985) A/C and the U-A patterns appear to meet criteria for inclusion in the Type D category (see Vondra et al., this volume). In contrast, the A/C and U-A patterns each appear to exclude many children whose behavior would meet criteria for the Type D category. Beyond some of the behavioral similarities of these categories, however, theoretical differences also underlie the discrepancies in classification criteria.

TABLE 2

CRITERIA FOR ATYPICAL ATTACHMENT CLASSIFICATIONS

Disorganized (Type D)	Avoidant/Ambivalent (Type A/C)	Unstable-Avoidant (Type U-A)
Strong or frequent manifestation of one or more of the following: 1. Sequential display of contradictory behavior patterns 2. Simultaneous display of contradictory behavior patterns 3. Undirected, misdirected, incomplete, and interrupted movements and expressions 4. Stereotypies, asymmetrical movements, mistimed movements, anomalous postures 5. Freezing, stilling, and slowed movements and expressions 6. Direct indices of apprehension regarding the parent 7. Direct indices of disorganization or disorientation	1. Moderate to high avoidance combined with moderate to high resistance during reunions 2. Moderate to high proximity seeking and contact maintenance, as is typical of securely attached infants	1. Marked avoidance in the first reunion (5–7 on Ainsworth's interactive rating scales), followed by at least a 4-point drop in avoidance in the second reunion (1–3 on the rating scales)

The Disorganized/Disoriented (Type D) Pattern

Main and Solomon (1986, 1990) researched the topic of atypical patterns and systematically recorded atypical Strange Situation behavior of 55 children who were judged not to fit either the Type A, B, or C categories. Their pool of Strange Situations was drawn from several research samples of varying degrees of social risk. From this research, they developed the criteria for the Disorganized/Disoriented, Type D pattern. The prevalence of Type D attachments has been shown to covary with the severity of social risk of the sample. Percentages of infants with Type D attachment have ranged in frequency from 10% to 33% among relatively low-risk samples (Ainsworth & Eichberg, 1991; Main & Solomon, 1990), to frequencies above 80% in high risk, particularly maltreated, samples (Carlson, Cicchetti, Barnett, & Braunwald, 1989a).

Main and Solomon (1990) have delineated seven indices of infant behavior that, when displayed in a strong or persistent manner in the presence of the caregiver during the Strange Situation, signify a Type D attachment. These criteria are summarized in Table 2 of this chapter and are reprinted in full in Table 3 in Pipp-Siegel et al. (this volume). These seven criteria include behavior and behavioral patterns spanning all three of the levels of analyses that have been described, the level of behavioral system coordination, the level of integration among emotion and interactive behaviors, and the level of discrete behaviors. Children assigned a Type D attachment classification include those who demonstrate behavior consistent with one of the traditional categories but also have clear or numerous indices of a Type D attachment, as well as those whose behavior is not consistent with classification as either Type A, B, or C.

One potentially controversial practice is to classify infants who demonstrate behavioral *patterns* consistent with secure, Type B attachments as insecure, Type D, based on discrete behavioral indices of disorganization. These attachments may represent one class of relationships that lie on the coding boundaries of disorganization and may, therefore, be coded differently in different laboratories, or by different coders in the same laboratory. Infants meeting the criteria for unstable avoidance (see below) are likely to fall into this group, since their interactive behavior in the second reunion often fits the description of a B4 or even B3 (secure) classification. Preliminary findings suggest, however, that Type D infants who can be forced into a secure classification have different caregiving experiences from securely attached, non-D infants (Ainsworth & Eichberg, 1991; Main & Hesse, 1990; O'Connor, Sigman, & Brill, 1987) and infants with Type D, forced insecure attachments (Lyons-Ruth et al., this volume; Lyons-Ruth, Repacholi, McLeod, & Silva, 1991; but see Vondra et al., this volume).

To account for the great diversity of behaviors common to infants with Type D attachments, Main and Solomon (1990) suggest that children classified with Type D attachments are unified by the absence of a "readily observable goal, intention, or explanation" (p. 122). In other words, infants with Type D attachments, in contrast to infants with Type A, B, or C attachments, are thought to lack a coherent strategy for coping with the arousal of their attachment system (Hertsgaard et al., 1995). But although infants with Type D attachments appear to lack a consistent behavioral strategy, they may have a consistent emotional experience—namely, fear (Main & Hesse, 1990). Fear of the caregiver is thought to underlie and explain the wide range of Type D indices. Fear in relation to the caregiver also may distinguish the Type D from all other patterns of attachment. Although the Type A and C patterns have been referred to as "anxious," fear and anxiety do not appear to be emotions typically aroused by separation in the Strange Situation. Shiller, Izard, and Hembree's (1986) analyses of infant facial affect have indicated that anger, not fear, is the emotion exhibited by infants with Type A, B, or C attachments during the Strange Situation separation episodes. Fear may be antithetical to the expression of anger (Tomkins, 1991) and the experience of a sense of security, and may interfere with the development of a consistent behavioral strategy for coping with the arousal of the attachment system. The introduction of fear as a primary affect within the attachment relationship may be particularly confusing to infants, resulting in a stressed infant showing signs of "disorganization" in the Strange Situation.

Being fearful of the attachment figure, or having an attachment figure who is frightened, is thought to be a common experience of children who develop Type D attachments. Research appears to support this hypothesis. Infants of abusive and neglectful mothers, infants of mothers who report elevated levels of psychiatric symptoms, and children whose parents have not resolved the loss of their own attachment figure, or who have not resolved a traumatic event, may be more likely to promote the development of a Type D attachment with their own infant (Ainsworth & Eichberg, 1991; Carlson et al., 1989a; Lyons-Ruth et al., 1991; Main & Hesse, 1990; Spieker & Booth, 1988). In one study, infants who experienced either lack of parental involvement or high hostile intrusiveness or a combination of both were at increased risk for Type D attachments (Lyons-Ruth et al., 1991). But more investigations focusing specifically on parental caregiving of infants with Type D attachments are needed. Lyons-Ruth and colleagues (this volume) present one of the first analyses of discrete parenting behaviors linked to the Type D attachment pattern (see also Schuengel, Bakermans-Kranenburg, & van IJzendoorn, 1999).

Only preliminary data are available that speak to the question of whether infants with Type D attachments differ from non-D infants in regard to temperament or neurologically based difficulties. Main and

Solomon (1990) found that 31 out of 34 infants demonstrated a Type D attachment specific to one parent but not the other, when each was observed with his or her child in the Strange Situation. They interpreted these findings in support of the idea that the Type D attachment is a characteristic of children's attachment relationship and not constitutionally based in children's physiology. Investigations of children with Down syndrome, however, indicate high proportions of unclassifiable attachments that are often D-like in appearance (see Atkinson et al., this volume). It also is unclear whether the behavioral indices characterizing Type D attachments have short-term stability and would be seen consistently across two assessments with the same caregiver. Data presented in this monograph do, in fact, suggest moderate stability at least in the *classification* of children considered atypical in their attachment at 12 months (Barnett et al., this volume; Vondra et al., this volume). Research is needed that studies directly whether factors constitutional to infants influence the development and expression of Type D attachments. Barnett et al. (this volume) examine emotional reactivity and the development of Type D attachments among low-income and maltreated toddlers. Atkinson and his colleagues (this volume) examine the contribution of child cognitive functioning to Type D, insecure, and unclassifiable attachments in a sample of children with Down syndrome.

A parallel form of the Type D attachment in the preschool period is thought to be the "controlling" pattern (Cassidy & Marvin, in collaboration with the MacArthur Working Group on Attachment, 1991). Main and Cassidy (1988) reported that 8 of 12 children classified as Type D at 12 months with mother tended to demonstrate controlling behavior at the age of 6 years. Wartner, Grossmann, Fremmer-Bombik, and Suess (1994) reported that 9 of 13 children classified as Type D in infancy demonstrated either controlling or unclassifiable behavior at the age of 6 years. Several studies of attachment patterns of 3- to 6-year-olds have reported widely varying numbers of children who demonstrate controlling patterns (e.g., Cicchetti & Barnett, 1991; Greenberg et al., 1991; Solomon et al., 1995; Wartner et al., 1994). These are viewed within the MacArthur and the Main and Cassidy (1988) systems to be manifestations of the Type D attachment in early childhood (i.e., 3–6 years of age). Two forms of the controlling pattern have been reported: controlling-caregiving and controlling punitive. Children also are known who mix controlling caregiving and punitive strategies, and external factors that might distinguish between the two varieties have not been identified. Common to both is that a parent-child role-reversal is present such that the child appears to be in authority. In the case of the controlling-punitive variety, the parent appears to be deferential to the child's hostility with the child angrily bossing the parent. In the case of the caregiving variety, the child appears to have assumed responsibility for the parent's emotional well-being, and appears to try to cheer, entertain, reassure, and comfort the

19

parent. If attachment disorganization is an antecedent of the controlling pattern, then it suggests transformations occur between the lack of an attachment strategy to one in which the child achieves a developmentally inappropriate degree of control. Perhaps the inconsistency and unpredictability thought to promote attachment disorganization in infancy leads the child to attempt to take control of the relationship in order to obtain some element of security during the preschool period.

In contrast to grouping children demonstrating controlling patterns into a single atypical group as in the MacArthur and the Main and Cassidy (1988) systems, Crittenden (1990–1995) views these strategies as extreme manifestations of Type A and Type C attachments (i.e., A3 = compulsive caregiving; A4 = compulsive compliance; and C3 = aggressive; C4 = helpless). Children who mix caregiving with punitive varieties are classified as A/C within Crittenden's Preschool Attachment Assessment (PAA: see Crittenden, this volume). Although these classifications can be considered "atypical" preschool attachments, in that they appear to be more anomalous and problematic relationships, like those designated as "controlling" in the MacArthur system, the difference from the normative forms of insecurity in the PAA (A1/2 and C1/2) is one of degree, not style. Because both of these preschool systems were developed by individuals who had familiarity with atypical infant attachments, patterns among preschool children and their mothers that were believed to reflect not simply insecurity, but relationship pathology, could be incorporated directly into the classification system. Hence, their "atypical" nature rests not in classification anomalies, but in their extremity and pathology.

The Avoidant/Ambivalent (Type A/C) Pattern

Based on reexamination of samples of children from economically disadvantaged backgrounds, including children who were abused and/or neglected, Crittenden (1985, 1988) identified an atypical pattern of attachment that she labeled "Ambivalent/Avoidant," or Type A/C. She observed that many of these maltreated children would have been classified as securely attached without the addition of the A/C classification to Ainsworth and colleagues' (1978) system. Type A/C attachments have been observed at frequencies from less than 10% of low-income but low-social risk dyads, to 32% of chronically underweight infants from impoverished families, to close to 60% of abused and neglected infants (Crittenden, 1988; Valenzuela, 1990).

The A/C attachment pattern is characterized by combinations of moderate to high avoidance and moderate to high resistance, along with the moderate to high proximity seeking and contact maintenance typical of securely attached infants. Many children with Type A/C attachments also exhibited uncommon Strange Situation behaviors such as "rocking and wetting" (Crittenden, 1988). Despite these discrete behaviors, children with A/C attachments are identified primarily at the level of their overall pattern of interactive behaviors. Thus, whereas all children classified as A/C fit criteria for inclusion in the D category (Spieker & Booth, 1988; Valenzuela, 1990), the reverse is not true.

Although both Crittenden's (1985, 1988) and Main and Solomon's (1990) atypical classifications share certain behaviors, the underlying strategies thought to guide these children's behavior differ. Whereas infants with the Type D pattern are viewed by Main and Solomon as lacking a coherent, organized strategy for managing attachment-related stress, Crittenden contends that toddlers and young children who demonstrate A/C attachments do exhibit an organized coping strategy (Crittenden, 1992a; Crittenden & Ainsworth, 1989). Just as infants with Type A, B, or C attachments are guided by anticipation of their caregiver's responses to their bids for comfort, children with A/C attachments may behave according to underlying expectations. Their expectations, however, may reflect the fact that they cannot predict their caregiver's mood and reactions. As a result, the internal models of infants with A/C attachments direct them to be alert and vigilant to their caregiver's signals of mood, availability, and actions, and to be prepared, moment to moment, to adjust their behavioral strategy accordingly (see Crittenden, this volume). In this manner, children who exhibit Type A/C attachments may be viewed as quite organized in their attachment strategies.

Crittenden (this volume) interprets many of the indices of attachment "disorganization" as evidence that an infant is actively processing environmental information, and adjusting his or her behavioral strategies in accordance with perceptions of the caregiver's behavior. For example, she hypothesizes that behaviors such as freezing and stilling function to give children additional time for assessing the emotional state of a potentially dangerous, and unpredictable, mother. Main and Solomon (1990) speculated that such behaviors occur when children are overwhelmed by distress or when approach and avoidance tendencies are simultaneously activated, mutually inhibiting one another. The debate, in other words, is whether such behaviors are signs of active coping or of breakdowns in coping. Crittenden also speculates that the signs of the Type D pattern found among children with a mental age of approximately 12 months are the result of developmental immaturity. With developmental advances in information processing and behavioral coordination, decisions about interactive styles with caregivers can be made more covertly.

The need for infants to be alert and flexible in behavior could be due to having experienced a great degree of unpredictability in interactions with their attachment figure. Although insensitive, the less than optimal

21

parenting of caregivers whose infants develop Type A or Type C attachments may be consistent in terms of the types of insensitivity they display (see Crittenden, this volume). In contrast, caregivers whose infants develop Type A/C attachments may demonstrate greater inconsistency and more severe insensitivity in their caregiving behaviors, mixing angry outbursts such as abuse episodes with the emotional withdrawal more characteristic of neglectful care (Crittenden, 1988).

The Unstable-Avoidant (Type U-A) Pattern

Lyons-Ruth and her colleagues (Lyons-Ruth et al., 1987; Lyons-Ruth, Zoll, Connell, & Grunebaum, 1986) identified an "Unstable-Avoidant" (Type U-A) attachment pattern in their research with high-risk infants. Archival analyses of additional samples indicated that the U-A pattern was particularly rare (approximately 3%) in low-risk dyads. The U-A pattern was observed at increased frequency among infants at high social risk, however, particularly among a sample of infants with maltreating caregivers (40%), and with caregivers who reported elevated levels of depressive symptoms (Lyons-Ruth, Connell, & Zoll, 1989). The majority of such infants would have been placed within the secure, Type B, pattern, if the U-A pattern were not considered.

The U-A pattern is characterized by a 4-point or greater decline in avoidance between the first and second Strange Situation reunions using Ainsworth et al.'s (1978) standardized interactive behavior scales. This entails a change across separations from marked avoidance to minimal or no avoidance in the second reunion. The U-A pattern, therefore, is identified solely at the level of interactive behaviors. Information concerning other aspects of an infant's behavior, in addition to the drop in avoidance, is needed to decide whether a child would meet criteria for the D or A/C patterns. Although none of the U-A attachments were classified as D (and many as secure) when Lyons-Ruth recoded her data for disorganization, it seems possible that many infants who demonstrate the U-A pattern also meet criteria for inclusion in these other atypical patterns. Every case of the small number of U-A attachments Vondra and her colleagues (this volume) reported included other behavioral indices of disorganization, and also could not be differentiated—on the basis of maternal report or observational data—from attachments designated as A/C. For example, the drop in avoidance often corresponds to an infant exhibiting an avoidant attachment strategy in the first reunion and then behaving in a fashion consistent with classification in the Type C category in the second reunion. Some infants adopt an avoidant strategy to cope with the first separation and reunion, but then behave as if they associated their avoidance with their caregiver's sudden (second) departure. With great distress over what may seem like abandonment, they give up avoidance as a strategy and, instead, seek proximity in the second reunion, often with distress and resistance.

Although Lyons-Ruth (1997, personal communication) reported that the unstable avoidance pattern was not observed among her sample of high-risk infants at 18 months, she noted that 60% of the small number of 12-month-olds given the U-A designation were coded as disorganized at 18 months. Vondra and her colleagues (this volume) observed the pattern both at 12 and at 18 months in their own sample of infants from low-income families, but, again, the numbers were small and the pattern did not show continuity over time (only 20% were coded as disorganized at 18 months).

Variability in both concomitant D behaviors and subsequent 18-month D classification does not lead to a clear interpretation of this pattern of behavior. Unpublished data from both 12- and 18-month assessments (Lyons-Ruth, 1997, personal communication), however, supports the risk-related nature of decreases in avoidance across reunions as compared to sustained levels of avoidance. When infants were scored for the difference in avoidance ratings from the first to second reunion, significant associations were obtained at both 12 and 18 months between increasing severity of maternal depressive symptoms and decreases in avoidance, $r(57) = .23$, $p < .05$, at 12 months; $r(74) = .28$, $p < .05$, at 18 months.

Whether the U-A pattern corresponds to an unstable representational model of the attachment figure or to an infant's processing of and reaction to new information is unknown. In any case, infants who demonstrate the U-A pattern appear unable to maintain an avoidant strategy under the stress of the second separation (Lyons-Ruth et al., 1987). Research suggests that the U-A pattern is related to having experienced more disturbed varieties of parenting than infants with Type A or other patterns of attachment (Lyons-Ruth et al., 1986, 1987, 1989). Why these parenting experiences would bring about unstable avoidance needs exploration.

THE PRESENT MONOGRAPH

The chapters gathered within address a number of questions discussed in this opening chapter. In general, they can be taken as a whole to support the construct validity of atypical attachments. Both convergent and discriminant validity for various forms of atypical attachments are presented. The diversity of forms these patterns assume during infancy and toddlerhood also are illustrated. Although the studies presented do not resolve the question of whether one or more patterns of atypical attachment should be adopted into the traditional classification system, they certainly highlight the importance of addressing this issue in the near future.

Several of the chapters address the role child factors may play in the formation of atypical attachments. Atkinson and his colleagues explore the potential contributions of child organic birth defects (i.e., Down syndrome and developmental delay) in the formation of atypical attachments. If child factors can have a main effect on the development of attachment security, then some of the basic underpinnings of attachment theory are challenged. Pipp-Siegel and her colleagues further address this issue by presenting the need and method for distinguishing symptoms of organically based neurological disorder from indices of relationship functioning. Barnett, Ganiban, and Cicchetti examine the role of child emotional reactivity on attachment disorganization and whether the Type D pattern in particular is linked with the development of emotional dysregulation.

Two chapters consider the types of experiences associated with the development of atypical attachments. Lyons-Ruth, Bronfman, and Parsons present a direct examination of Main and Hesse's (1990) specific hypothesis that maternal frightened and frightening behavior promotes the formation of a Type D attachment. Vondra and her colleagues focus more broadly on the larger ecosystem of stresses and supports surrounding the parent-child relationship.

The question of stability, change, and developmental transformation of atypical attachments also is addressed across a number of chapters. Barnett et al. present data on stability of the Type D pattern across three assessment points from 12 to 24 months child age. Vondra et al. report on the stability of a variety of atypical patterns from 12 to 18 months and, importantly, consider sources of stability and change. Crittenden provides a theoretical examination of the role child maturation and development may play in transforming traditional and atypical attachments across early childhood. Her developmental analysis provides a broader context for understanding the relation and distinction between traditional and atypical varieties of attachment. Finally, Barnett, Butler, and Vondra discuss and integrate the chapters of this *Monograph* and make suggestions for future research.

II. NEUROLOGICAL ASPECTS OF THE DISORGANIZED/DISORIENTED ATTACHMENT CLASSIFICATION SYSTEM: DIFFERENTIATING QUALITY OF THE ATTACHMENT RELATIONSHIP FROM NEUROLOGICAL IMPAIRMENT

Sandra Pipp-Siegel, Clifford H. Siegel, and Janet Dean

One major assumption of attachment theory is that attachment status reflects an important component of the relationship between infant and mother. Until recently, attachment studies have relied upon the traditional Ainsworth (Ainsworth, Blehar, Waters, & Wall, 1978) classification system to assess infant's attachment to the primary caregiver (i.e., secure, insecure-avoidant, insecure-ambivalent). Use of this category system, however, led to a surprisingly large number of maltreated infants being classified as secure, a finding that contradicts expectations arising from attachment theory. Further, Main and Weston (1981) reported that approximately 13% of 12- to 18-month-old infants in their nonmaltreated middle-class sample did not fit into the three existing classifications, and so were labeled "unclassifiable."

To address these issues, further categories have been proposed beyond the original three, and Barnett and Vondra (this volume) provide an excellent review of the different schemes that have been proposed to enable a more complete categorization of infants' behavior in the Strange Situation, the laboratory paradigm used to assess attachment status (Ainsworth & Wittig, 1969). The focus of this chapter is the category of "disorganized/disoriented" (D), developed and validated by Main and Solomon (1986, 1990). The criteria behaviors for this category are clearly articulated, and evidence for construct validity has been presented. Maltreated infants, for example, have a higher probability of being classified as D compared to nonmaltreated infants, with an incidence as high as 82% (Carlson, Cicchetti, Barnett, & Braunwald, 1989b).

In their article describing the procedures for identifying D status, Main and Solomon (1990) raised the question of whether some behaviors considered as indices of disorganization and disorientation may be related to neurological abnormalities, and explicitly stated that the "sample being studied should be one in which subjects are presumed neurologically normal" (1990, p. 146). And, several investigators have noted the difficulty of using the D category with neurologically impaired infants (Capps, Sigman, & Mundy, 1994; Rogers, Ozonoff, & Maslin-Cole, 1991; Thompson, Cicchetti, Lamb, & Malkin, 1985; Vaughn et al., 1994; see Atkinson et al., this volume, for a review of this issue). Others, however, have applied the D classification to children who are neurologically impaired. The percentage of children with disorganized/disoriented attachment was significantly higher for children with neurological abnormalities compared to those without neurological abnormalities (van IJzendoorn, Goldberg, Kroonenberg, & Frenkel, 1992; van IJzendoorn, Schuengel, & Bakersmans-Kranenburg, 1999). In a meta-analysis devoted to ascertaining the causes of D attachment status, van IJzendoorn and his colleagues (1999) reported that, compared to 15% of Ds in middle-class samples, a significantly higher percentage of D attachment was found in children with diagnoses of autism and Down syndrome (35%), in premature children (24%), and in children whose mothers abused alcohol and drugs (43%). Children with nonneurological, severe physical problems (e.g., congenital heart disease, cleft palate, 20%) and children whose mothers were depressed (19%), however, did not evidence a significantly higher percentage of D status compared to controls.

The purpose of this chapter is to examine possible neurological causes of the various indices of D attachment status. We briefly describe Main and Solomon's system of attachment categories and the criteria for assessing disorganized and disoriented behavior, then point out which of these behaviors also may be a result of neurological abnormalities. We suggest a strategy for differentiating neurological risk status from disorganized/disoriented attachment status, thus providing guidelines for obtaining a "differential diagnosis" between behaviors that presumably reflect attachment and those that may reflect neurological abnormalities. Finally, preliminary data are provided examining the incidence of neurological indices in neurologically impaired children compared to children with nonneurological physical conditions.

THE DISORGANIZED/DISORIENTED ATTACHMENT CATEGORY

Contradictions exist in the literature on the strategy of using the D category for samples of neurologically impaired infants and children. One strategy was to assign the U, or unclassifiable, category to all children who may be neurologically impaired. Because of the neurological impairments of Down syndrome children, for example, Vaughn and his colleagues (1994) followed the lead of Main and Solomon (1990) and decided that "cases that might otherwise have been coded as Insecure-Disorganized were assigned instead to the U" (p. 100), or the insecure-unclassifiable category. It should be noted, however, that while Vaughn et al. (1994) categorized all infants whose behavior reflected unclassifiable or disorganized/disoriented behavior as U, they felt that differentiation between the two categories would be useful. The strategy used by Atkinson and his colleagues (this volume) was to assign the D category conservatively.

Main herself scored the attachment behavior in a set of autistic and mentally retarded children (Capps et al., 1994). In this case, all autistic children were assigned a primary classification of D. In further analysis of the data, Capps et al. found that the attachment status changed when stereotypic behaviors were assumed to be characteristic of autism and not the attachment relationship. Of the 15 children previously classified as D, 3 were considered to be true Ds, "indicating the presence of disorganized/disoriented behaviors other than stereotypies characteristic of autism" (1994, p. 255).

This study and the meta-analyses performed by van IJzendoorn et al. (1999) point to the importance of determining which behaviors reflect neurological impairment and/or attachment-related behaviors. Capps et al. highlighted one behavior—stereotypies—observed in the Strange Situation that may be due to neurological impairment associated with autism. Neurological impairment, however, can manifest itself in behaviors other than stereotypies, and autism reflects only one diagnosis of neurological impairment. For these reasons, we believe it is important to specify those behaviors specified by Main and Solomon (1990) that may reflect neurological abnormalities as well as disorganized/disoriented attachment. First, a detailed description of the behaviors leading to a D classification will be presented.

Main and Solomon (1990) broadly defined disorganized/disoriented attachment behavior to be inexplicable in the immediate context or explicable only if an assumption is made that the infant is afraid of the parent. As a result of extensive work with a large number of videotapes of reunions of infants and mothers in the Strange Situation, Main and Solomon (1986, 1990) identified specific behaviors that may be observed when infants have a disorganized/disoriented attachment relation to their caregiver. The complete list of D behaviors identified by Main and Solomon (1990) is reproduced in Table 3. As can be seen from this table, they described seven major headings to define the D attachment status. These consist of: (a) Sequential display of contradictory behavior patterns; (b) Simultaneous display of contradictory behavior patterns; (c) Undirected, misdirected, incomplete, and interrupted movements and expressions; (d) Stereotypies, asymmetrical, mistimed movements, and anomalous postures; (e) Freezing, stilling, and slowed movements and expressions; (f) Direct indices of apprehension regarding the parent; and (g) Direct indices of disorganization or disorientation.

Each one of these headings includes a variable number of subcategories. A count of the explicit behaviors that are described in this table totals 66 behaviors that contribute to a determination of a disorganized/disoriented attachment. Of these 66 behaviors, any one of 22 behaviors are normally in and of itself sufficient to place an infant into a primary D attachment status. These behaviors are italicized in Table 3, and include behaviors such as "Infant rises or begins approach immediately upon reunion, but falls

TABLE 3

Indices of Disorganization and Disorientation Described in Table 1
(Main & Solomon, 1990).

I. Sequential Display of Contradictory Behavior Patterns

A. Very strong displays of attachment behavior or angry behavior suddenly followed by avoidance, freezing, or dazed behavior. For example:

1. In the middle of a display of anger and distress, the infant suddenly becomes markedly devoid of affect and moves away from the parent.

2. *Immediately following strong proximity seeking and a bright, full greeting with raised arms, the infant moves to the wall or into the center of room and stills or freezes with a "dazed" expression.*

3. *Infant cries and calls for the parent at the door throughout separation: immediately upon reunion, however, the infant turns about the moves sharply away from the parent, showing strong avoidance.*

B. Calm, contented play suddenly succeeded by distressed, angry behavior. For example:

1. *Infant calm and undistressed during both separations from the parent, but becomes extremely focused upon the parent, showing highly distressed and/or angry behavior immediately upon reunion.*

II. Simultaneous Display of Contradictory Behavior Patterns

A. The infant displays avoidant behavior simultaneously with proximity seeking, contact maintaining, or contact resisting. For example:

1. While held by or holding onto parent, infant shows avoidance of parent such as the following:

   (a) Infant sits comfortably on parent's lap for extended period but with averted gaze, ignoring parent's repeated overtures;
   (b) infant holds arms and legs away from the parent while held, limbs stiff, tense, and straight;
   (c) infant clings hard to parent for substantial period while *sharply* averting head/gaze. (Note: Disorganized only if infant is clinging hard while sharply arching away. Many infants look away or turn heads away while holding on lightly after a pick-up.)

2. Infant approaches while simultaneously creating a pathway which avoids or moves away from parent, and this cannot be explained by a shift of attention to toys or other matters. Thus, from its inception the infant's "approach" seems designed to form a parabolic pathway.

3. *Movements of approach are repeatedly accompanied by movements of avoidance such as the following:*

   (a) *infant approaches with head sharply averted;*
   (b) *infant approaches by backing toward parent;*
   (c) *infant reaches arms up for parent with head sharply averted or with head down.*

4. *Distress, clinging or resistance is accompanied by marked avoidance for substantial periods, such as the following:*

   (a) *infant moves into corner or behind item of furniture while angrily, openly refusing or resisting parent;*
   (b) *infant cries angrily from distance, while turning in circles and turning away from parent.* (Note: Arching backward with flailing arms, and throwing self backward on floor are part of normal infant tantrum displays and are not necessarily considered disorganized.)

5. *Extensive avoidance of parent is accompanied by substantial distress/anger indices, such as: infant silently averted head and body away from parent who is offering or attempting pick-up but makes stiff, angry kicking movements and hits hand on floor.*

B. Simultaneous display of other opposing behavior propensities. For example:

1. Infant's smile to parent has fear elements (*very strong index* if marked, see no. VI).

2. *When in apparent good mood, infant strikes, pushes or pulls against the parent's face or eyes. These usually subtle aggressive movements are sometimes immediately preceded by a somewhat **dazed expression**, or may be accompanied by an **impassive expression**.*)

III. Undirected, Misdirected, Incomplete, and Interrupted Movements and Expressions

A. Seemingly undirected or misdirected movements and expressions. For example:

1. Upon becoming distressed, infant moves away from rather than to parent. (Note: Do not consider brief moves away from parent disorganized when an infant has been crying and displaying desire for contact for a long period, and parent has failed to satisfy infant. Infant may briefly move away while crying in response to frustration in these circumstances, coming back to parent to try again, without being disorganized.)

2. Infant approaches parent at door as though to greet parent, then attempts instead to follow stranger out of the room, perhaps actively pulling away from

the parent. (This pattern seems more misdirected or redirected than undirected; see no. VII for similar behavior.)

3. Initiation of extensive crying in parents' presence without any move toward or look toward the parent. (Note: This is not necessarily disorganized if parent is already nearby and attentive. It also is not disorganized if the infant, having already been crying and focused on the parent for an extended period, simply does not look at or move closer to the parent for a few seconds.)

4. Any marked failure to move toward the parent when path is not blocked and infant is clearly frightened.

5. Similarly, expression of strong fear of distress regarding an object while staring at it, without withdrawing from it or looking toward parent.

6. *Extensive or intense expressions of fear or distress accompanied or followed by moves away from rather than to parent, as infant appears frightened of stranger in parents' presence, moves away and leans forehead on wall.*

7. *Infant cries at stranger's leave-taking, attempts to follow her out of room. (This behavior pattern may be more misdirected or redirected than undirected; see also no. VII.)*

B. Incomplete movements. For example:

1. Movements to approach parent are contradicted before they are completed, for example, infant moves hand toward parent and withdraws hand quickly before touching parent, without rationale. Or repeated, hesitant, stop-start approach movements (or reach movements) toward parent.

2. Exceptionally slow or limp movements of approach to parent, as though the infant is resisting the movements even while making them ("underwater" approach movements).

3. *Exceptionally slow, limp, movements of striking at, pushing at, or pulling at the parent's face, eyes or neck ("underwater" movements). The subtle but definite aggressive intent is almost indiscernible because of the incomplete, slow nature of the movements. See also no. V.*

C. Interrupted expressions or movements. For example:

1. After a long period of contented play, sudden out-of-context crying or displays of distressed anger without rationale.

2. *Infant interrupts approach to parent on reunion with a bout of angry behavior, directed away from the parent, then continues approach. As, begins strong approach upon reunion but interrupts approach to look away and strike hand on floor with angry sounds, then completes full approach.*

3. *Infant rises or begins approach immediately upon reunion, but falls prone in "depressed" (huddled) posture.*

IV. Stereotypies, Asymmetrical Movements,
Mistimed Movements, and Anomalous Postures

A. Asymmetries of expression or movement. For example:

1. Asymmetries of movement on approach to parent (asymmetrical creeping, heavy or fast on one side only), with or without sudden, unpredictable changes of direction.

2. Asymmetries of facial expression directly upon the appearance of the parent, for example, an extremely swift "tic" which lifts only the left side of the facial musculature.

B. Stereotypies. For example:

    1. Extended rocking, ear pulling, hair twisting, and any other rhythmical, repeated movements without visible function. (Note: Do not include "stereotypies" that make sense in the immediate context, as rubbing eyes in a tired infant, or some initial ear pulling or hair pulling in the stranger's presence.)

    2. Marked stereotypies while being held by the parent. (Do _not_ include rubbing eyes if infant has been crying, or brief continuation of previous stereotypies while in arms in an infant who showed the same stereotypies during separation.)

C. Assumption of anomalous postures. For example:

    **1. Repeated assumption of uninterpretable postures, as, head cocking with arms crooked over head.**

    2. Assumption of huddled, prone, depressed posture for more than twenty seconds, unless infant is clearly tired.

    3. Any posture stereotyped for a particular baby, as closing eyes and holding hands forward at shoulder height for several seconds in response to each reunion.

D. Mistimed movements. For example:

    1. Unpredictable bouts of activity or movement which seem to lack normal preparation time for initiation, and/or which have a jerky, automaton-like (unmonitored) quality. For example, a sudden burst of jerky arm and leg activity in an infant who had been sitting tense and immobilized a second prior.

V. Freezing, Stilling, and Slowed Movements and Expressions

Freezing is identified as the holding of movements, gestures, or positions in a posture that involves active resistance to gravity. For example, infant sits or stands with arms held out waist-high and to sides. _Stilling_ is distinguished from freezing in that infant is in comfortable, resting posture which requires no active resistance to gravity. Freezing is considered a stronger marker of disorientation than stilling.

A. Freezing and stilling suggestive of more than momentary interruption of activity. For example:

    **1. Freezing lasting twenty seconds or more, and stilling lasting thirty seconds or more, accompanied by dazed or trance-like facial expression. For example, freezing accompanied by tense, smooth closing of the lids or by lifeless stare.**

    **2. Interrupting a bout of resistant or distressed behavior, freezing (ten or more seconds) or stilling (twenty or more seconds) is accompanied by a dazed or trance-like expression.**

    **3. Freezing lasting twenty-five seconds or more, and stilling lasting thirty-five seconds or more, while held by parent unless infant has recently been engaged in hard crying (below).** (Notes: [1] Context should be considered. [2] Do not consider stilling during the first thirty seconds of reunion if the infant is being held by parent, has been crying hard, and is clearly simply in transition from crying. [3] Infant should not be considered to be freezing or stilling if infant is watching something with lively interest, as, watching stranger demonstrate working of a toy. [4] The C2 infant is passive by definition: general passivity should not be confused with stilling.)

B. Slowed movements and expressions suggesting lack of orientation to the present environment. For example:

    1. Markedly apathetic or lethargic movements, as though infant is without purpose in movement forward.

    2. Slack, depressed, dazed, or apathetic facial expression especially when unexpected, as accompanying approach to parent on reunion ending in raised arms. (Note: Consider only expressions specified above. Neutral or impassive expressions are not considered indicative of disorientation with respect to the current environment.)

VI. Direct Indices of Apprehension Regarding the Parent

A. Expression of strong fear or apprehension directly upon return of parent, or when parent calls or approaches. For example:

    1. Immediate responses to noting parent's entrance such as the following:

        (a) jerking back, with fearful expression;
        (b) flinging hands about, over, or in front of face, or over mouth, with fearful expression;
        (c) dashing away from the door/parent upon reunion, with hunched or tucked head and shoulders.

    2. Other expressions of fear or apprehension soon following reunion, such as *fearful facial expression on pick-up.*

B. Other indices of apprehension regarding the parent. For example:

    1. Moving behind chair or behind furniture without immediate rationale (pursuit of toy, interest in object behind chair, or brief exploration), especially when infant is then out of reach or out of sight of parent.

    2. Following a hesitant, seemingly cautious approach to the parent with a rapid, tense "away" movement.

    3. Offering objects to the parent with tense arm and over an unusual distance, as though avoiding parental "reach" space.

    4. Raising or tensing shoulders when approaching or in contact with parent.

    5. Highly vigilant posture or appearance when in presence of parent. Movements or posture tense, infant gives impression of being hyperalert to parent even or especially when parent positioned behind her.

VII. Direct Indices of Disorganization or Disorientation

A. Any clear indices of confusion and disorganization in first movement of reunion with parent. For example:

    1. Raising hand or hands to mouth directly upon the return of parent without accompanying confused, wary, or fearful expression. (Do not include thumb or finger sucking, putting objects in mouth, or removing objects from mouth. Do not include if hands already near face.)

2. *"Greeting" stranger brightly at the movement of reunion with parent, that is, approaching stranger with raised immediately as parent enters.* (Note: Distinguished from the bright or happy look to stranger made by many infants at the movement of the parent's return, often accompanied by pointing to parent to further mark the event.)

3. *Flinging hands over, about, or in front of face directly upon return of the parent and in clear response to return of parent.*

4. *Raising hand or hands to mouth directly upon the return of the parent with a clearly confused or wary expression.*

5. *Confused or confusing sequences of very rapid changes of affect in first few seconds of reunion with parent, as (a) rapid movement of withdrawal, (b) accompanied by confused cry-laugh, (c) succeeded by approach movement.*

B. Direct indices of confusion or disorientation beyond the first movements of reunion with the parent. For example:

1. Fall while approaching parent when infant is good walker. Similar unexplained falls when parent reaches for infant, or when parent calls from outside of door.

2. **Disorganized wandering, especially when accompanied by disoriented expression.**

3. Rapidly pursuing parent to door, protesting departure, then smiling as though in greeting as door closes.

4. **Disoriented facial expression. Sudden "blind" look to eyes, where infant has previously used eyes normally.**

Note: From "Procedures for Identifying Infants as Disorganized/Disordered During the Ainsworth Strange Situation," by M. Main and J. Solomon, 1990, in M. Greenberg, D. Cicchetti, and E. M. Cummings (Eds.), *Attachment in the Preschool Years: Theory, Research, and Intervention* (pp. 136–140), Chicago: University of Chicago Press. Copyright 1990 by University of Chicago Press. Reprinted with permission. As in the original, italics mark very strong indices, which in themselves are usually sufficient for D category placement. Text that is both boldfaced and underlined denotes behavior that may reflect neurological impairmaent (boldfacing and underlining added by authors of current chapter).

prone in 'depressed' (huddled) posture" or "Immediate responses to noting parent's entrance such as the following: (a) jerking back, with fearful expression; (b) flinging hands about, over or in front of face, or over mouth, with fearful expression; (c) dashing away from the door/parent upon reunion, with hunched or tucked head and shoulders."

Other behaviors are considered to be less indicative of disorganized or disoriented behavior. Any one of these behaviors by itself is not enough to consider a primary D classification. The behaviors listed in Table 3 that are *not* italicized are in this category. These include, for example, "In the middle of a display of anger and distress, the infant suddenly becomes markedly devoid of affect and moves away from the parent" or "Infant approaches parent at door as though to greet, then attempts instead to follow stranger out of the room, perhaps actively pulling away from the parent." These lesser indicators can together add up to form a primary D classification only if they are frequent enough, intense enough, or clearly lacking in rationale.

To determine whether an infant has a disorganized or disoriented attachment relation to his primary caregiver, a "D index" is assigned from 1 to 9. Each odd rating is labeled. For example, "1" is labeled "No signs of disorganization/disorientation," "5" is labeled "Moderate indices of disorganization/disorientation which are not clearly sufficient for a D category placement," and "9" is labeled "Definite qualification for D attachment status." In general, a D index of 6 or above is considered to reflect unambiguous D status, an index of 4 and below reflects a non-D primary classification, and an index of 5 is considered to be ambiguous, with careful consideration of the behaviors required to determine primary classification. If a primary attachment category of D is assigned, a secondary attachment status also is determined. An infant will be assigned a D/A code if, for example, the D index is above 6 (and perhaps 5) and criteria also are met for avoidant reunion behavior. When the D index, however, is below 4 (and perhaps 5), an attachment status other than D is assigned, e.g., A, B, C, U_{ABC}. (According to Main and Solomon, the U_{ABC} category reflects "a failure to fit to the A, B, C criteria" [1990, p. 154] and enables one to distinguish "between infants who meet D criteria *while being readily classifiable in the* A, B, C *system* from infants who meet D criteria and are *unclassifiable* with respect of A, B, C" [1990, p. 154, italics in original].)

POSSIBLE NEUROLOGICAL SYMPTOMS OR CONDITIONS CONTRIBUTING TO A D STATUS

A number of different medical conditions involve neurological impairment, including autism, cerebral palsy, Down syndrome, epilepsy, Tay-Sachs disease, and so on (see Menkes, 1995). In order to remain true to Main and Solomon's Table 1, however, we identified several different medical *symptoms*—independent of the potential medical condition that might give rise to these symptoms—that may reflect disorganized/disoriented attachment behavior. These conditions include: chorea, dyspraxia, dystonia, focal seizures, hypotonia, stereotypies, and tics. Behaviors that may reflect the neurological symptoms are both boldfaced and underlined in Table 3. It should be noted that the medical conditions to be discussed are rare in the general population, and that the behaviors described in Table 3 are observed with greater frequency when special populations are selected for study.

Involuntary movements can represent tics, chorea, or choreoathetosis. *Tics*, defined as repetitive involuntary movements, would probably be easily observable as such. Tics are familiar to most observers as sudden repetitive jerky movements, yet they can involve any muscle group and are not always jerky. Because of this and the fact that some children (but not infants) often learn to fashion tics into seemingly purposeful movements, they can occasionally be difficult to discern. Most often, though, the repetitive occurrence of the movements distinguishes tics from normal motor behavior. Other involuntary movements, such as *chorea* or *choreoathetosis*, occur with less frequency than tics. Choreiform movements are unrelated and unpatterned behaviors, and almost never appear as a part of a coordinated activity (Lees, 1985). These movements can be slow or rapid, as well as repetitive or singular. The same muscle groups can be involved from one movement to the next, leading to a repetition that could make the movement easier to recognize as a neurological abnormality. With choreiform movements, however, the repetition can be spaced out over much longer time intervals than with tics, and as such might not be repeated within the time frame of the Strange Situation paradigm. Also, choreoatheoid movements can affect different muscle groups from one movement to the next and might thus be harder to differentiate from other activity. Choreiform disorders in infancy can be inborn or a result of trauma (Aicardi, 1992; Drake, Jackson, & Miller, 1987; Kurland & Shoulson, 1983; Lance, 1977). Involuntary movements with a neurological basis such as tics and choreiform disorders often occur more in anxiety provoking situations, and thus could occur with greater frequency in particular interactional contexts.

Other behaviors, such as averting or turning the head sharply, could occur in slower involuntary movement disorders such as the *dystonias*, which are more sustained involuntary torsions or tensions of a muscle (Lees, 1985). While the individual usually experiences a dystonia as a stiffness or pain in the involved muscle, this stiffness or tension might not be evident to an observer, who instead might only see a movement of whatever part of the body is controlled by the stiffening muscle. Conditions that can produce dystonic movements include benign paroxysmal torticollis and symptomatic paroxysmal dystonia (Aicardi, 1992), as well as nonneurological conditions, for example, Sandifer's syndrome, which involves contortions of the neck and trunk because of hiatal hernia (Sutcliffe, 1969). Dystonias are not always part of an illness; they can also occur transiently (Angelini, Rumi, Lamperti, Nardocci, 1988). Other conditions, such as hyperekplexia (Sander, Layzer, & Goldsobel, 1980) could include combinations of dystonic or stiff posturing and sudden unexplained movements. Hyperekplexia results in movements that can be abnormally violent, and the child can appear frightened and tense during infancy (Gordon, 1993).

Seizures may influence a number of behaviors described as possible D indices. Focal myoclonic seizures, involving sudden jerking of focal muscles, are rare in infancy. When myoclonic seizures do occur they are usually generalized and involve the whole body, and rarely involve single muscle groups in infancy (Aicardi, 1986). Sudden stilling with trancelike expression could be an indication of petit mal seizures or variations of such.

Misguided movements, such as the infant reaching past the parent, could occur in the *dyspraxias*, disorders of movement coordination and planning unrelated to demonstrable sensory or motor deficits. Developmental dyspraxia, which might be related to variability in the myelination of higher cortical pathways, can take multiple forms and can occur in the absence of any other neurological problems (Cermak, 1985; Miller, 1986).

Stereotypies are common in infants and children with *pervasive developmental disorders*, such as autism or Asperger's syndrome. These disorders would need to be ruled out if these behaviors are used to classify children as disorganized or disoriented.

Possible Dual Indices

Behaviors that may reflect dual causation—disorganized or disoriented attachment to the primary caregiver and/or neurological impairment in the infant—are the underlined and boldfaced behaviors in Table 3. In subsequent discussion, these behaviors are given the shorthand of "dual indices." It should be noted that dual indices may include those behaviors that are sufficient by themselves for a primary D classification (and are noted in Table 3 by italicized font) or include lesser behaviors that by themselves are not sufficient for a primary D classification.

The behaviors described in three categories or headings in Table 3 do not describe patterns of behavior that may be due to neurological impairment. Main and Solomon's (1990) descriptions of sequential (heading I) and simultaneous (heading II) display of contradictory behavior patterns and the descriptions of direct indices of apprehension (heading VI), thus, unambiguously reflect infants' attachment related behavior.

The third heading in Table 3 describes movements and expressions that are undirected, incomplete, or interrupted. All three examples of incomplete movements described in this section may reflect neurological impairment. Index III.B.1. refers to stop, start, approach, or reach movements toward parents and can reflect chorea, whereas exceptionally slow or limp movements (III.B.2. and III.B.3.) may reflect hypotomia or dyspraxia. In general, the three examples all describe behavior directed at the parent. If they are observed in a tape, it will be important to examine minutely all other aspects of the tape in order to determine whether these behaviors also are observed independent of the parent. Of course, if they are only exhibited toward the parent there is a greater likelihood of the behavior being attachment related.

The fourth heading regarding stereotypies and atypical movements and postures contains descriptions of a number of behaviors that could reflect neurological deficits. The two stereotypies noted by Main and Solomon

(1990) include rhythmical, repeated movements without visible function both alone (IV.B.1.) or while being held by parent (IV.B.2.). Stereotypies are common in infants and children with pervasive developmental disorders, and may be observed throughout the Strange Situation. Some stereotypic behaviors in an infant with autism (such as hand-flapping), for example, may represent a greeting response to the mother instead of an index of disorganized/disoriented attachment to her (Rogers, personal communication).

Asymmetry of movement (IV.A.1.) may represent cerebral palsy or dyspraxia, but would generally be observed in all behavior, not just that directed toward the parent. Asymmetry of facial expressions (IV.A.2.) may represent tics, as noted by Main and Solomon (1990), or may represent muscle weakness. Anomalous postures (IV.C.1.) may reflect dystonia. Finally, mistimed movements that are jerky or unpredictable may be due to chorea, tics, or dyspraxia, and the presence of these conditions should be determined before using these indices as an indication of a primary D classification.

Freezing and stilling, behaviors described under the fifth heading, may be caused by seizure disorders. These behaviors are described in indices V.A.1., V.A.2., and V.A.3. As described by Main and Solomon (1990), each one of these indices varies in time from 10 to 30 s. It is unclear why these times were chosen, but in general, petit mal seizures are rapid in nature, generally less than 10 s, while other types of seizures can last more than 30 min (Menkes, 1995).

The seventh and final category regards direct indices of disorganization or disorientation. Disorganized wandering (VII.B.2.) is characteristic of mentally retarded children and to be attachment related must not be observed in other episodes besides the reunion episodes to be coded as D. Finally, disoriented facial expression (VII.B.4.) could reflect a petit mal seizure.

Percentage of D Indices Related to Possible Neurological Impairment

Main and Solomon (1990) suggested that the seven headings listed in Table 3 reflect important subcategories of D behaviors, but should be considered as examples only. As a result, other behaviors that are not explicitly listed in Table 3 also may reflect D attachment. Because of this, it is unclear how to calculate the percentage of behaviors that may reflect either disorganization in the attachment relationship or neurological impairment in the infant.

If we confine ourselves to behaviors listed only in Table 3, however, the percentage of underlined and boldfaced behaviors in this table may be calculated in a number of ways: (a) First, one may calculate the percentage by the number of the major headings. "Neurological" indices are contained primarily in three of the seven major headings, including (III) Undirected, incomplete and interrupted movements and expressions, (IV) Stereotypies, asymmetrical movements, mistimed movements, and anomalous postures, and (V) Freezing, stilling, and slowed movements and expressions. Three out of a possible seven major categories, or 43%, thus may include behaviors reflecting either neurological impairment or disorganized attachment; (b) Alternatively, examination of the specific behaviors described in Table 3 shows that 14 out of a total of 66, or 21%, of the behaviors listed by Main and Solomon (1990) were judged to include behaviors that could be dually caused by either neurological impairment or the attachment relationship; and (c) A final way to analyze these data is to examine the proportion of the behaviors that are italicized and so are presumed to be behaviors that could singly be sufficient for D categorization. At the level of the individual example of behavior, 5 out of 33 of the italicized behaviors, or 15%, may be dually caused.

Thus, depending upon the criteria used to determine the percentage of "neurological" D behaviors, the percentages range from 15% to 43%. These are not negligible percentages and highlight the importance of differentiating the causes of behavior observed in the Strange Situation.

"DIFFERENTIAL DIAGNOSIS" IN ATTACHMENT CLASSIFICATION

The above discussion of the intersection between neurological problems and D attachment characteristics raises two questions. The first question regards *when* one should be sensitive to possible neurological indices. The frequency of any of the above medical conditions is low. When examining medical conditions that have neurological components, for example, the prevalence ratings are as follows: mental retardation (approximately 1.0% of population, American Psychiatric Association, 1994), pervasive developmental disorders, including autism (5 cases/1,000 children; Menkes, 1994); cerebral palsy (2 cases/1,000 children, Paneth & Kieley, 1984). In a low-risk population, therefore, sensitivity to possible neurological contributions to disorganized/disoriented attachment status may be unnecessary.

There are two instances, however, when careful consideration of D indices is warranted. The first instance is if infants and children with neurological conditions are to be targeted for study. Secondly, high-risk populations are often at higher risk for neurological impairment. Premature birth is associated with increased probability of neurological impairment and occurs in 9.7% of the U.S. population (National Center for Health Statistics, 1988). Other conditions that are associated with neurological disorder in high-risk populations include exposure to teratogens, head trauma that may result from maltreatment, and malnutrition.

The second question regards *what* strategy an investigator should use if he or she decides to ask the question of whether disorganized/disoriented behavior is the result of the relationship, neurological impairment, or both. Five possible approaches are described below.

(a) One possibility is to consign the "neurological Ds" to error variance. Especially when the target sample is a low-risk sample, an investigator could simply tolerate that disorganized/disoriented attachment strategies may reflect heterogeneous causes, including maltreatment, unresolved mourning of the caregiver for his or her parents (Main & Hesse, 1990), and/or neurological impairment. Of course, it is important to consider carefully what is consigned to error variance as a function of the hypothesis that the investigator is testing. If the hypothesis to be tested is that a component of the parent/child interaction mediates D attachment status and unresolved mourning of the caregiver for his or her parents, then confusing the potential causes of a child's attachment status obviously would be foolish.

(b) A second approach is to screen low-risk samples for certain events that sometimes lead to neurological impairment. In this case, samples could be constructed to exclude, for example, infants who are prenatally exposed to teratogens, born prematurely, and/or who are born with extremely low birthweights.

(c) A third possibility is to compare the child's behavior within the episodes of the Strange Situation by *comparing* the child's behavior during interactions with the parent and with the stranger. If behaviors that have a possible neurological cause are observed only with the mother, then one could count these behaviors toward the final attachment rating. The mother, however, is present alone for 57% of the Strange Situation, the stranger present alone for only 29%, and both are present 14%, and so there is a higher probability that *any* behavior will be observed more with mother than stranger. Alternatively, if behaviors that may be dually caused are observed in the presence of both stranger and mother, a somewhat higher probability obtains that the behavior in question is neurological in nature. As one reviewer correctly pointed out, an additional strategy is to calculate a proportional index. A comparison could be made between: (a) the number of times neurological D indices are observed when the infant is with *mother* divided by the amount of time mother and infant are together in the Strange Situation, and (b) the number of times neurological D indices are observed when the infant is with the *stranger* divided by the amount of time stranger and infant are together in the Strange Situation.

(d) The most substantive approach is to go beyond the attachment paradigm itself. Two possible strategies may be used. First, one could obtain information concerning the neurological impairments that are typical of children with certain diagnoses. This, in fact, was the strategy chosen by Capps et al. (1994) in their study of attachment in autistic children. A group of behaviors, stereotypies, was ruled out as an index of disorganized/disoriented attachment. As a result, children were judged to be securely attached if their reunion behavior was judged to be secure even with the presence of stereotypic behavior. The difficulty with this group approach is that there is marked heterogeneity in children who are diagnosed with the same disorder. Some children show just enough symptoms to meet diagnostic standards and other children are more profoundly affected. In the case of autism, for example, autism is differentiated from Asperger's Disorder (American Psychiatric Association, 1994). Although both disorders share qualitative impairment in social interaction, children with Asperger's do not demonstrate impairment in communicative ability. An alternative strategy is to interview each primary caregiver about his or her individual child's special behavior. This approach has the potential advantage of being able to provide more specific information regarding which behaviors may be attachment-related *for that infant* and which behaviors may represent neurological deficits exhibited in the child's general functioning. Hand-flapping, for example, may represent a greeting response to the mother for one autistic child, but for another autistic child it may be exhibited only when the child is anxious or stressed, and for another child may be a general stereotypic behavior in many situations. Information at the individual level enables different inferences to be made about the same behavior across different children (Rogers, personal communication).

(e) A more powerful approach is to obtain more complete medical information for each individual child. When behaviors occur that may reflect neurological impairment, we suggest that the preference be to obtain relevant medical information pertaining to the individual child. This could include using the infant's medical history as known by the parent, a review of hospital and outpatient medical records, and/or a complete neurological evaluation. The latter would be most telling, as it would include a careful history-taking as well as a *current* neurological examination. In general, history-taking includes a family medical history and a complete developmental history of the infant. A family medical history is important because conditions that are heritable may be found. A complete developmental history, including pregnancy, birth, and the neonatal period, provides information on factors that may influence the developing central nervous system. The neurological exam could further determine whether certain infant behaviors were actually signs of neurological dysfunction, and whether further tests were needed to pinpoint certain disorders (e.g., EEG, MRI).

Ruling Out Neurological Abnormalities

It is important to examine the constellation of indices used in assigning a primary D attachment rating in order to rule out neurological impairment as a possible cause for disorganized or disoriented behavior in the Strange Situation. In general, the assumption that a D classification results from the quality of the attachment relationship alone will be warranted if a primary D classification is observed *without* the inclusion of any of the dual indices that are underlined and boldfaced in Table 3.

If, however, the behaviors that constitute the judgment to assign a child to the D category include the neurological indices, the second step is to examine the type of behaviors that are included. If a D is assigned on the basis of both an italicized neurological indicator *and* an italicized nonneurological indicator, a D classification should be assigned on the basis of quality of the relationship with questions regarding neurological involvement. If the neurological index is the only italicized indicator noted, one should examine medical information or—if the child has a diagnosed condition, such as mental retardation or autism—obtain information from primary caregivers regarding the typical behavioral repertoire for that individual child. After examination of this information, decisions can be made whether the observed behavior for that child represents quality of attachment or neurological impairment.

Alternatively, infants can obtain a D classification when the lesser, non-italicized indicators are frequent enough, intense enough or clearly lacking in rationale. In this case, it is crucial to determine whether any of the "neurological indices" are included to determine a primary D classification. A very careful coding of all behaviors observed in the Strange Situation will enable the coder to determine if the "neurological indices" noted are due to reunions or are observed more generally. Again, medical information and an assessment of parental report of individual behaviors that may be characteristic of each individual child also would be useful.

EMPIRICAL EVIDENCE

In an initial study that examined attachment behavior and noted the neurological signs described in the present manuscript, Barnett and his colleagues (in press) calculated the percentage of neurological indices in children with cerebral palsy and children with a nonneurologically based birth defect (i.e., facial cranial abnormalities). This study was especially well-designed, in that the children with cerebral palsy were compared to a group with nonneurological birth defects (instead of a sample of children without any medical conditions). Any differences between the two groups, therefore, would be due to neurological impairment and not to a diagnosed medical condition. The investigators found that children with cerebral palsy exhibited significantly more neurological D indices than did children with facial cranial abnormalities. Moreover, the two groups did not differ on the number of nonneurological D indices. These data provide preliminary evidence that the neurological indices noted in the present manuscript reflect behavior that stems from neurological disorder.

The Barnett et al. (in press) study, however, did not use strategies (d) and (e) outlined above, and so definite understanding of how neurological disorders influence assigning D type status has still not been empirically tested. Without the use of these strategies, Barnett and his colleagues reported no significant differences in attachment status between children with neurologically and nonneurologically based birth defects, even though children with cerebral palsy evidenced significantly more neurological D indices than children with facial cranial abnormalities. As a result, it will be important to validate the present approach of classifying behaviors that could reflect both disorganization due to parental (or environmental) factors and neurological (or child) factors.

WHEN BEHAVIORS ARE MULTIPLY DETERMINED

In this chapter, we framed the question as "Does neurological disorder *or* history of interactions between infant and parent cause disorganized and disoriented behavior?" Framing the question as an either/or question, however, prematurely forecloses our understanding of the relation between neurological development and interactions between infants and their caregivers.

Evidence is beginning to accrue that infants' developing neurological system and aspects of interactions between infants and primary caregivers are interdependent. Biobehavioral organization has been shown to be different between infants who are securely and insecurely attached; infants who are categorized as disorganized/disoriented have been shown to have significantly higher cortisol levels than securely attached infants (Hertsgaard, Gunnar, Erickson & Nachmias, 1995; Spangler & Grossman, 1993). The failure of the attachment system to buffer the stress response may either influence or reflect differences in biological functioning between disorganized/disoriented and securely attached infants.

High-risk infants present a particular dilemma in determining the variables that lead to or sustain disorganized/disoriented attachment. Research on attachment status and prenatal substance abuse is a case in point. Infants who were prenatally exposed to PCP and cocaine, for example, were much more likely to be insecurely attached (with a predominant classification of D) than a carefully selected control group (Rodning, Beckwith, & Howard,

1991). And, infants who were prenatally exposed to drugs demonstrated disorganized functioning in unstructured play *and* the Strange Situation, although the disorganization was more prominent during more structured assessments.

Prenatal exposure to teratogens may influence neurological integrity as well as reflect maternal characteristics that lead to less than optimal parenting skills. Studies are beginning to unravel the relation between infant neurological impairment, maternal characteristics, and infant outcome. Through the technique of path analysis, for example, O'Connor, Sigman, and Kasari (1992) investigated how alcohol use during pregnancy begins a cascade of changes that results in less than optimal attachment. Prenatal alcohol consumption was related to negative affect in the infant. Negative affect, in turn, was related to qualities of the mother-infant interaction. Maternal interaction, in turn, was related to infant attachment status. This model fits the data better than other models that included mothers' *post*natal alcohol consumption or models that assumed direct pathways between prenatal alcohol consumption and the other three variables (infant negative affect, maternal interaction, and infant attachment). Prenatal substance abuse, therefore, may influence the neurological integrity of the infant that, in turn, initiates a series of changes in the quality of the mother-infant relationship.

Infants who are neurologically impaired also may be at higher risk for maltreatment from caregivers. Disorganized and disoriented behavior in the Strange Situation may reflect an infant version of posttraumatic stress disorder (PTSD). PTSD is one possible result of parental maltreatment (among other causes) and a number of authors suggest that PTSD symptoms influence neurological functioning (Kolb, 1987; van der Kolk, 1988). Since infants' central nervous system is immature, the effects of maltreatment may be more powerful during this time period (Drell, Siegel, & Gaensbauer, 1993).

In a clinical, high-risk sample with multiple risk factors, the direction of causality may be complex, and it may be difficult to disentangle relational history from prior or resulting neurological development. Interactions between infants and parents may be influenced by the neurological condition of the infant *and* these interactions may influence the development of the immature neurological system. The resulting neurological impairment may then have further influences on parental interactions that, in turn, sustain a particular pathway of neurological functioning. In these cases, coders may decide that a D classification is due both to qualities of the attachment relationship *and* characteristics of the infants' neurological system. Such complexity further underlines the need for caution in interpretation of D indices that reflect neurological impairment.

FUTURE RESEARCH

In the present chapter, we noted possible D signs that have the potential to represent a child's neurological impairment as well as attachment related behaviors. Empirical validation of these potential "neurological D" signs was evidenced in a report showing that children with neurologically based birth defects had significantly more neurological D signs than children with nonneurologically based birth defects (Barnett et al., in press). Further research should be directed toward replicating the above findings, both with children diagnosed with cerebral palsy (as in the Barnett et al. study), and also with children with other medical conditions that involve neurological impairment (e.g., Down syndrome and autism).

Further, several strategies were described to ascertain with greater certainty whether a child should be assigned a primary disorganized/disoriented attachment classification. Other researchers have taken into account the context of a child's capacities when coding behavior in the Strange Situation, and have therefore adjusted the criteria for assessing D behaviors to the sample (Capps et al., 1994). We attempted to provide a template that specifies explicit rules for adjusting how to code behavior in the Strange Situation by the five strategies outlined above. This template has the promise of providing researchers with guidelines regarding potential adjustments when assessing children with known or suspected neurological impairment. A further research direction is to test the efficacy of using these strategies. One potential research design is to compare (a) children who are at high risk due to *neurological impairment,* (b) children who are at high-risk due to *environmental* factors (e.g., as a function of parental maltreatment), and (c) children who are at high risk as a function of both *neurological impairment and environmental* risk. This design will enable an assessment of the validity of the present system of differentiating indices that may be due to disorganized/disoriented attachment and/or neurological factors in the child.

One of the most exciting questions regards the interplay between neurological development and quality of the attachment relationship. Traditionally, attachment theorists often focus on interactions between infants and their mothers or maternal characteristics as explaining differences in child outcome to the relative exclusion of neurological considerations. One of the aims of this chapter is to emphasize the importance of addressing the issue of neurological contributions to the disorganized/disoriented attachment category, especially in high-risk children.

III. MATERNAL SENSITIVITY, CHILD FUNCTIONAL LEVEL, AND ATTACHMENT IN DOWN SYNDROME

Leslie Atkinson, Vivienne C. Chisholm, Brian Scott, Susan Goldberg, Brian E. Vaughn, Janis Blackwell, Susan Dickens, and Frances Tam

A principal hypothesis of attachment theory is that parental sensitivity influences the quality of parent-child attachment (Ainsworth, Blehar, Waters, & Wall, 1978; Bowlby, 1969). This association has been verified meta-analytically (de Wolfe & van IJzendoorn, 1997). By demonstrating that intervention aimed at maternal sensitivity may increase the probability of secure attachment, van IJzendoorn, Juffer, and Duyvesteyn (1995) showed that the link between these two constructs might be a causal one. Nevertheless, in a review of the sensitivity-attachment literature, Schneider-Rosen and Rothbaum (1993) pointed out that there remains relatively little research addressing maternal precursors of security, considering the detail with which theorists have described the experiential origins of attachment relationships.

The dearth of predictive research with atypical samples confirms this observation (van IJzendoorn, Goldberg, Kroonenberg, & Frenkel, 1992). This paucity handicaps theorizing in so far as atypical samples provide the greatest yield of atypically attached individuals (e.g., Crittenden, 1985; Radke-Yarrow, Cummings, Kuczynski, & Chapman, 1985; Vaughn et al., 1994). Only through the longitudinal study of atypical attachment can we fully encompass the human attachment experience. Furthermore, Schneider-Rosen and Rothbaum (1993) argued that the modest association between parental sensitivity and attachment security indicates the need for an interactional approach to attachment security; we must move beyond main effects to investigate both parental and child contributions to the relationship. In assessing interactional hypotheses, the use of atypical samples is indicated for two reasons. First, in the single longitudinal investigation of an atypical sample, the data linking maternal sensitivity and quality of attachment were ambiguous. Studying low birthweight, preterm infants, Goldberg, Perotta, Minde, and Corter (1986) predicted that mothers of secure (B2, B3) children would prove more sensitive than mothers of "marginally secure" (B1, B4) youngsters, and that mothers of insecure (A, C) infants would be least sensitive. These hypotheses were verified with the 6-week data. But the 3-, 6-, and 9-month observations revealed a tendency for mothers in the marginally secure group to present less sensitively than mothers of insecure babies, although mothers of the secure group consistently proved most sensitive. These ambiguous findings suggest the need for further longitudinal research with atypical samples, utilizing more complex hypotheses.

A second reason for using atypical samples to study interactional hypotheses lies in the fact that such samples may facilitate distinction of mother and child contributions (Ganiban, Barnett, & Cicchetti, in press). Samples can be chosen that best elucidate the impact of those mother or child factors under consideration. The focus of the present study involves the contribution of child cognitive/adaptive functioning to attachment security. Theorists (Bowlby, 1969; Case, 1996; Main, Kaplan, & Cassidy, 1985; Waters, Kondo-Ikemura, Posada, & Richters, 1995) have long acknowledged the integral role of cognition in the formation of attachment relations. At the level of "goal corrected behavior," intelligence presumably helps in balancing attachment needs and exploratory proclivities while interacting with an only somewhat predictable mother and an environment in constant flux. At the representational level, Bowlby (1969) discussed "internal working models." These are not mere reproductions of past experience; reality is not simply "apprehended." As their name implies, "working" models are active constructions that are restructured in response to environmental, affective, and cognitive change (Case, 1996; Main, Kaplan, & Cassidy, 1985). Again, intellectual capacity is presumably instrumental in these constructions and reconstructions. It is possible, however, that empirical concentration on normally intelligent children has disguised the fundamental contribution that intelligence makes to the formation of an organized attachment pattern, or to organized patterns as we currently conceptualize them.

For these reasons, we chose to investigate the contribution of intelligence to attachment security using a sample of children with Down syndrome (DS). Such a sample provides both etiological homogeneity and functional heterogeneity (Cicchetti & Beeghly, 1990), albeit at the price of generalizability, given that DS is only one form of mental retardation. Moreover, we already know that samples with DS include a large percentage of children (by some estimates, about 50%) who are atypically attached (van IJzendoorn et al., 1992; Vaughn et al., 1994).

Specifically, we evaluated the influence of child intellectual/adaptive functioning and maternal sensitivity, and their interaction, on attachment security. One test of whether assessments of attachment are valid among atypical samples involves evaluating whether the same correlates characterize attachment for these groups as is the case in normative samples. To the extent that maternal sensitivity is related to attachment security among children with DS, attachment assessments can be considered to have convergent validity. To the extent that measures of developmental functioning are associated with attachment security, attachment instrumentation lacks discriminant validity. Perhaps most important, though, insofar as sensitivity and developmental competence interact to influence attachment security, to that extent we can begin to understand the atypical nature of attachment in DS.

Attachment and Down Syndrome

Investigators have both denied and affirmed the validity of the Strange Situation in the context of DS.

The Strange Situation Is Invalid With DS. Initial Strange Situation studies of infants/toddlers with DS (Berry, Gunn, & Andrews, 1980; Cicchetti & Serafica, 1981; Serafica & Cicchetti, 1976) revealed a consistent pattern of findings: (a) When compared to children without developmental disability, children with DS were less likely to signal attachment needs, approach their mothers, or make physical contact on reunion; (b) nevertheless, children with DS evinced awareness of episodic changes in the Strange Situation; (c) while the distress of children with DS was comparatively muted, (d) the organization of their responses was similar to those of children without DS (for further discussion of these findings, see Ganiban et al., in press). None of the early investigators explicitly commented on the validity of the Strange Situation with DS, but the fact that they did not offer security classifications may reflect reservations.

Thompson, Cicchetti, Lamb, and Malkin (1985) confirmed and expanded the above findings, offering attachment classifications in a footnote. The distribution they found (19% avoidant, 69% secure, 12% ambivalent) was similar to that reported for typical samples. Nevertheless, Thompson et al. refrained from interpreting the classificatory data, expressing concern about the potentially confounding effects of neurological deficit (see also Pipp-Siegel, Siegel, & Dean, this volume).

Vaughn and his colleagues (1994) reported on three samples with DS, including the children coded by Goldberg (1988) and the sample used in the present study (at first assessment). Vaughn et al. found that, among children who were classifiable according to the traditional ABC scheme, the distribution of classifications was not unlike that of a nonhandicapped control sample. When Unclassifiable (U) youngsters, with heterogeneous forms of atypical behavior, were included in the comparison, however, only 46% of the DS sample was considered secure (B), significantly fewer than the 60% secure in the nondisabled comparison sample. Because of the large proportion of U children (42%, compared with 3% for the control sample) and the small percentage of B youngsters, Vaughn et al. speculated that the Strange Situation may not be valid with DS samples.

Evaluating 34 atypical samples against 21 samples of typical mother-child dyads, van IJzendoorn et al. (1992) found that the sample with DS (one of three samples from the Vaughn et al., 1994, study) was the only "child problem" group that deviated significantly from the norm. This deviation was attributable to the many "unclassifiable, D-like" (p. 853) relationships. Van IJzendoorn et al. (1992) hypothesized that "limited behavioral and cognitive abilities . . . preclude accurate use of the [Strange Situation] classification scheme" (p. 853).

The Strange Situation Is Valid With DS. Despite cautions, many investigators, in some cases the same investigators, have argued or implied that the Strange Situation is valid with DS. As mentioned, Thompson, Cicchetti et al. (1985) expressed reluctance to interpret their classificatory data. Noting the analogous organization of attachment in children with and without DS, however, Cicchetti and Beeghly (1990) observed that most children with DS are securely attached. Based on the large number of Unclassifiable children, van Ijzendoorn, Goldberg et al. (1992) and Vaughn, Goldberg et al. (1994) warned that the Strange Situation may be invalid in the context of DS. Nonetheless, while acknowledging classificatory difficulties, Goldberg (1988) concluded, "the procedure can readily be used" (p. 182). Or again, while Vaughn et al. (1994) questioned the validity of the Strange Situation with this population, they also argued that the Unclassifiable toddlers were bona fide insecure ("Insecure- unclassifiable"), often meeting "disorganized" (D; Main & Solomon, 1990) criteria. Thus, while investigators recommended caution with reference to the Strange Situation and DS, they were not entirely convinced by the caveat. Of course, the crucial shortcoming with respect to validity judgments, negative or positive, lies in the fact that all observations have been confined to the Strange Situation itself, without reference to home behavior of mother or infant (Thompson et al., 1985; Vaughn et al., 1994).

Hypotheses

Based on the aforementioned considerations, we evaluated the following hypotheses: (a) Maternal sensitivity is related to attachment security as measured in the laboratory (with the Strange Situation) and at home (with the Attachment Q-set; Waters & Deane, 1985). Positive findings will extend a central hypothesis of attachment theory (regarding the longitudinal relations between maternal sensitivity and attachment security) beyond typical samples; (b) Strange Situation classifications are related to secure base behavior in the home (as measured with the Attachment Q-set; Waters & Deane, 1985). Pertinent to Hypotheses a and b, the Strange Situation was originally validated with reference to infant and maternal behavior at home. Positive findings will indicate that observations of muted secure base behavior and atypical attachment (reviewed above) are not simply artifacts of the Strange Situation ecology and are relevant, on a daily basis, to the developing mother-child relationship; (c) Child adaptive and cognitive functioning is related to Strange Situation classifications and Attachment Q-set scores. Positive findings could invalidate the Strange Situation and the Q-set for use with developmentally delayed samples, or dramatically change the way these instruments are used in the context of developmental disability. Positive findings also would indicate the importance of cognitive functioning in the typical and atypical manifestation of attachment relationships; (d) The interaction of maternal sensitivity and child adaptive/cognitive functioning predicts attachment security, such that both sensitive mothering and relatively high cognitive functioning are prerequisite to secure attachment. Crittenden (this volume) forwarded such a hypothesis in her survey of attachment and intellectual deficits.

We measured four constructs over a 2-year period—maternal sensitivity, child cognitive functioning, child adaptive functioning, and attachment security. All constructs were assessed at least twice.

METHODS

Participants

Participants (also described elsewhere; Atkinson et al., 1995) were 53 infants/toddlers (31 boys, 22 girls) with chromosomally confirmed DS and their mothers. Dyads were recruited from four early intervention programs in and around Toronto over a 2-year period. In the agency where the project was based, we solicited mothers' participation by phone. Of 51 mothers contacted, 39 (76%) participated. In the case of the other clinics, we requested that program directors ask interested parents to contact us. This resulted in 17 more participants, but refusal rate is unknown.

Children were between 14 and 30 months chronological age at first observation (M = 19.00, SD = 4.55). This age variability was necessary to obtain a sample size adequate for analysis of unevenly distributed classificatory data. Approximately 7 months later, at the time of the first Strange Situation, the youngsters earned Bayley mental age equivalents of between 12 and 23 months ($M = 16.24$, $SD = 3.71$; mean Bayley Mental Developmental Index = 49.50, $SD = 15.46$). At the time of the second Strange Situation, the children's chronological ages ranged from 29.98 to 57.43 months ($M = 42.21$, $SD = 7.83$). The Vineland age equivalent varied between 12.00 and 45.50 months ($M = 22.72$, $SD = 6.72$; mean Vineland Adaptive Behavior Composite = 62.00, $SD = 9.55$; we do not offer Bayley age equivalents, as 19 children exceeded ceiling at the 42-month assessment).

The mothers' mean age on first visit was 33.04 years ($SD = 6.44$). Family socioeconomic status was determined according to mother's or father's occupation, whichever was higher, using an index for occupations in Canada (Blishen, Carroll, & Moore, 1987). This index has a mean of 42.74 ($SD = 13.28$). The mean of the present sample was 47.65 ($SD = 13.19$). With reference to employment, 22 (42%) mothers were full-time homemakers, 9 (17%) were employed part-time, and 25 (47%) held full-time positions outside the home. In seven cases (12.5%), mother was a single parent. With reference to siblings, 12 (21.4%) of the children had none, 27 (48.2%) had one, 12 (21.4%) had two, and 5 (9.0%) had three or more at the start of the study.

Sample size varies across analyses for several reasons. Technical/procedural difficulties spoiled three of the 26-month Strange Situations and two of the 42-month procedures. At various points over the 2-year study, 12 families discontinued their involvement (seven families relocated, four wished to terminate, and one child died; we found no significant differences, across a variety of demographic and attachment variables, between these families and families who continued to completion). At the 26-month assessment, we could not elicit the cooperation of one child to complete the Bayley; at the 42-month assessment, we were unsuccessful with three youngsters. Three children were excluded from analysis because of low functional level and one because of autistic features.

Procedures

This study involved four sets of home observations and two laboratory visits over two years (see Table 4 for overview).

Strange Situation. The children's behavior in the Strange Situation (Ainsworth et al., 1978) was coded into the patterns A, B, C, D, and U. Children classified U were a heterogeneous group; they were coded U if

TABLE 4

OUTLINE OF PROCEDURE

Location	Procedures
19 months	
Home	Feeding sensitivity observation
	Nonfeeding sensitivity observation while mother
	responded to demographics interview
	Vineland Adaptive Behavior Scales
23 months	
Home	Feeding sensitivity observation
	Nonfeeding sensitivity observation while mother
	completed variety of inventories
	Vineland Adaptive Behavior Scales
26 months	
Lab	Strange Situation
	Nonfeeding sensitivity observation while mother
	completed inventories
	Vineland Adaptive Behavior Scales
Home	Bayley Scales of Infant Development
42 months	
Home	Bayley Scales of Infant Development
	Vineland Adaptive Behavior Scales
	Attachment Q-set
	Maternal Behavior Q-set
	Strange Situation

their behavior did not resemble any of the four defined profiles, at least to some extent. Many, but not all, youngsters classified as U did not show concern, or even evidence of noticing, that their mothers had left the room. Or, if they were disturbed at separation (especially in Episode 6), they became calm in the presence of the stranger. For these children, it was difficult to describe the relationship with mother as "special" in any way. Mothers and strangers might be treated similarly. In typically developing children, this pattern would be consistent with the Avoidant classification, but for the children with DS, interaction with mother was not avoided especially, it simply was not sought out. Again, children classified as U were heterogeneous, differing from recognized classifications in different ways.

Because children with DS may show disorganized/disoriented behavior due to neurological deficit, the D classification was assigned conservatively. Children were classified D only where they met three or more of the Main and Solomon (1986, 1990) criteria (for listing, see Pipp-Siegel et al., this volume; e.g., fearful facial expression at reunion, elevated evidence of freezing, backwards approach, falling on approach, using markedly different strategies across the Strange Situation [e.g., avoidance on first reunion with mother, resistance on second reunion], stereotypies in reunion episodes but not in other episodes). Pipp-Siegel and her colleagues (this volume) discussed the danger of miscoding neurological signs as indices of D. They noted, for example, that freezing may be indicative of petit mal seizures; hitting at the face, if conceptualized as a misguided movement, may reflect dyspraxia (see also Ganiban et al., in press). So, although we emphasized (a) nonneurological, (b) convergent, and (c) extreme signs of D, we cannot guarantee that coding in the present study was not confounded by neurological involvement. For the purposes of future research, we endorse the strategies recommended by Pipp-Siegel et al. to reduce misclassification (see Barnett et al., in press, for empirical illustration of Pipp-Siegel et al.'s system).

Based on 15 randomly selected tapes, two coders (B. Vaughn, S. Goldberg) obtained 73% agreement (Cohen's $\kappa = .53$, $z = 2.26$, $p = .01$) when all classifications were included, 80% ($\kappa = .61$, $z = 2.44$, $p < .01$) when tapes were scored Secure (B) versus nonsecure (A, C, D, U). The same coders reported A, B, C reliability figures of 75% and 85% using two other samples with DS (Vaughn et al., 1994). Coders were blind to all other observational data.

Attachment Q-Set. After training with the 90-item Attachment Q-set (Waters & Deane, 1985) for 3 months, two or three observers visited the study mothers and their children at home for two, 2-hr periods. Visits were made approximately 1 week apart. Observations of the first five families were discussed at length by two or three observers and ratings were made by consensus. For reliability purposes, two observers sorted 33 Q-sets independently. Interobserver agreement (r) for the Attachment Q-set varied between .60 and .91, with a median of .77. All observers were blind to Strange Situation findings, but one of the observers had participated in the Ainsworth sensitivity ratings (see below), introducing the possibility of bias. Very similar intercorrelations were found regardless of which observer's ratings were used, however, suggesting that observer bias did not contribute significantly to variable interrelations. The mean Attachment Q-set scores of the two observers who made all visits were used in the analyses.

Maternal Sensitivity. We assessed sensitivity six times over the 2-year period, in different locations (in and around the home and in the laboratory), in different contexts (in unstructured interaction, during feeding, while mother was being interviewed, and while she was completing paper-and-pencil measures), and with different observational procedures.

The five mother-child observations (two at 19 months, two at 23 months, and one at 26 months) prior to and immediately after the first Strange Situation were videotaped and scored by two or three raters according to scales developed by Ainsworth, Bell, and Stayton (1971). The scales include numerous discrete behaviors, but we confined our analyses to four general constructs: maternal sensitivity (mother responds promptly and appropriately to child's signals), acceptance (mother values the child's will), cooperation (mother's interventions are minimally intrusive), and accessibility (mother is psychologically available as needed). The concurrent ratings of these variables correlated highly (.63 to .93, median = .80) in the present sample, suggesting they do not measure distinct constructs. We therefore averaged the scores to form a single sensitivity composite for each observation. Three raters independently coded 22 randomly selected tapes. Interobserver reliability (r) varied between .92 and .94. Because two of the raters coded all tapes, they were not blind to earlier sensitivity ratings. The third rater was blind, however, and the high reliability between all three raters attenuates the possibility of bias.

The Ainsworth sensitivity ratings remained stable across all five observations (r = .39 to .81, median = .70). For the purposes of measurement reliability and parsimony of presentation, and because initial analyses showed little difference in the predictive capacity of the various ratings, we combined all Ainsworth ratings into a single composite.

The Maternal Behavior Q-set (Pederson et al., 1990), used at 42 months only, focuses on maternal responsiveness to child signals. Maternal Behavior Q-sort scores have been related to Strange Situation and Attachment Q-set findings (Moran et al., 1992; Pederson et al., 1990). In the present sample, Maternal Behavior Q-sort scores correlated .68 with the composite Ainsworth sensitivity rating. Maternal Behavior Q-sort observations were made concurrently with Attachment Q-set observations and using the same procedures, as described above. Interobserver reliability (r) for the Maternal Behavior Q-sort varied between .54 and .95 (median = .81).

Developmental/Adaptive Scales. Children's cognitive functioning was assessed with the Mental and Psychomotor Development components of the Bayley Scales of Infant Development (Bayley, 1969). Because concurrent administrations of these scales were highly correlated (.53 at 26 months, .66 at 42 months) and because analyses using both scales yielded similar findings, we only report findings based on the mental component.

At the 42-month assessment, 19 children exceeded Bayley ceiling. Rather than confound results with the introduction of a second instrument, or reduce the generalizability of findings by excluding these children from analyses, we employed raw scores. While raw scores are not a measure of intelligence, discounting, as they do, age of the child, they nevertheless represent level of cognitive development; children who earn higher scores are more cognitively adept than children who earn lower scores, regardless of age. We acknowledge, though, that the use of raw scores does not address the issue of ceiling effects; findings with respect to cognitive functioning

53

at the 42-month Strange Situation may be conservative. Nevertheless, the issue of ceiling effects did not apply to the 26-month assessment; insofar as the 26-month and 42-month findings were comparable, we can be assured that ceiling effects did not distort 42-month findings too dramatically. All assessments were augmented with the Vineland Scales of Adaptive Behavior (Sparrow, Balla, & Cicchetti, 1984) administered to the mother.

RESULTS

The 26-month Strange Situation distribution was: 21 (40%) B, 4 (8%) avoidant (A), 2 (4%) ambivalent (C), 1 (2%) D, and 25 (47%) U. At 42 months, classifications were 19 (47.5%) B, 3 (7.5%) A, 0 C, 5 (12.5%) D, and 13 (32.5%) U. The mean Attachment Q-set score was .19, SD = .22, range = −.38 to .56.

Given small cell sizes due to classification of participants into five groups, all analyses were conducted twice. Following Vaughn et al. (1994), we compared children who showed an optimal attachment-exploratory balance or smoothly functioning secure base behavior (B) to those who did not (A, C, D, U). But because the status of the U classification is uncertain (it is not clear whether U implies *in*security or just lack of secure base behavior, i.e., *non*security), we repeated all analyses, comparing Secure children with Unclassifiable youngsters (and excluding the A, C, and D classifications due to small combined sample size). We reasoned that if the mothers of U children were less sensitive than mothers of Secure youngsters, such a finding might suggest actual insecure attachment, rather than just an absence of secure base behavior. A finding that Unclassifiable children are cognitively less adept than their Secure peers might suggest that the U classification reflects cognitive impairment rather than attachment security. This second set of analyses (comparing Secure to Unclassifiable youngsters and excluding A, C, and D) involved the loss of 5 or 7 dyads, depending on the analysis, with consequent decrease in statistical power.[1]

Maternal Sensitivity

Table 5 shows mean sensitivity scores for dyads classified Secure, Unclassifiable, and Insecure (combined A, C, D) in the Strange Situation

---

[1] We also completed a third set of analyses, comparing Secure youngsters to Unclassifiable + disorganized children. Because the pattern of findings closely replicated that of the Secure versus Insecure + Unclassifiable results, the former are not reported here.

TABLE 5

SENSITIVITY AND STRANGE SITUATION CLASSIFICATIONS

Classification	Ainsworth Rating				MBQS			
	N	Mean	SD	t	N	Mean	SD	t
26-month Strange Situation								
Secure	21	5.99	1.54		17	.61	.18	
Insecure	7	5.09	1.61		5	.23	.57	
Unclassifiable	25	5.23	1.19		23	.40	.34	2.53*
Insecure + Unclassifiable	32	5.13	1.25	2.23*	28	.37	.38	2.84**
42-month Strange Situation								
Secure	19	6.29	1.19		18	.62	.18	
Insecure	8	4.89	1.67		8	.33	.32	
Unclassifiable	13	5.06	1.29	2.57*	13	.41	.40	
Insecure + Unclassifiable	21	4.97	1.45	2.92*	21	.38	.37	2.65*

Note. t = t-value comparing designated group with Secure group; MBQS = Maternal Behavior Q-sort (Pederson et al., 1990).

*$p < .05$. **$p < .01$.

at mean ages 26 and 42 months. In the case of the 26-month Strange Situation, we included both prior/concurrent sensitivity ratings and sensitivity ratings made subsequent to the Strange Situation in order to facilitate data interpretation (i.e., to assess the relation between sensitivity and attachment security not only in terms of its statistical significance, but also in terms of its consistency). In all instances, mothers of Secure children were most sensitive, mothers of Insecure children least sensitive. Mothers of Secure children invariably proved significantly more sensitive than mothers in the Insecure + Unclassifiable (A, C, D, U) group.

Findings were less consistent when mothers from the Secure group were compared to mothers in the Unclassifiable (U) group, although it must be remembered that the loss of seven or eight children (depending on analysis) reduced analytic power. Maternal Behavior Q-sort scores were significantly higher for mothers whose children were classified Secure, as opposed to Unclassifiable, in the 26-month Strange Situation; Ainsworth sensitivity ratings were significantly higher in mothers whose children were classified Secure, versus Unclassifiable, in the 42-month Strange Situation. Ainsworth ratings were not significantly related to 26-month classifications, however, nor were Maternal Behavior Q-sort scores significantly associated with 42-month security classifications (although in both cases, the associations approached significance, $p < .10$).

We also analyzed relations between maternal sensitivity and Attachment Q-set scores. In the first set of analyses, all cases were included. In the second set, we removed children whom had been coded Insecure (A, C, D) in the

42-month Strange Situation. This permitted analysis similar to the Secure-Unclassifiable comparisons outlined above. The Ainsworth sensitivity rating did not significantly predict Attachment Q-set score ($r = .23$, ns, when all children were included in the analysis; $r = .16$, ns, when Insecure children removed). To assess the relation between Maternal Behavior Q-sort and Attachment Q-set scores, we correlated the Maternal Behavior Q-sort score of each rater with the Attachment Q-set rating of the other (following Pederson et al., 1990). With all children included in the analysis, $r = .51$, $p < .0005$; with the Insecure (A, C, D) youngsters removed, $r = .38$, $p < .05$. The mothers of Secure children appear more sensitive than the mothers of the Insecure + Unclassifiable and Unclassifiable youngsters.

Table 6 summarizes the findings as effect sizes. Where the Secure group was compared to the Insecure + Unclassifiable group, effect sizes ranged from .23 to .50, median = .42. Where Secure children were compared to Unclassifiable youngsters, effect sizes varied between .16 and .42, median = .385. According to Cohen (1988), an effect size of .30 is medium strength, .50 is strong. By these criteria, the median effect sizes in this study are medium-strong.

Developmental Functioning

Table 7 shows mean Bayley scores by attachment classification. Concurrent 26-month Bayley and Strange Situation assessments were not related. However, 26-month Bayley scores significantly predicted 42-month attachment classification. This finding was replicated with the concurrent 42-month Bayley and Strange Situation assessments and with the Attachment Q-set (Table 8). Secure youngsters earned higher Bayley scores than did Insecure + Unclassifiable and Unclassifiable children.

The effect sizes linking Bayley scores and attachment security are highly variable (Table 8). When all children are included in the analyses, effect sizes

TABLE 6

MATERNAL SENSITIVITY AND ATTACHMENT SECURITY: EFFECT SIZES

Sensitivity Measure	Effect Size (r)		
	26-month SS	42-month SS	AQS
Secure vs. Insecure + Unclassifiable			
Ainsworth rating	.30	.43	.23
MBQS	.41	.44	.50
Secure vs. Unclassifiable			
Ainsworth rating	.28	.42	.16
MBQS	.39	.41	.38

Note. SS = Strange Situation; AQS = Attachment Q-set (Waters & Deane, 1985); MBQS = Maternal Behavior Q-sort (Pederson et al., 1990).

TABLE 7

BAYLEY MENTAL DEVELOPMENT SCORES AND STRANGE SITUATION CLASSIFICATIONS

Classification	26-Month Bayley				42-Month Bayley			
	N	Mean	SD	t	N	Mean	SD	t
26-month Strange Situation								
Secure	20	53.80	12.64					
Insecure	6	51.00	15.44					
Unclassifiable	21	47.57	18.56	1.25				
Insecure + Unclassifiable	27	48.33	17.69	1.18				
42-month Strange Situation								
Secure	18	59.06	16.40		16	144.94	9.38	
Insecure	6	44.50	14.07		6	133.83	13.64	
Unclassifiable	10	38.20	9.98	3.65**	11	125.45	19.27	3.51**
Insecure + Unclassifiable	16	40.56	11.65	3.75**	17	128.41	17.53	3.35**

Note. Means and standard deviations for 42-month Bayleys are in raw score format; t = t-value comparing designated group with Secure group; MBQS = Maternal Behavior Q-sort (Pederson et al., 1990).

**p < .01.

TABLE 8

BAYLEY MENTAL SCORES AND ATTACHMENT SECURITY: EFFECT SIZES (r)

Attachment Measure	Effect Size (r)	
	26-month Bayley	42-month Bayley
Secure vs. Insecure + Unclassifiable		
26-month SS	.03	
42-month SS	.36*	.52**
AQS	.34*	.28
Secure vs. Unclassifiable		
26-month SS	.01	
42-month SS	.47*	.57**
AQS	.35*	.57**

Note. SS = Strange Situation; AQS = Attachment Q-set (Waters & Deane, 1985); 42-month Bayley are Bayley Mental Development raw scores.

*p < .05. **p < .01.

range from r = .03 to .52, median = .34. When the analyses include only Secure and Unclassifiable youngsters, effect sizes range from .01 to .57, median = .47. The median effect sizes are moderate and strong, respectively, and appear roughly comparable to the effect sizes linking sensitivity and attachment security (see Table 6).

We also analyzed the relations between Vineland Adaptive Behavior Composite, as derived at 19, 26, and 42 months, and concurrent or subsequent attachment quality. Of 16 analyses, only one proved significant; the

42-month Composite was significantly associated with the 42-month Attachment Q-set score when all children (Secure and Insecure + Unclassifiable) were included in the analysis ($r = .37$, $p < .05$). The lack of findings vis-á-vis the Vineland might appear anomalous, given the expectedly significant correlations between Bayley and Vineland indices (26-month Bayley correlated with 26-month Vineland at $r = .30$, $p < .05$; 42-month Bayley correlated with 42-month Vineland at $r = .54$, $p < .001$). Nevertheless, it is statistically explicable. To illustrate, if the correlation between Bayley and Vineland is .54, and that between Bayley and Attachment Q-set is .57 (Table 8), then the correlation between the Vineland and the Attachment Q-set can vary between −.38 and 1.00. (Stanley & Wang, 1969).

SENSITIVITY, DEVELOPMENTAL LEVEL, AND ATTACHMENT SECURITY

Having examined maternal sensitivity and developmental functioning separately, we scrutinized their joint effect on attachment security with a set of 5 regression analyses (forward stepwise logistic regression, likelihood ratio selection, in the case of the Strange Situation; forward stepwise multiple regression in the case of the AQS). Each analysis included three independent variables (viz., maternal sensitivity, child competence, and the sensitivity × competence interaction) predicting concurrent and/or subsequent attachment security. The five analyses were as follows: (a) The mean Ainsworth sensitivity rating, the 26-month Bayley Mental Development Index, and their interaction, were used to predict 26-month Strange Situation classifications; (b) These same predictor variables were regressed against 42-month Strange Situation classifications; (c) They also were regressed against 42-month Attachment Q-set scores; (d) Maternal Behavior Q-sort scores, 42-month Bayley Mental raw scores, and their interaction were used to predict 42-month Strange Situation; (e) They also were used to predict Attachment Q-set results. Due to small sample size, we did not exclude Insecure (A, C, D, U) children from any of these analyses.

In each equation, a single predictor met the inclusion criterion ($p < .05$), or almost did so, while the other two predictors met the criterion for exclusion ($p > .10$). Thus, (a) logistic regression analysis showed a possible relation between the interaction of Ainsworth sensitivity rating and Bayley Mental Development Index in predicting 26-month Strange Situation classification (64.01% cases correctly classified, $B = .004$, $SE\ B = .003$, Wald($1df$) = 2.68, $p = .10$); (b) This same sensitivity by mental competence interaction was significantly related to 42-month Strange Situation classification (73.53% cases correctly classified, $B = .02$, $SE\ B = .01$, Wald($1df$) = 7.89, $p = .005$). (c) And again, multiple regression showed that this same interaction was significantly associated with Attachment Q-set score ($B = 6.18E\text{-}04$, SE

$B = 2.26\text{E-}04$, $\beta = .41$, $R^2 = .17$, $p < .01$). In addition, (d) the interaction of Maternal Behavior Q-set score and 42-month Bayley Mental raw score significantly predicted concurrent Attachment Q-set findings ($B = .003$, $SE\ B = 6.68\text{E-}04$, $\beta = .55$, $R^2 = .30$, $p = .0003$). The single exception to these interactional findings involved the fact that (e) 42-month Bayley Mental raw scores significantly predicted concurrent Strange Situation findings (68.75% cases correctly classified, $B = .12$, $SE\ B = .04$, $Wald(1df) = 7.00$, $p < .01$). Although not entirely consistent, these regression equations, each of which included two main effects (Bayley score, maternal sensitivity rating) and their interaction, overwhelmingly indicated that the combination of relatively high cognitive competence and maternal sensitivity were most advantageous for attachment outcomes.

STABILITY AND CONSISTENCY OF ATTACHMENT SECURITY

The data offer little evidence of stability in attachment security from 26 to 42 months. Whether the entire sample is used, or only the Secure and Unclassifiable children, a nonsignificant 62% of the children receive consistent Strange Situation classifications (for Secure vs. Insecure + Unclassifiable dyads, $\kappa = .23$, $z = 1.45$, ns; for Secure vs. Unclassifiable dyads, $\kappa = 26$, $z = 1.44$, ns; the percentage of stable dyads was comparable in the Secure, Insecure + Unclassifiable, and Unclassifiable groups). Furthermore, while there is some evidence for the stability of security from the 26-month Strange Situation to the Attachment Q-set where Secure and Unclassifiable dyads are concerned, $t(38) = 1.70$, $p < .05$, one tailed, this finding was not replicated with reference to Secure and Insecure + Unclassifiable dyads, $t(41) = 1.19$, ns. Given the small sample sizes involved and the slight inconsistencies in the data, we refrain from drawing any conclusions about the stability of attachment in DS (although see Ganiban et al., in press, for discussion). It should be noted, however, that the 62% stability figure found here is comparable to the percentages cited by various other investigations (for discussion, see Belsky, Campbell, Cohn, & Moore, 1996; Mangelsdorf et al., 1996). Vaughn, Egeland, Waters, and Sroufe (1979), for example, reported exactly this stability figure in their high-risk Minnesota sample.

A significant association did emerge when concurrent Strange Situation and Attachment Q-set findings were analysed. Children classified Secure in the Strange Situation at 42 months obtained higher ratings than their Insecure + Unclassifiable, $t(37) = 3.43$, $p < .0005$, and Unclassifiable, $t(29) = 2.50$, $p < .01$, peers on the Attachment Q-set. Effect sizes were strong, $r = .49$ and $.42$, respectively. Children who display secure behavior in the laboratory are more likely to do so at home.

59

DISCUSSION

We assessed four hypotheses: (a) maternal sensitivity, (b) child function-ing, and (c) the interaction of these factors are related to attachment security, and (d) attachment classification in the laboratory is associated with secure base behavior at home. Each of these hypotheses will be considered in turn.

Maternal Sensitivity and Attachment Security

A minority of children with DS exhibited secure behavior (40%) and a high proportion were Unclassifiable (47%) in the Strange Situation at 26 months (13% showed clear signs of insecure attachment). A similar distribu-tion held when the children were assessed an average of 16 months later (47.5% B, 32.5% U, 20% insecure).

Classifications from both Strange Situations, as well as scores from the Attachment Q-set conducted at mean age 42 months, were related to measures of maternal sensitivity taken over a 2-year period under varying conditions. Mothers of Secure children were more sensitive than mothers in the Insecure + Unclassifiable (A, C, D, U) group and the Unclassifiable (U) group. Median effect sizes linking sensitivity and attachment security were medium-strong ($r = .42$ and .385 when Secure children were compared to Insecure + Unclassifiable and Unclassifiable children, respectively).

The data indicate that maternal sensitivity and attachment security are linked among children with DS and that this association holds for children of all classifications. The finding is particularly important for children who are considered Unclassifiable. As discussed above, there has been confusion as to whether this form of attachment is an artifact of the nonstressful nature of the Strange Situation for these children, or whether it reflects maternal behavior in the home (Vaughn et al., 1994). The data reviewed thus far support the latter conclusion, although further evidence indicates that the relation between maternal sensitivity and attachment security cannot be explained adequately with a simple main effects model, as discussed below.

Child Adaptive/Cognitive Functioning and Attachment Security

Crittenden (this volume) posed the question of whether attachment organization covaries with intellectual functioning. Previous investigators refrained from classifying or interpreting the Strange Situation behavior of children with DS for fear that it might be confounded by impaired develop-ment. The present findings answer the question and support the caution. Mental functioning, as assessed with the Bayley, predicted concurrent and subsequent behavior in the Strange Situation; lower functioning individuals were less frequently classified secure than were higher functioning children. This represents a confound, to be sure, making the Strange Situation difficult to use for the purposes of inferring quality of prior caregiver-child interaction.

But cognitive functioning also correlates with Attachment Q-set scores, indicating that the cognitive confound is not merely an artifact of laboratory ecology, as discussed above. It cannot be argued, for example, that the behavior of children with DS in the Strange Situation simply reflects a failure to experience separation or stranger anxiety. Lower functioning individuals also showed less secure behavior in the home, on a day-to-day basis, than did comparatively competent children.

The question becomes, why do so few of these children manifest secure attachment behaviors, either in the laboratory or in the home? One possibility is that the difficulty reflects behavioral incompetence on the part of the child. Puzzling over the muted Strange Situation responsivity of another sample with DS (mean age = 33.5 months), however, Serafica and Cicchetti (1976) pointed out that the children were capable of the signaling and approach behaviors necessary to using the mother as a secure base. The same could be said of the current sample. The sufficiency of their behavioral repertoire was further verified by the Vineland Adaptive Behavior Scales. Indeed, at the 42-month assessment, the children's mean behavioral age equivalent was close to that of a 2-year-old. So, the failure of these children to display strong secure base behaviors does not reflect behavioral deficit. This may be why the links between Vineland and attachment indices were weak.

One might then ask, does the muted display of secure base behavior reflect the cognitive limitations integral to DS? Pondering this issue, Serafica and Cicchetti (1976) noted that much younger samples have mastered object permanence, the basic cognitive prerequisite to secure base behavior. Our own data present a paradox. On the one hand, the youngsters in this sample do have sufficient cognitive capacity to form goal corrected partnerships. Indeed, the mean Bayley mental age at 42-month assessment was 18.95 months (with no one scoring below the 12-month level and 19 children excluded from this analysis because they exceeded the Bayley ceiling age equivalent of 30 months). On the other hand, the significant and consistent correlations between Bayley score and attachment status reflect the fact that more cognitively competent children were more likely to form secure attachments. This paradox may suggest that something more than the basic competence to coordinate with mother is requisite to the maintenance of intimate relationships. This "something" may be distinct from cognition (otherwise the basic cognitive prerequisites would suffice to engender goal-corrected partnerships), yet related to cognition (as suggested by the significant correlations between Bayley scores and quality of attachment). In the following section, we discuss two related correlates of cognition that might explain the aforementioned paradox, inefficient affective signaling and insufficient motivation.

SENSITIVITY, COGNITION, AND SECURITY

Regression analyses showed that the interaction between maternal sensitivity and child cognitive functioning predicted attachment security: relatively high levels of both increased the probability of secure attachment and deprivation of either attenuated that probability. This interactional finding is especially noteworthy because, for a variety of methodological and statistical reasons, interaction effects are difficult to demonstrate in field studies, even when there are strong theoretical reasons for believing they exist (MacCallum & Mar, 1995; McClelland & Judd, 1993).

It has been argued that infants with developmental disabilities may not "provide the stimuli and responses necessary to support sensitive interaction with their caregivers" (Moran et al., 1992, p. 439; see also Stone & Chesney, 1978). This hypothesis appears probable in light of delays/deficits in a host of communicatory modes and attachment-related behaviors, for example, looking, eye contact, vocalizations, crying, smiling, turn taking, laughter, maternal referencing, initiative taking, approach, and language (Berger & Cunningham, 1986; Bridges & Cicchetti, 1982; Cicchetti & Sroufe, 1976; Crown, Feldstein, Jasnow, Beebe, & Jaffe, 1992; Cytryn, 1975; Emde & Brown, 1978; Emde, Katz, & Thorpe, 1978; Gunn, Berry, & Andrews, 1982; Rothbart & Hanson, 1983; Sorce & Emde, 1982; Sorce, Emde, & Frank, 1982; Stoel-Gammon, 1990).

More specifically, Emde et al. (1978; see also Ganiban et al., in press) showed that there is more uncertainty or noise in the *emotional* signaling of infants with DS than is the case for nonhandicapped children. This noise renders their communication difficult to interpret. Harding (1984) argued that maternal attributions of meaning influence the frequency and quality of mothers' responses to their children, thereby facilitating synchronous mother-child interaction. The significance of affective communication to the attachment relationship is illustrated in some earlier Strange Situation observations.

> In the sense elaborated by Bowlby . . . the attachment system fails to achieve its set goal of contact and arousal reduction for the children with Down syndrome. Even when the DS children made approaches with appropriate signals for contact, mothers and strangers rarely completed the contact, presumably because the child was not able (at her or his prevailing level of arousal) to accompany the approach with

distress signals . . . that typically elicit being picked up. (Vaughn et al., 1994, p. 105)

A second, related, hypothesis is motivational in nature. It may be that the behavioral skills necessary to coordinate with mother are distinct from those requisite to the maintenance of intimate relationships. Fogel (1993) discussed intimacy as shared meaning that is created through coregulated interactions (p. 90) involving, inter alia, thought and memory. Moreover, the creation of meaning is the motivation for communication and for the persistence of relationships over time (p. 89; see Crossley, 1996, for similar treatment of shared meaning). One possibility is that, for some children with DS (specifically, those coded U), cognitive limitations undermine the development of shared meanings and consequent motivation to form goal-corrected partnerships (which is most powerfully signaled through affective display). Such a hypothesis would explain why these children, who are motorically and cognitively capable of secure base behavior, evince it relatively rarely. Longitudinal work is necessary to assess the role of developing cognitive capacity in the ontogeny of attachment relationships (see also Crittenden, this volume).

Now, we are not suggesting that the same transactional hypotheses apply to all mother-child dyads. It is possible that children with DS, who are either unresponsive or who do not seem to react in profoundly different ways to mother and stranger (i.e., children coded Unclassifiable), constrain parental sensitivity. In other cases (i.e., Insecure toddlers) insensitivity on the part of the caregiver may restrict the development of competent secure base behavior. Even in the case of unresponsive children, however, it is important to note that some (sensitive) mothers of infants with severe mental handicaps can interpret extremely subtle cues (Yoder & Feagans, 1988). Within this single population, the interactional links between maternal sensitivity, cognitive development, and child attachment security may vary with dyad. Moreover, the cognition/sensitivity dynamic may change with the developing capabilities of the child, such that secure base behavior becomes more evident with age. Further longitudinal study of this variation may illuminate the respective roles of caregiver and child, both handicapped and nonhandicapped, in the development of attachment relationships (Crittenden, this volume; see also Pipp-Siegel et al., this volume, for discussion of the transactional nature of attachment security in samples with neurological impairment).

STRANGE SITUATION AND ATTACHMENT Q-SET

It was necessary to evaluate the Strange Situation behavior of children with DS against observations in the home because the Strange Situation was designed to reflect home interaction. When children with DS reacted in muted fashion to the Strange Situation, many investigators (e.g., Berry et al., 1980; Vaughn et al., 1994) assumed that the procedure did not elicit the same quality of attachment behavior as might be exhibited under more ecologically valid conditions. Investigators argued that the Strange Situation imposed less stress on children with DS than on their nonhandicapped peers, such that the former sought less comfort from their mothers.

The present data suggest that the attachment behavior shown in the laboratory is a fair reflection of secure base behavior at home. In fact, the effect sizes linking Attachment Q-set and Strange Situation findings in this sample (.42 and .49 when Secure children were compared to Insecure + Unclassifiable youngsters and Unclassifiable youngsters, respectively) are substantially larger than those typically reported. Thus, van IJzendoorn, Vereijken, and Riksen-Walraven (in press) reported a combined effect size of .23 in their meta-analysis of Attachment Q-set, Strange Situation convergence studies.[2] The present findings indicate that the majority of youngsters with DS had not developed smoothly functioning secure base behavior, even by toddlerhood and the preschool years. This state of affairs pertains both to emergency responses (as measured in the Strange Situation) and to more routine circumstances, where attachment and exploration is relatively stress-free (as evaluated with the Attachment Q-set).

Moving beyond within-sample comparisons, we point out that while children classified Secure in the Strange Situation were rated higher than their Insecure + Unclassifiable and Unclassifiable peers in the Attachment Q-set, the Secure children's scores were still lower than those reported for samples of typical children. Thus, the Secure children in the present sample obtained a mean Attachment Q-set score of .30. This is substantially lower than the .50 Security score reported by Vaughn and Waters (1990) for nonhandicapped Secure children and is comparable to the security scores of nonhandicapped avoidant and ambivalent youngsters (.23 and .25, respectively). Moran et al. (1992) made a similar observation, indicating that the mean Attachment Q-set score of their sample with developmental delay (.27) was substantially smaller than that of a nonhandicapped sample they had assessed earlier (.40; Pederson et al., 1990). The observation that secure children with DS may show less competent secure base behavior than secure, nonhandicapped youngsters suggests that cognition may explain between-sample variation in attachment behavior, as well as within-sample

[2] Van Ijzendoorn et al. (1999) suggested that convergent validity between Attachment Q-set and Strange Situation may be greatest where the children are older, observers (as opposed to family members) make the Q-set ratings, and observation periods are relatively long. This study meets all three of these criteria.

differences. The present findings suggest that even secure children with DS may not fully benefit from a well equilibrated attachment-exploration system. In the context of this volume, these findings suggest that secure attachment in DS may, in itself, be "atypical." Further work is required to determine how secure base behavior, as manifested in atypical samples, differs from secure base behavior as displayed by more typical samples.

FUTURE RESEARCH ON ATYPICAL ATTACHMENT

Attachment security in DS is related to the interaction of maternal sensitivity and cognitive competence. Further longitudinal work is needed to answer questions regarding the implications of this finding for the future socioemotional development of children with DS. For example, Crittenden (this volume) queried whether children with extreme developmental disabilities (who are often considered Unclassifiable with regards to attachment) reorganize to form more sophisticated strategies as they mature. If so, what forms do these reorganizations take? Are they similar to the attachment patterns of younger children, or are they "organized" but qualitatively different from the strategies adopted by individuals without DS? As the caregiver-child relationship itself matures, does the relative influence of mother's sensitivity and child's competence change? What are the implications of the competence-sensitivity interaction for the child's development outside the home, for example, in the formation of friendships?

As Cicchetti and Serafica (1981) observed, "the developmental psychologist concerned with this group is in the unique and enviable position of being able to examine more closely the interaction between nature and nurture in the developing organism" (p. 47). Traditionally, theory has focused on maternal sensitivity as the major influence on attachment security. As research moves towards an emphasis on cognitive factors (van IJzendoorn, 1995), work with samples where both sensitivity and cognition are salient may play an increasingly informative role. Similarly, as we start to explore issues of stability (van IJzendoorn, 1995) and instability (van IJzendoorn et al., 1995) in the intergenerational transmission of attachment security, the study of populations where child characteristics obviously influence the process and/or outcome of that transmission may contribute disproportionately to theory.

More generally, this chapter has two broad implications: (a) The study of atypical populations may provide a rich and diverse source of atypical attachment patterns. In the present case, we were able to explore some of the precursors and correlates of Unclassifiable attachment. Moreover, the heterogeneity of the children so classified presents potential for further exploration based on a refined taxonomy; (b) In explaining atypical attachment, we

65

may have to reach beyond those constructs that traditionally have been central to attachment theory (e.g., sensitivity) to incorporate broader psychological (and other) constructs (in this case, developmental competence). This will serve to extend the nomothetic net of attachment theory, ultimately deepening our understanding of attachment, both typical and atypical, and our comprehension of broader developmental processes.

IV. MATERNAL FRIGHTENED, FRIGHTENING, OR ATYPICAL BEHAVIOR AND DISORGANIZED INFANT ATTACHMENT PATTERNS

Karlen Lyons-Ruth, Elisa Bronfman, and Elizabeth Parsons

A central question in the study of atypical attachment relationships in infancy is whether interactive processes between caregiver and infant are associated with the infant's display of disorganized strategies (Main & Hesse, 1990). Attachment theory locates one central influence on the infant's attachment strategies in the interplay between parent and infant over the 1st year, especially in the degree of sensitive responsiveness to the entire range of the infant's affectively charged communications (Ainsworth, Blehar, Waters & Wall, 1978). Linkages between appropriate parental responsiveness and secure infant attachment strategies have been supported in a number of empirical studies (Ainsworth et al., 1978; Belsky, Rovine, & Taylor, 1984; Grossmann, Grossmann, Spangler, Seuss, & Unzner, 1985; Londerville & Main, 1981; van IJzendoorn, 1995). These earlier studies, however, were undertaken prior to the discovery of the disorganized/disoriented infant attachment pattern. They explored the relation between maternal behavior and the three organized infant attachment strategies only (ambivalent/avoidant/ secure). With the increasing recognition that a sizable proportion of infants from families with serious social risk factors display disorganized forms of attachment strategies, the question of whether disorganized behaviors emerge in the context of particular patterns of parent-infant interaction also must be addressed.

The issues of whether and how mother-infant interactive processes are related to disorganization of infant attachment patterns gains additional importance from recent findings that early disorganized or controlling attachment strategies are related to oppositional or hostile-aggressive behaviors up to age 7 (Lyons-Ruth, Alpern, & Repacholi, 1993; Lyons- Ruth, Easterbrooks, & Cibelli, 1997; Shaw, Keenan, Owens, Winslow, Hood, & Garcia, 1995; see Lyons-Ruth, 1996, for review). Additional work has related disorganized or controlling attachment patterns during preschool to concurrent oppositional or externalizing behavior (Greenberg, Speltz, DeKlyen & Endriga, 1993; Moss et al., 1996, 1998; Solomon, George, & DeJong, 1995; Speltz, Greenberg, & DeKlyen, 1990). Others have described the coercive cycles observed between oppositional preschoolers and their mothers by the time of clinic referral (Campbell, 1991; Patterson, 1982). Less well understood is the extent to which parental coercion develops in response to a temperamentally aggressive or difficult-to-discipline child (Patterson, 1982) or whether the coercive process has deeper historical roots in intergenerationally transmitted patterns of relationship (Elder, Caspi, & Downey, 1986). Observing maternal interactive behavior in infancy and toddlerhood, before the establishment of coercive cycles, can shed light on the extent to which atypical early caregiving contributes to the developmental pathway leading to externalizing syndromes.

A number of studies have related an increased incidence of disorganized infant attachment behaviors to serious maternal risk factors such as maltreatment, depression, adolescent parenthood, or alcohol consumption (Carlson, Cicchetti, Barnett, & Braunwald, 1989b; Crittenden, 1985; Hann, Castino, Jarosinski, & Britton, 1991; Lyons-Ruth, Connell, Grunebaum, & Botein, 1990; O'Connor, Sigman, & Brill, 1987; Teti, Gelfand, Messinger, & Isabella, 1995). Other studies have examined the process of mother-child interaction among these dyads. Several studies have examined interaction during infancy (Hann et al., 1991; Lyons-Ruth, Repacholi, McLeod, & Silva, 1991; Spieker & Booth, 1988) and at least three other studies have explored mother-child interaction at later ages, either among children classified as disorganized during infancy (Main, Kaplan, & Cassidy, 1985) or among children classified as disorganized or controlling at later ages (DeMulder & Radke-Yarrow, 1991; Solomon, George, & Ivins, 1987). The few existing studies provide some support for the hypothesis that less optimal patterns of interaction characterize dyads that include a disorganized infant. Because of the mixed findings and the wide range of parental behaviors and child ages assessed, however, no clear picture emerges of the maternal behaviors involved.

A robust empirical link *has* been established between parental responses to the Adult Attachment Interview and infant disorganized attachment patterns. In a meta-analysis, van IJzendoorn (1995) reported an average effect size of .31 between infant disorganization and classification of responses to the Adult Attachment Interview as unresolved with respect to loss or trauma. Unresolved status is indexed by lapses in the monitoring of reasoning or discourse during loss or trauma-related portions of the interview. Main and Hesse (1990; Hesse, 1996) relate such lapses to the segregation or dissociation of traumatic material in an encapsulated system of consciousness separate from normal processing.

The major theory-based hypothesis that has been advanced regarding mother-child interactive processes among infants with disorganized attachment strategies is Main and Hesse's (1990) formulation regarding frightened or frightening parental behavior. According to Main and Hesse, "the traumatized adult's continuing state of fear together with its interactional/behavioral concomitants (frightened and or frightening behavior) is the mechanism linking unresolved trauma to the infant's display of disorganized/disoriented behaviors" (p. 163). When the current study was designed, Main and Hesse's (1990) hypothesis regarding the central etiological role of frightened or frightening maternal behavior had not been empirically tested. Main and Hesse (1992), however, had developed a coding protocol for assessing frightened or frightening behavior.

We would argue that two related hypotheses regarding parental correlates of disorganized infant attachment patterns also are implicit in the attachment literature. The first hypothesis, which we termed the "failure of repair" hypothesis, is that parental interactive behaviors that exceed the tolerance limits for supporting an organized infant attachment strategy should lead to infant disorganization. That is, parental behavior must be responsive enough that an organized infant strategy "works." For example, an ambivalent infant strategy, to be stable, must work well enough to elicit care ultimately from a reluctant or preoccupied caregiver. Should the rejecting or unresponsive parental responses associated with infant avoidant or ambivalent attachment strategies become even more unresponsive to infant affective communications, the avoidant or ambivalent strategy should break down. The mother's repeated failure to alter her caregiving behavior toward the infant in the face of clear and repeated infant cues should lead to disorganization of infant strategies whether the unresponsive maternal behavior is withdrawing, role-reversing, controlling, or rejecting in form. The derailment of communication between parent and infant in attachment-eliciting contexts should be fear-arousing in itself because the infant will have little sense of influence over the caregiver at times of heightened fear or stress. Lyons-Ruth and colleagues have related such parental failures of response theoretically to the parent's self-protective mechanisms associated with unresolved loss and trauma and Main and Hesse's (1990) "continuing state of fear" (Lyons-Ruth & Block, 1996; Lyons-Ruth, Bronfman, & Atwood, in press).

The second hypothesis, the "competing strategies" hypothesis, posits that a parent who is experiencing a continuing state of fear around attachment needs is likely to experience and display competing parental attachment tendencies toward the infant, much as the disorganized infant displays competing or contradictory attachment behaviors toward the parent.

Caregiving behaviors likely to both reject and heighten infant attachment affects would be examples of behaviors that combine competing dismissing and involving strategies, such as ignoring the infant's distress while asking the infant for a kiss. These three hypotheses (fear-related behavior, failure of repair, and competing strategies) are not mutually exclusive and may be describing interrelated aspects of the parent-child interaction experienced by disorganized infants.

The research base on disorganized infant attachment behaviors indicates that behaviorally differentiated infant subgroups can be identified within the larger disorganized attachment category. Therefore, the different caregiving hypotheses also may be describing aspects of disrupted caregiving that are differentially salient for one or another disorganized infant subgroup. Lyons-Ruth, Repacholi, McLeod, and Silva (1991) reviewed studies that used the disorganized classification system and also reported the data on alternate forced classifications for all disorganized infants. This review revealed that a majority of infants from low-risk samples who were classified in the D category displayed disorganized forms of secure strategies without marked avoidance or resistance (D/Forced Secure or DS; Lyons-Ruth et al., 1991). In contrast, a majority of infants from families with more serious psychosocial risk factors displayed disorganized forms of avoidant or ambivalent strategies (D/Forced Insecure or DI). Analyses *within* a low SES cohort also have confirmed the association between increased incidence of maternal depression, psychiatric hospitalization, or infant maltreatment and increased incidence of DI, but not DS, strategies (Lyons-Ruth et al., 1991).

Disorganized forms of secure approach (DS) strategies and disorganized forms of avoidant or ambivalent behavior (DI) have different correlates in maternal childhood history. DS infant attachment strategies have been associated with maternal histories of loss of a parent in childhood, particularly unresolved losses as coded on the Adult Attachment Interview (AAI; Ainsworth & Eichberg, 1991; Lyons-Ruth et al., 1991; Main et al., 1985). In contrast, DI infant attachment strategies have been associated with a maternal history of foster care, family violence, or abuse (Lyons-Ruth et al., 1991; Lyons-Ruth & Block, 1996). Therefore, the maternal behaviors associated with these disorganized infant subtypes may also differ.

In designing the current study, we noted that the anecdotal observations of frightened or frightening maternal behavior cited by Main and Hesse (1990) are often examples drawn from maternal behavior in the Strange Situation. The Strange Situation has several advantages over other possible assessment settings for evaluating attachment-relevant maternal behavior. Following George and Solomon (1996), we conceptualize the maternal caregiving system as the parental complement to the infant attachment system, that is, the set of parental responses activated to respond to the infant's tendency to seek proximity, contact or comfort when stressed. The Strange Situation is currently the best validated assessment technique specifically designed to activate the infant attachment behavioral system. Attachment behaviors also can be observed at home but are attenuated by the familiarity of the setting (Ainsworth, Blehar, Waters, & Wall, 1978). In addition, at home, attachment-eliciting situations that are responded to by caregiver and infant with distancing and avoidance are more difficult to detect. Infant distancing and avoidance, as well as other attachment-related behaviors, are codable in the Strange Situation because of the known normative eliciting properties of that setting. Thus, we reasoned that maternal attachment-related caregiving responses might best be observed under conditions when the infant's attachment system was known to be aroused. Therefore, we elected to code maternal caregiving behavior in the Strange Situation as a first test of whether particular maternal caregiving responses were associated with the appearance of disorganized forms of infant attachment strategies.

Strange Situation videotapes from an ongoing longitudinal study of infants at social risk were coded for maternal behavior. Infant attachment behavior from these assessments had been coded in an earlier phase of the study (Lyons-Ruth, Connell, Grunebaum, & Botein, 1990). These infant attachment classifications were related both to concurrent family risk factors and to later childhood outcomes, and similar relations between attachment classifications, family risk factors, and childhood outcomes have been found in other studies of both low- and middle-income families, as noted above. Therefore, the infant attachment data from this sample were well supported empirically as a validating criterion for the maternal behavior data.

Because the infants' attachment behaviors also are evident in the Strange Situation, a maternal coding instrument was developed that was closely tied to clearly described maternal behaviors, and coders were used who were not developmental psychologists and were not familiar with the coding procedures for infant attachment behaviors. The cross-situational stability of aspects of maternal interaction observed in the Strange Situation also was assessed in relation to maternal behaviors at home. Maternal behaviors at home had been coded in the infant phase of the study before disorganized attachment behaviors had been described in the literature (Lyons-Ruth, Connell, Zoll, & Stahl, 1987; Lyons-Ruth, Repacholi, McLeod, & Silva, 1991). Therefore, the home coding protocol had emphasized aspects of maternal behavior associated with secure attachment, such as sensitivity, warmth, verbal communication, and tender touching, and did not attempt to include a full array of atypical maternal behaviors now thought to be associated specifically with disorganization.

The current study addressed three questions. First, do mothers of infants who display disorganized attachment strategies behave differently toward their infants than mothers of infants who display organized strategies? Second, do mothers of D infants behave similarly to one another or do DS and DI infant subgroups have different correlates at the level of maternal behavior? Finally, can we demonstrate cross-situational stability for maternal behaviors observed in the Strange Situation?

METHODS

Participants

Participants in the study were 65 low-income mothers and infants (39 boys, 29 firstborns) participating in an ongoing longitudinal study for whom videotaped Strange Situation attachment assessments were available at 18 months of age. Approximately half the sample had been referred to a home-based intervention service because of concerns about the quality of the caregiving environment. The other half of the sample were low income women matched to the referred group on infant age, gender, and birth order, per person family income, and maternal education, age, and ethnicity. Therefore the sample was designed to overrepresent mother-infant dyads considered at risk by area social and health service providers. Sixty-six percent were supported by government assistance and 45% were single parents. Forty-seven percent had their first child before age 20. Sixty-two percent were high school graduates. Nineteen percent of mothers were Black or Hispanic. Nine infants in the sample (14%) were being followed by state social service workers for neglect of the target child or an older sibling. Additional descriptive information is available in Lyons-Ruth, Connell, Grunebaum, and Botein (1990).

Originally 71 families had been videotaped in the Strange Situation (Lyons-Ruth, Connell, Grunebaum, & Botein, 1990) but tapes for six subjects had technical problems that precluded recoding for maternal behavior. One additional tape with areas of sound failure in the first two episodes was not included in the initial analyses relating maternal behavior to infant attachment due to the compromised quality of the maternal data. This tape was judged adequately codeable to contribute to later multivariate analyses once validity of the maternal codes had been analyzed. Of the 64 uncompromised tapes, 11 tapes were used for scale development and 53 were used for validation analyses of infant-mother correspondence. In analyses subsequent to the validation analyses, codes from all 65 tapes were included.

PROCEDURES

Infant Attachment Security. At 18 months of age, mothers and infants were videotaped in the Ainsworth Strange Situation (Ainsworth et al.,

1978). In this procedure the infant is observed in a playroom during a series of eight 3-min episodes in which the mother leaves and rejoins the infant twice. Videotapes were coded for infant attachment behaviors and for the three attachment classifications as described by Ainsworth and her colleagues (1978) and for disorganized/disoriented behaviors as described by Main and Solomon (1990). Pearson correlations between two coders on 12 tapes for the infant attachment behaviors described by Ainsworth et al. (1978), including avoidance, resistance to mother, resistance to stranger, proximity-seeking, contact-maintaining, and crying, ranged from .97 to .72, with a mean of .86. The three original attachment classifications (secure, avoidant, ambivalent) were assigned by both a computerized multivariate classification procedure developed on the original Ainsworth data (Connell, 1976; see Lyons-Ruth, Connell, Zoll & Stahl, 1987, for additional details; see also reference in Richters, Waters, & Vaughn, 1988) and a coder trained by M. Main. Agreement between the two sets of classifications was 86%. Seventy-five percent of the disagreed-upon tapes were later found to meet criteria for the disorganized/disoriented classification. Agreement on the disorganized classification between M. Main and a second coder for 32 randomly selected tapes was 83%, κ = .73. Coder reliability for the 9-point Level of Disorganized Behavior Scale was r = .84.

Infants who were classified as insecure but *not* disorganized were all in the avoidant classification. Of four infants classified as ambivalent at 18 months, all also met criteria for the disorganized/disoriented category and were classified as disorganized. The distribution of attachment classifications was as follows: Secure n = 22, Avoidant n = 13, Disorganized n = 30 (D Forced Secure = 10, D Forced Insecure = 20).

Atypical Maternal Behavior in the Strange Situation. An initial coding system for maternal behavior observed in all episodes of the Strange Situation was first developed on 11 randomly selected Strange Situation videotapes (four Secure, one Avoidant, five D [Forced Avoidant], one D [Forced Ambivalent]). The tapes were viewed blind to infant attachment classification and assigned blind-coded maternal classifications by the third author (EP), a clinical psychology student who worked with adult trauma patients and who was untrained in infant attachment classification. These initial blind classifications were retained so that subsequent to the validation analyses blind-coded data would be available for these pilot tapes as well. Infant attachment classifications were then reviewed and the coding indices were refined nonblind to capture variation in maternal behaviors related to infant disorganization.

These atypical behavior codes were then reorganized by the second author (EB) for ease of coding and expanded to include all items from Main & Hesse's (1992) coding instrument, entitled Frightening, Frightened,

73

Dissociated, or Disorganized Behavior on the Part of the Parent, which describes proposed behavioral indices of frightened or frightening behavior. Items from Sroufe, Jacobvitz, Mangelsdorf, DeAngelo, and Ward's (1985) Boundary Dissolution Scales and Spousal Behavior Scales relevant to infants and toddlers also were added to expand the role confusion codes because indices of role confusion were important aspects of the pilot tapes.

The resulting coding protocol yielded the following measures: (a) frequency of total atypical behaviors, with six subtotals for affective communication errors, role confusion, negative-intrusive behavior, disorientation, withdrawal, and controlling behavior; (b) one qualitative 3-point scale for failure of repair, or the extent of maternal inability to modify her behavior based on repeated infant signals; (c) one qualitative 7-point scale for level of disrupted communication; and (d) a bivariate classification for disrupted or not disrupted affective communication (defined as scores of 5–7 on the Level of Disrupted Communication Scales; Bronfman, 1993). The qualitative scale and classification were included to allow coders to weigh the seriousness of the atypical behaviors observed. Possibly only a few instances of atypical behavior would be displayed but those instances might be disturbing enough to yield a high coder rating on qualitative rating scales. The coding protocol for total atypical behaviors provided a list of codable behavioral examples for each of the six subtypes of atypical behavior, although coders could add additional behaviors that fit the general descriptors for each subtype. Table 9 displays behavioral examples for the five subtypes of atypical behavior that were reliably coded (see below). Full coding procedures are available in Bronfman, Parsons and Lyons-Ruth (1993).

Two new raters were then trained on the 11 pilot tapes using the coding manual. In the training phase, coders first coded each tape blind to both mother and infant attachment classification, then discussed the coding. The primary coder's (EB) frequencies and ratings, as coded blind prior to discussion, were retained. Because the third author (EP) had refined the coding scales based on review of the infant attachment data, however, only her initial blind classifications are completely blind for the 11 pilot tapes.

After training on the 11 pilot tapes, 15 additional tapes, randomly selected from all remaining tapes, were coded by both coders to assess reliability. Intraclass correlation coefficients for the measures were as follows: Total Atypical Behavior Score $r_i = .67$, Affective Communication Errors Subscore $r_i = .75$, Role Confusion Subscore $r_i = .76$, Negative-Intrusive Behavior Subscore $r_i = .84$, Disorientation Subscore $r_i = .73$, Withdrawal Subscore $r_i = .73$, Controlling Behavior Subscore $r_i = .31$, Failure of Repair Scale $\kappa = .74$, Level of Disrupted Communication Scale $\kappa = .93$, Disrupted Communication Classification Agreement = 87%, $\kappa = .73$. Since the Controlling Behavior subscore did not reach reliability, those scores were deleted

TABLE 9

DIMENSIONS OF DISRUPTED MATERNAL AFFECTIVE COMMUNICATION

---

1. Affective Errors

   a. Contradictory cues, e.g., invites approach verbally then distances.

   b. Nonresponse or inappropriate response, e.g., does not offer comfort to distressed infant.

2. Disorientation (items from Main & Hesse, 1992)

   a. Confused or frightened by infant, e.g., exhibits frightened expression.

   b. Disorganized or disoriented, e.g., sudden loss of affect unrelated to environment.

3. Negative-Intrusive Behavior (including frightening items, Main & Hesse, 1992).

   a. Verbal negative-intrusive behavior, e.g., mocks or teases infant.

   b. Physical negative-intrusive behavior, e.g., pulls infant by the wrist.

4. Role Confusion (includes items from Sroufe et al., 1985; Main & Hesse, 1992).

   a. Role-reversal, e.g., elicits reassurance from infant.

   b. Sexualization, e.g., speaks in hushed intimate tones to infant.

5. Withdrawal

   a. Creates physical distance, e.g., holds infant away from body with stiff arms.

   b. Creates verbal distance, e.g., does not greet infant after separation.

---

from the Total Atypical Behavior score and were not used further. Reliability of the Total Atypical Behavior Score with Control items deleted, $r_i = .75$.

The three-level Failure of Repair Scale was originally included to focus the coders' attention on the conceptual importance of this construct in assessing parental behavior. In Parsons' (1991) original work, she had counted the numbers of repeated infant signals and maternal nonresponses in extended sequences in which the infant's communication was never heeded. This proved too cumbersome a procedure for large-scale coding and the attempt to reduce the measure to a three-level scale was not felt to be particularly satisfactory. Because this three-level measure was relatively poorly delineated and proved to be highly correlated with the more fine-grained Level of Disrupted Communication Scale, $r = .73$, it was not analyzed separately here.

Due to the complexity of the coding protocol, separate counts of the behaviors on the Main and Hesse (1992) coding instrument for frightened or frightening behavior (FR) were not initially maintained. Given the interest in those behaviors, however, coding protocols were reviewed again after the initial study was completed and separate counts were generated for the frightened, frightening, dissociated, and role reversed behaviors included in the Main and Hesse (1992) instrument. When considered separately, these codes also achieved adequate reliability as assessed by intraclass correlation: FR (total frightened or frightening behaviors) $r_i = .80$; FR^+ (total frightened, frightening, role reversed, and dissociated behaviors) $r_i = .79$; frightened behavior $r_i = .76$; frightening behavior $r_i = .65$; dissociated behavior $r_i = .65$; role reversed behavior $r_i = .58$. Analyses of Main and Hesse's (1992) frightened or frightening behaviors subset are presented after the analyses of the original set of variables.

Maternal Behavior at Home. Two weeks prior to the Strange Situation assessment, naturalistic mother-infant interaction was videotaped at home for 40 min. Maternal behavior was coded in 10 4-min intervals on 12 5-point rating scales and one timed variable. This coding was carried out during the initial phase of the longitudinal study before infant disorganized attachment patterns had been described and the coding scheme focused on the maternal behaviors that had correlated with secure or insecure infant attachment in previous literature. Behaviors coded included sensitivity, warmth, verbal communication, quality and quantity of comforting touching (physical contact in the service of communicating affection, "touching base," or reducing distress), quality and quantity of caretaking touching, interfering manipulation, covert hostility, anger, disengagement, flatness of affect, and time out of room, rounded to the nearest half minute. (For additional description, see Lyons-Ruth, Connell, Zoll, & Stahl, 1987.) Coders were blind to all other data on the families. Interobserver reliabilities, computed on a randomly selected 20% of the 40-min videotapes, yielded intraclass correlations ranging from .76 to .99. Principal components analyses of the scales yielded two main factors. Factor 1, labeled maternal involvement, accounted for 38% of the variance and included negative loadings (> .50) for maternal disengagement and flatness of affect and positive loadings (> .50) for maternal sensitivity, warmth, verbal communication, and quantity of comforting touch. Factor 2, labeled hostile intrusiveness, accounted for 26% of the variance and included negative loadings (> .50) for quality of comforting touch and quality of caretaking touch and positive loadings (> .50) for covert hostility, interfering manipulation, and anger (Lyons-Ruth, Zoll, Connell & Grunebaum, 1989). These two factor scores were used for data analysis. Home data were missing for one subject.

Infant Negative Affect at Home. Two measures of infant affect during naturalistic observation at home also were coded from the home videotapes by different coders than those who coded maternal behaviors: (a) the number of 20-s intervals in which the infant displayed distress; and (b) the total times anger toward mother, anger toward sibling, displaced anger, and resistance to contact were exhibited (Lyons-Ruth & Block, 1996). Twenty minutes of the 40-min home videotape were coded for infant affect, selecting every other 4-min period for coding. Intraclass correlations between two coders on 20 tapes were as follows: distress $r_i = .74$, anger toward mother $r_i = .77$, anger toward sibling $r_i = .92$, displaced anger $r_i = .92$, and resistance to mother, $r_i = .79$. Infant affect data were missing for two subjects.

Demographic Risk. Nine demographic variables were coded from maternal interviews: mother's minority status (Black or Hispanic), whether mother was a high school graduate, per person weekly income (including government assistance [AFDC] and food stamps), mother's age at birth of the target child, child's birth order, mother's age at the birth of her first child, whether mother was a single parent, whether the family was supported by government assistance, and the number of siblings under age 6.

A cumulative demographic risk score was also computed from maternal interview data by summing the presence of the following factors: mother minority status, no high school diploma, AFDC recipient, no male partner, mother under 20 at birth of first child, more than two children under age 6.

Severe Psychosocial Risk. Severe maternal psychosocial risk was coded as positive if the mother had a documented history of child maltreatment and/or a history of inpatient psychiatric care. Sixteen mothers were coded as positive.

RESULTS

Analytic Strategy

Of the six possible contrasts among infant attachment subgroups, the two questions of primary theoretical interest were, first, whether maternal behavior among disorganized infants differed from maternal behavior among organized infants and, second, whether maternal behavior among DS infants displaying predominantly approach behavior (forced secure subclassification) differed from maternal behavior among DI infants displaying prominant avoidant or resistant behavior (forced insecure subclassification). Given modest cell sizes, planned contrasts were used to test these two primary questions, using T statistics with unequal variance assumptions, with effect sizes evaluated by the eta statistic. Less central comparisons among subgroups were evaluated by post hoc tests protected for multiple comparisons among means (Duncan's Multiple Range Tests). The five subtypes of maternal behavior were analyzed only if differences in the overall frequency of atypical maternal behavior were significant. Cell sizes were too small in the disorganized subgroups to evaluate gender by subgroup interactions, so the interaction between gender and overall attachment disorganization was examined in a separate analysis.

Intercorrelations of Atypical Maternal Behaviors

Table 10 displays the intercorrelations among the five subscores for maternal atypical behavior. The low to moderate intercorrelations indicate that the subscores are not redundant with one another but tap relatively discrete dimensions of maternal behavior. All subscores correlated positively with the total atypical behavior score, however, $rs = .33$ to $.74$.

Do Mothers of Disorganized Infants Behave Differently Than Mothers of Organized Infants?

Atypical Maternal Behavior by Level of Infant Disorganization. The frequency of atypical maternal behavior was significantly correlated with the 9-point scale for level of disorganized attachment behavior displayed by the infant, $r = .39$, $p < .01$. The rated level of disrupted affective communication also was significantly associated with the level of infant disorganization, $r = .42$, $p < .001$, as was the maternal classification as disrupted, $\eta = .31$, $p < .05$. Given the significant associations between infant disorganization and these summary measures, the five subtypes of atypical maternal behavior also were analyzed. Three of the five subtypes were significantly related to level of infant disorganization, including affective communication errors, $r = .32$, $p < .01$, disorientation, $r = .31$, $p < .01$, and negative-intrusive behavior, $r = .31$, $p < .01$.

Atypical Maternal Behavior by Infant Disorganized Attachment Classification. Table 11 displays the mean frequencies and ratings for maternal behavior scores by infant attachment classification, along with effect sizes and significance levels. The first set of analyses assessed whether mothers whose infants displayed disorganized attachment strategies behaved differently

TABLE 10

CORRELATIONS AMONG THE SUBSCORES FOR MATERNAL ATYPICAL BEHAVIORS

Subscore	Disorientation	Negative-intrusive behavior	Role confusion	Withdrawal
Affective errors	.33	.39	.14	.44
Disorientation		.33	.21	.14
Negative-intrusive behavior			.53	−.14
Role confusion				−.26

Note. $N = 53$.

TABLE 11

INFANT ATTACHMENT STATUS AND MATERNAL ATYPICAL BEHAVIOR SCORES

Maternal Atypical Behavior Scores	Infant Attachment Classification				Strength of Association	
	Organized		Disorganized			
	Secure	Avoidant	Forced secure	Forced insecure		
					Org vs. Dis	DS vs. DI
n	18	11	10	14		
Total atypical behaviors	16.00	12.91	16.30	28.71	.34*	.44*
Affective errors	4.94	2.27	5.40	7.14	.28*	.22
Disorientation	1.83	2.73	2.60	5.14	.25	.32
Negative-intrusive behavior	1.89	1.45	1.30	4.93	.27	.49**
Role confusion	3.39	4.91	2.40	9.00	.18	.42*
Withdrawal	3.94	1.55	4.60	2.50	.06	−.44*
Level of disrupted communication	3.28	3.36	3.40	4.93	.31*	.54**
Maternal disrupted classification						
Not disrupted	67%(12)	64%(7)	70%(7)	21%(3)	.24	.49*
Disrupted	33%(6)	36%(4)	30%(3)	79%(11)		

Note. Strength of association is assessed by η statistic, with significance level assessed by *t*-test, except for maternal classification where strength of association is assessed by Φ, with significance assessed by χ^2 or Fisher's Exact Test.

*p <.05. **p <.01.

toward their infants than did mothers of infants displaying organized strategies. Consistent with predictions, mothers of disorganized infants displayed more atypical maternal behaviors in interaction with their infants, $T(44)$ = 2.43, $p < .02$. Given the significantly elevated total scores, the five scores for subtypes of atypical maternal behavior were then analyzed to see which behaviors contributed to the discrimination between organized and disorganized attachment groups. Only the subscores for affective communication errors separately differentiated mothers of organized and disorganized infants, $T(49) = 2.03$, $p < .05$, as shown in Table 11.

The rated level of disrupted communication displayed by mothers in the Strange Situation also was significantly associated with infant disorganized classification, $T(40) = 2.15, p < .04$. The association between maternal classification (Disrupted/Not Disrupted) and infant classification (D/not D) did not quite reach significance, $\chi^2 (1, N = 53) = 3.01, p < .08$. Proportions in each group are shown in Table 11.

Do Mothers of DS Infants Behave Differently Than Mothers of DI Infants?

The second set of analyses assessed whether mothers of infants who displayed disorganized forms of secure behavior (DS) behaved differently than mothers of infants who displayed disorganized forms of insecure (avoidant or ambivalent) behavior (DI). These analyses revealed substantial differences in maternal behavior *within* the disorganized infant group, with mothers of DI infants displaying significantly more atypical behaviors than mothers of DS infants, $T(22) = 2.49$, $p < .02$. Mothers of DI infants were also rated higher on level of disrupted communication $T(15) = 2.80$, $p < .01$, and were more likely to be classified disrupted, Fisher's Exact Test ($N = 24$), $p = .04$, as shown in Table 11.

When the atypical behavior subscores were analyzed, the two D subgroups did not differ significantly in frequency of affective communication errors or in frequency of disoriented behaviors. As was shown in Table 10, scores for role confusion and negative-intrusive behavior were strongly correlated, and mothers of DI infants displayed significantly higher rates of both types of behavior than did mothers of DS infants, negative-intrusive, $T(21) = 2.92$, $p < .01$, role confusion $T(16)$, $= 2.52$, $p < .02$. In contrast, mothers of DS infants exhibited significantly higher rates of withdrawal, $T(13) = 2.10$, $p < .05$.

Given the significant differences obtained in maternal behavior *within* the overall D group, post hoc tests were conducted to compare atypical maternal behaviors of DS and DI subgroups separately to the two organized groups, Duncan's Multiple Range Tests, all $p < .05$. Behaviors of mothers of disorganized-insecure infants differed from the behaviors of mothers in both organized groups, with mothers of DI infants displaying more frequent total atypical behaviors, receiving higher ratings on level of disrupted communication, and being classified more often as disrupted with Φ or η values indexing strength of association ranging from .43 to .55. In addition, mothers of DI infants displayed more disorientation and more role confusion than mothers of secure infants, and mothers of DI infants displayed more affective communication errors than mothers of avoidant infants. In contrast, mothers of infants displaying disorganized forms of secure strategies (DS) displayed more affective communication errors and more withdrawing behaviors than mothers of avoidant infants, but not more than mothers of secure infants. Differences between mothers of avoidant and DI infants were not due to the presence of three DI infants with ambivalent rather than avoidant subclassifications. With mothers of those three infants excluded, all significant differences between mothers of avoidant and disorganized-avoidant infants remained the same, effect sizes .43 to .58.

Given the substantial differences obtained in the interactive behaviors of mothers of DS and DI infants, it also was of interest to refine the analysis of these dyadic patterns by examining more directly the specific infant behaviors exhibited in the Strange Situation in relation to the five dimensions of maternal behavior. Table 12 displays the associations between the five dimensions of maternal behavior and the five central infant behaviors coded as part of the standard scoring for the Strange Situation. Only one subgroup of disorganized infants was included with both groups of organized infants in each analysis. Only one disorganized subgroup was included in each analysis, because it was important to assess whether particular maternal behaviors were correlated with similar infant behaviors across both DS and DI subgroups or whether infant subgroup differences were based partly on different infant responses to similar maternal behaviors. All organized infants were included in both sets of analyses to maintain adequate score variability on maternal and infant measures.

Table 12 reveals several findings of interest. As previously noted, there were two maternal scores on which the two D subgroups did not differ: maternal affective communication errors and disorientation. Each of these maternal behaviors had similar correlates in infant behaviors regardless of the disorganized subgroup included in the analysis, except in the case of infant resistance. In both sets of analyses maternal affective communication

TABLE 12

CORRELATIONS BETWEEN TYPES OF MATERNAL ATYPICAL BEHAVIORS
AND TYPES OF INFANT ATTACHMENT BEHAVIORS

| Infant Attachment Behaviors | Atypical Maternal Behaviors | | | | |
	Affective communication errors	Disorientation	Negative-intrusive behavior[c]	Role confusion[c]	Withdrawal[c]
Infants with organized and disorganized-secure classifications only[a]					
Disorganization	.27*	.24	.10	−.05	.28*
Avoidance	−.25	.26*	.13	.16	−.25
Resistance	.08	.09	.26*	−.02	−.03
Proximity-seeking	.40**	−.07	.17	−.06	.15
Crying	.46**	−.18	.13	−.17	.23
Infants with organized and disorganized-insecure classifications only[b]					
Disorganization	.35**	.34**	.43**	.26*	.05
Avoidance	−.14	.29*	.28*	.31*	−.21
Resistance	.28*	.30*	.14	.09	.00
Proximity-seeking	.31*	−.15	−.09	−.18	.21
Crying	.45**	−.24	−.04	−.07	.25*

[a] $N = 39$; 14 infants classified disorganized-insecure omitted from analyses.

[b] $N = 43$; 10 infants classified disorganized-secure omitted from analyses.

[c] For the DS subgroup negative-intrusive behavior and role confusion were not elevated and for the DI subgroup withdrawal was not elevated (see Table 11), which is likely to have mitigated the relations between those maternal variables and infant behavior in the relevant columns above.

*$p < .05$. **$p < .01$.

errors were correlated with increased infant disorganization, increased proximity-seeking, and increased crying. Infant resistance appeared to be a more individually variable response to maternal affective communication errors, and infants who displayed resistance in combination with crying, proximity-seeking, and disorganization were forced-classified in the DI subgroup, as would be appropriate, and infants who did not display resistance forced-classified in the DS group. In contrast to affective errors, maternal disorientation was significantly associated with increased avoidance in both subgroups. Maternal disorientation also was positively associated with infant disorganization in both subgroups, but the correlation only reached significance for the DI subgroup. Again, infant resistance appeared to be a more individually variable response to maternal disorientation and infants who displayed resistance in combination with avoidance were forced-classified in the DI subgroup.

The patterning of infant behavior to the other three maternal behaviors, withdrawal, negative-intrusive behavior, and role confusion was different for the DS and DI subgroups, but these differences most likely reflected the significant differences in those maternal behaviors exhibited by mothers in the two subgroups. Mothers in the DI subgroup did not show elevated rates of withdrawal, resulting in less variability for the DI analyses, and mothers in the DS subgroup did not show elevated rates of role confusion and negative-intrusive behavior (see Table 11), reducing variability in maternal behavior for the corresponding DS analyses.

For the DI analyses, where elevated levels of maternal negative-intrusive behavior and role confusion occurred, these maternal behaviors were correlated with increased scores for infant disorganization and infant avoidance but not with increased infant resistance. Infant resistance (without disorganization) only emerged as a correlate of maternal negative-intrusive behavior in the DS analyses, where lower levels of negative-intrusive behavior were present. In the DS analyses, where elevated levels of maternal withdrawal occurred, heightened maternal withdrawal was associated only with increases in infant disorganized behaviors, unaccompanied by avoidance, resistance, or proximity seeking. At the milder levels observed in the DI analyses, maternal withdrawal was associated only with increased infant crying.

In summary, these analyses reveal four dyadic correlational patterns contributing to the DI and DS subgroups. In the first pattern, infants displaying disorganized forms of avoidance are more likely to have mothers who exhibit negative-intrusive and role-confused behavior. In the second pattern, infants who display disorganized forms of proximity seeking, forms that may include resistant behavior, are more likely to have mothers who display elevated rates of affective communication errors. In the third pattern, infants who display disorganized forms of mixed avoidance and resistance are more likely to have mothers who exhibit disoriented behavior at high levels. The milder levels of disorientation occurring among mothers in analyses including the DS group (see Table 11) appear to be reliably associated only with infant avoidance. Finally, infants who show disorganized behaviors alone, without associated avoidance, resistance, or proximity-seeking (e.g. dazed wandering, putting head down on the floor) are more likely to have withdrawing mothers.

These significant relations between maternal and infant behaviors do not appear to represent necessary dependencies of one partner's behavior on the other's. One could envision, for example, maternal withdrawal leading to infant avoidance or maternal role confusion leading to increased crying and infant resistance. Instead, these relations begin to sketch out profiles of mother-infant relational organization within the disorganized spectrum.

Subsequent to the validation analyses for the coding system presented above, maternal behavior scores for the 11 pilot subjects and the one subject with partial sound failure on the tape (infant classified avoidant) were added to the database to contribute to analyses with other variables. For the full cohort, relations between maternal and infant attachment data were very similar to those shown in Table 11. The association between maternal D classification and infant D classification, however, reached significance for the full sample with the blind-coded pilot classifications added, $\chi^2(1, N = 65) = 6.62, p < .01, \Phi = .32$.

Given the significant results of the overall analyses, a final review of the coding protocols was conducted to see whether a smaller set of maternal behaviors could be identified that were particularly highly associated with disorganized infant behavior. Code sheets were reviewed with knowledge of infant classification to identify maternal behaviors that occurred at least three times more often among mothers of disorganized infants and that were displayed by at least three mothers. Table 13 lists those behaviors and Table 14 displays their associations with infant attachment classifications. This was a nonblind, optimizing analysis so the results need to be validated in other samples. Results suggest, however, that simpler and more powerful coding protocols for identifying high-risk interactive behaviors could emerge from continued refinements of the coding system. Based on the results in this sample, selecting mothers who displayed none of these serious interactive errors and mothers who displayed four or more would result in relatively pure subgroups of disorganized and nondisorganized infants, with a 9% false negative rate and a 16% false positive rate, as shown in Table 14. It also is notable that the DS subgroup is better discriminated by this set of maternal behaviors.

TABLE 13

SERIOUS INTERACTIVE ERRORS: MATERNAL ATYPICAL BEHAVIORS THAT WERE PARTICULARLY
FREQUENT AMONG MOTHERS OF INFANTS DISPLAYING DISORGANIZED ATTACHMENT STRATEGIES

Does not attempt to soothe the infant when distressed (Aff. Err.)
Laughs while infant crying or distressed (Aff. Err.)
Directs inauthentic "over bright" affect towards infant (Aff. Err.)
Fails to set appropriate limits (Aff. Err.)
Invites approach and then distances (Aff. Err.)
Uses friendly tone while maintaining threatening posture (Aff. Err.)
Directs infant to do something and then not to do it (Aff. Err.)
Does not offer comfort when infant falls (Aff. Err.)
Exhibits frightened expression (Disorient.)
Exhibits sudden change of mood unrelated to the environment, including loss of affect
    (Disorient.)
Handles infant as though inanimate (Disorient.)
Exhibits "haunted" or frightened voice (Disorient.)
Hushes crying infant (Intrus.)
Uses loud or sharp voice (Intrus.)
Speaks in hushed intimate tones to the infant (Role Conf.)
Pulls infant by the wrist (Intrus.)
Mocks/teases infant (Intrus.)
Removes toy despite infant engagement (Intrus.)
Withholds toy from infant (Intrus.)
Holds infant away from body with stiff arms (Withdrawal)

Note. Subscore to which item contributed indicated in parentheses. Aff. Err. = Affective Communication Errors, Disorient. = Disorientation, Role Conf. = Role Confusion, Intrus. = Negative-Intrusive Behavior. All listed behaviors were three times more prevalent among mothers of disorganized infants and were displayed by at least three mothers.

TABLE 14

NUMBER OF MOTHERS DISPLAYING SERIOUS INTERACTIVE ERRORS
BY INFANT ATTACHMENT CLASSIFICATION

Number of Serious Maternal Interactive Errors	Infant Attachment Classification			
	Organized		Disorganized	
	Secure	Avoidant	DS	DI
n	22	13	10	20
0	12	8	2	0
1–3	7	4	3	4
4+	3	1	5	16

Frightened or Frightening Behavior—Separate Analyses

Our coding protocol was not initially set up to yield separate analyses of the frightened or frightening behaviors on the Main and Hesse (1992) coding inventory. Due to the interest generated by Main and Hesse's (1990) hypotheses regarding this class of maternal behaviors, however, separate counts were generated for the frightened, frightening, dissociated, and role-reversed behaviors included in the Main and Hesse (1992) inventory and a second set of analyses was conducted. In reporting these results, the symbol FR refers to frightened or frightening behaviors only; FR$^+$ refers to all four classes of behavior on the Main and Hesse protocol.

Descriptively, 20 mothers, or 31% of the sample, displayed no FR$^+$ behaviors during the Strange Situation and 65% of their infants were securely attached. A majority of mothers who displayed any FR$^+$ behavior displayed more than one type, however, and this was true in all attachment subgroups. Forty-nine percent of mothers displayed frightening behavior, 43% displayed frightened behavior, and 28% and 14% exhibited dissociated or role-reversed behavior, respectively. Role-reversed and dissociated behavior almost never occurred in the absence of other FR$^+$ behaviors, 0% and 3%, respectively, partly because they were displayed less frequently than frightened or frightening behavior. Frightening, dissociated, and role-reversed behaviors were significantly intercorrelated, rs ranging from .32 to .38, all ps < .01, but frightened behavior was independently distributed, rs ranging from .16 to .00.

Using the same planned comparisons and post hoc follow-up tests as before, total frightened or frightening behaviors showed the same relation to infant disorganized attachment classification as did total atypical behavior. Frightened or frightening maternal behaviors (FR) discriminated infants classified as disorganized, $T(45) = 2.32$, $p < .03$, $\eta = .32$, $N = 65$. In addition, mothers whose infants were classified DI exhibited more FR behavior compared to each of the other attachment groups, Duncan's ps > .05, with means of 1.95 (secure), 2.0 (avoidant), 2.3 (DS), and 5.6 (DI). The same results were obtained using the FR$^+$ score (frequency of dissociated and role-reversed behaviors added to the total FR score). Mothers of DI infants also displayed more dissociative behaviors than mothers of secure infants and displayed more frightening behaviors than mothers of secure or avoidant infants, Duncan's $p < .05$, but did not differ from other groups in frequencies of frightened or role-reversed behavior, although means of the DI subgroup were highest on all scores. Similar to results of the total atypical behavior scores, mothers of DS infants did not differ from mothers of organized infants in any of these analyses.

As shown in Table 15, however, a more subject-based analysis of patterns of behavioral organization across all four types of FR$^+$ behavior yielded different results. These analyses revealed that, as a group, mothers of DS infants did display a distinct pattern of behavior that distinguished them both from mothers of organized infants and from mothers of DI infants. Mothers of DS infants were more likely than other mothers to exhibit frightened behavior at moderate but not extreme levels and without associated elevations in frightening, dissociated, or role-reversed behavior. This was

85

TABLE 15

THE PROPORTIONS OF INFANTS IN EACH ATTACHMENT CLASSIFICATION WHOSE MOTHERS
DISPLAYED A PARTICULAR PATTERN OF FRIGHTENED OR FRIGHTENING BEHAVIOR

Maternal Frightened or Frightening Behavior	Infant Attachment Classifications			
	Secure	Avoidant	Disorganized	
			DS	DI
n	22	13	10	20
No FR+ behavior[a]	.59 (13)	.23 (3)	.20 (2)	.10 (2)
Mild frightened pattern[b]	.14 (3)	.23 (3)	.50 (5)	.10 (2)
Mild frightening, dissociated, or role-reversed pattern[c]	.18 (4)	.46 (6)	.20 (2)	.25 (5)
High frightened, frightening, dissociated or role-reversed behavior[d]	.09 (2)	.08 (1)	.10 (1)	.55 (11)

Note. N = 65, cell *n*s in parentheses.

[a] *FR+* refers to all behaviors on the Main and Hesse (1992) coding protocol.

[b] No single *FR+* score over 4; frightened behavior score within one point of frightening score; no dissociation or role reversal scored.

[c] No single *FR+* score over 4; frightening behavior predominates or dissociation or role reversal scored.

[d] Scores over 4 on any single type of *FR+* behavior.

termed a fearful-inhibited pattern. Fifty percent of mothers of DS infants displayed this pattern of behavior, compared to 14% and 23% of mothers of secure and avoidant infants, respectively, and 10% of mothers of DI infants. Consistent with previous linear analyses, higher levels of frightened behavior, as well as frightening, dissociated or role reversed behaviors, were displayed by mothers of DI infants, as also shown in Table 15. Because of small expected cell sizes, Table 15 was collapsed into two orthogonal two-way tables to test whether mothers of DS infants differed separately from mothers of organized infants and from mothers of DI infants, DS versus Org/Fearful versus all other, Fisher's Exact Test ($N = 45$), $p = .05$, $\Phi = .32$; DS versus DI/Fearful versus all other, Fisher's Exact Test ($N = 30$), $p = .03$, $\Phi = .44$.

Therefore, effects associated with frightened maternal behavior were nonlinear. Milder levels of frightened maternal behavior, occurring in the absence of frightening, dissociated, or role-reversed behavior, were associated with disorganized-secure infant attachment behavior. In contrast, higher-intensity frightened behavior or frightened behavior co-occurring with heightened frightening, role-reversed, or dissociated behavior was associated with disorganized-insecure infant behavior.

These analyses also revealed that maternal frightened and maternal dissociated behaviors had different correlates in infant behavior and should not be combined in a single score as was done in the disorientation subscore of our atypical behavior coding protocol. Dissociated maternal behaviors were related to DI infant behavior, whereas effects of fearful maternal behaviors depended on both the intensity of the fearfulness and the presence of other FR+ behaviors.

In addition, it is important to note that the FR$^+$ behaviors on the Main and Hesse (1992) protocol constituted only 17% of the behaviors coded in the larger study as atypical. With all FR$^+$ behaviors removed from the total atypical behavior score, the remaining atypical behaviors still reliably discriminated mothers of organized and disorganized infants, $T(46) = 2.69$, $p < .01$, $\eta = .36$, $N = 65$. In addition, DS and DI mothers did not differ reliably in the display of the remaining atypical behaviors, $T(21) = 1.89$, $p < .07$, as they had in the display of FR$^+$ behaviors. These findings indicate that FR$^+$ behaviors are embedded in a broader context of disrupted affective communication between mother and infant.

Is There Cross-Situational Stability for Maternal Behaviors Observed in the Strange Situation?

In order to assess whether maternal atypical behavior in the Strange Situation was situation-specific or whether it was predictive of similar interactive behavior in other settings, maternal atypical behavior in the Strange Situation was correlated with maternal behavior observed at home. Maternal behavior at home had been coded earlier in the study before infant D behavior had been described (Lyons-Ruth, Connell, Zoll, & Stahl, 1987). Prior analyses of maternal behavior at home had yielded two orthogonal summary factor scores, one indexing degree of involvement with the infant and one indexing extent of hostile-intrusive behavior. These dimensions were similar to two of the subscores contributing to the measure of total atypical maternal behavior in the Strange Situation; the score for withdrawal and the score for negative-intrusive behavior. The other three atypical behavior subscores did not have counterparts in the coding system used for home behavior (role confusion, disorientation, affective communication errors). Both maternal withdrawal and maternal negative-intrusive behavior in the Strange Situation were significantly correlated with similar behaviors observed at home, SS Withdrawal by Home Involvement, $r = -.29$, $p < .02$, $N = 64$, SS Negative by Home Hostile-Intrusive, $r = .33$, $p < .01$, $N = 64$.

Correspondence in maternal behavior across settings also was assessed at a more general level of analysis. For the home data, a single global dichotomous classification code (Optimal/Non-Optimal maternal behavior) had also been created (see Lyons-Ruth et al., 1991). This code had been created from the two factor scores by designating mothers in the "best" one third of the sample on both factor scores (high in involvement/low intrusiveness) as showing optimal behavior. Mothers who showed optimal behavior at home were significantly more likely to be classified Nondisrupted in the Strange Situation, $\chi^2(1, N = 64) = 3.95$, $p < .05$, $\Phi = .25$, with 82% of optimal mothers classified in the Nondisrupted group in the Strange Situation, compared to

49% of nonoptimal mothers. These significant relations between maternal behaviors at home and maternal interaction in the Strange Situation increase confidence that the maternal behaviors coded in the present study were representative of the mother's behavior more generally and were not particular to the constraints of the laboratory situation or to the infants' behaviors in the Strange Situation.

Maternal behavior displayed in the Strange Situation also was significantly related to infant affect displayed at home. Because our only a priori hypothesis regarding infant affect was that more disrupted maternal communication should be associated with less optimal infant affect regulation, the two measures of infant affect at home were analyzed in relation to the maternal level of disrupted communication rating. Increased infant distress at home was associated with higher levels of maternal disrupted communication in the Strange Situation, $r = .25$, $p < .05$, $N = 63$; infant anger/resistance at home was not, $r = .07$, ns. To examine the specific maternal behaviors contributing to the association with infant distress at home, distress was analyzed in relation to the five maternal atypical behavior scores shown in Table 11. Only the subscore for affective communication errors predicted infant distress at home, $r = .30$, $p < .02$, $N = 63$.

Given the relation between maternal behavior in the Strange Situation and infant distress at home, it also is notable that infant distress at home was related to the infant's display of disorganized attachment behavior in the Strange Situation, $F(1, 67) = 4.31$, $p < .05$, $\eta = .25$, while infant anger/resistance at home was not, $F(1, 67) = .01$, ns. ($N = 69$ for these analyses not involving maternal behavior). Frequency of infant distress at home was equally elevated in the two disorganized subgroups, with means of .51 ($n = 10$) and .53 ($n = 23$) for DS infants and DI infants, respectively, compared to a mean of .24 ($n = 36$) for infants displaying organized strategies. Regression analysis further indicated that maternal D behavior and infant D behavior were redundant in predicting infant distress at home, with infant D behavior failing to account for additional variance in infant distress after maternal D behavior was entered, maternal D $F(1, 61) = 4.21$, $p < .04$, infant D Fchg (2, 60) = 2.53, ns. The relation between infant disorganization and infant distress, however, indicates that increased infant distress at home should be viewed as one correlate of a disorganized attachment relationship rather than simply as a correlate of less optimal maternal behavior.

Demographics, Severe Psychosocial Risk, Infant Gender, and Atypical Maternal Behavior

Demographic factors were not associated with maternal D classification, probably because the sample was homogeneous in low socioeconomic status and because matching of referred and nonreferred mothers on SES variables mitigated relations between SES variables and other risk factors. Demographic factors alone also have failed to predict other outcomes in this sample (Lyons-Ruth et al., 1990; Lyons-Ruth et al., 1991). The measure of cumulative demographic risk did not approach significance, $F(1, 63) = .59$, *ns*. Among the nine separate variables assessed (mother's age at birth of first child, mother's age at birth of this child, per person weekly income, AFDC status, mother's minority status, mother's education, single parent, number of children under 6, infant birth order), the only significant association was in a direction opposite to that expected, in that mothers with more children under 6 were *less* likely to be classified as disrupted, $\tau = -.26$, $p < .02$, perhaps because they were more experienced parents. Having more children under six did not lessen the incidence of infant disorganization in the Strange Situation, however, $\tau = -.03$, *ns*, so number of children could not account for the earlier relations reported between maternal behavior and infant disorganization. There also were no differences by infant gender, with mothers of boys and mothers of girls equally likely to be classified as disrupted (46% both sexes). Mothers who had a history of psychiatric hospitalization or child maltreatment *were* more likely to be classified disrupted, $\chi^2(1, N = 65) = 5.00$, $p < .03$, $\Phi = .28$. Sixty-nine percent of the 16 mothers in this group were classified disrupted, as compared to 37% of other mothers. Again, however, the maltreatment/hospitalization variable was not powerful enough to account for infant disorganization directly, $\chi^2(N = 65) = 1.37$, *ns*.[1]

Although there was no main effect of infant gender on maternal behavior, infant gender also was assessed as a potential moderator of the relation between disrupted maternal communication and infant D classification, because at least one study has reported a higher incidence of disorganized attachment behavior among boys (Carlson et al., 1989b). Perhaps male infants are more likely to become disorganized in the presence of disrupted maternal communication than are girls.

In earlier published analyses of all 71 infant attachment tapes, a strong trend toward a gender difference in infant attachment classification did not reach significance because the two sexes were equally likely to be classified secure, 30% (m) versus 36%(f); Lyons-Ruth et al., 1991).[2] Further analyses,

---

[1] Lyons-Ruth et al. (1991) did find an association between maternal psychosocial problems, a variable that included maternal depressive symptoms and clinical referral for supportive services as well as maltreatment and hospitalization, and the DI subtype of infant disorganization, but the association was significant only among families who did not receive home-visiting services (see also Lyons-Ruth et al., 1990).

[2] In the current sample of 65, the gender effect on disorganized infant classification did reach significance, because the six tapes of the original 71 that could not be recoded for maternal behavior included a higher proportion of *D* females (2 *D* girls and 1 *D* boy), $\chi^2(1, N = 65) = 4.13$, $p < .05$.

however, revealed a significant gender difference *among insecure infants only*, with insecure girls more likely to be classified avoidant (50%), while insecure boys were more likely to be classified disorganized (82%) rather than avoidant (18%), $\chi^2(1, N = 48) = 5.61$, $p < .02$, $\Phi = .34$. In addition, using the scaled (1–9) scores for overall level of infant disorganized behavior (rather than the final infant classifications), there was a robust gender effect in the full sample, $F(1, 69) = 8.50$, $p < .01$, $\eta = .33$, indicating that boys displayed more disorganized attachment behaviors in general whether or not they were classified as D. Therefore, although an overall gender effect on classification failed to reach significance in the full sample, our data show some influence of male gender consistent with that in the Carlson et al. (1989b) study.

A hierarchical log-linear analysis testing for the significance of the moderator (interaction) effect of infant gender on the relation between maternal classification and infant classification did not reach significance, $\chi^2(1, N = 65) = .265$, *ns*, indicating that the maternal effect on infant disorganized classification and the gender effect on infant disorganized classification (which was marginal in this sample overall) are best viewed as additive. Maternal disrupted classification doubled the rate of infant disorganization, and male gender almost doubled the rate, as shown in Figure 1. Using the

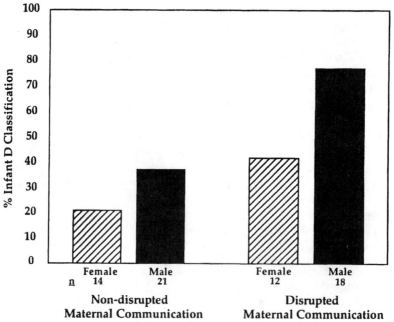

FIGURE 1. Infant disorganized attachment by maternal disrupted communication and infant gender

scaled score for infant disorganization, which was more sensitive to infant gender effects, similar results were obtained: Infant gender, $F(1, 61) = 9.08$, $p < .01$, $\eta = .34$; maternal D, $F(1, 61) = 10.70$, $p < .01$, $\eta = .36$; infant gender × maternal D, $F(1, 61) = .06$, ns, multiple $R = .50$, $R^2 = 25\%$.

DISCUSSION

The results of the validity study indicate that mothers whose infants are classified disorganized exhibit an elevated level of atypical maternal behaviors in the Strange Situation. When the subtypes of atypical maternal behaviors were examined, mothers whose infants were classified disorganized were particularly likely to display more affective communication errors, errors that included offering contradictory messages in their own communications as well as responding inappropriately or not at all to clear communications by the infant. In addition, the findings underscored the presence of distinct maternal subgroups within the overall disorganized classification. The two D subgroups did not differ significantly in rates of affective communication errors or in rates of disoriented behaviors. Mothers of DI infants, however, displayed significantly higher frequencies of negative-intrusive behaviors and role confusion, as well as higher overall frequencies of both FR$^+$ behaviors and total atypical behaviors, compared to mothers of DS infants and to mothers of infants with organized attachment strategies.

In contrast, mothers of infants with DS classifications showed a significantly elevated rate of withdrawing behaviors compared to mothers of DI infants and maternal withdrawal correlated with infant disorganization in analyses with DI infants excluded. On analyses of Main and Hesse's (1992) inventory of frightened and frightening behaviors, mothers of DS infants displayed a behavioral pattern of predominant mild fearfulness that significantly distinguished them both from mothers of organized infants and mothers of DI infants. This combination of fearful behavior and withdrawal bears at least surface similarity to the "helpless" stance described by George and Solomon (1996) as characterizing the behavior of mothers whose 6-year-olds were classified as displaying a controlling attachment strategy (the later counterpart of infant disorganization). Clearly, further work is needed to describe maternal caregiving in the DS subgroup, particularly since a majority of disorganized infants in lower risk samples have displayed DS behavior. Jacobvitz, Hazen, and Riggs (1997) and Schuengel and his colleagues (in press) also have reported elevated rates of frightened and frightening behavior among DI mothers, using maternal unresolved AAI classifications as the basis for the DS/DI distinction rather than infant classifications.

The associations obtained in the present study do not rule out the possibility that the mother's display of atypical behavior occurs because the infant's disorganized attachment behavior or the infant's distress at home is so difficult to read or to manage. The coding protocol, however, emphasized the parent's repeated failures to respond appropriately to clear infant signals, and coders did not experience difficulty making judgments about the communicative intentions of the 18-month-olds in the study. Reading through the list of serious interactive errors in Table 13 also reveals the unambiguous nature of many of the infant affective cues in question, for example, laughs while infant distressed, does not offer comfort when infant falls, removes toy despite infant engagement. Many of the maternal role-reversing and disoriented behaviors also had an out-of-context quality that appeared uncorrelated with the infant's current behavior. In addition, although the stranger's behavior vis- -vis the infant in the Strange Situation was not coded, casual inspection suggests that atypical behaviors of the kind detailed in the coding protocol were uncommon in the stranger's interactions with the infant even when the infant was displaying difficult behavior. Comparisons of mother-infant and stranger-infant interaction might be informative in future studies.

In general, parental attempts to modify their behavior based on infant cues, even when the infant's cues were ambiguous, could be clearly discriminated from parental behavior that was unresponsive or intrusive. Thus, the present results document a parental contribution to the disorganized attachment relationship that appears not to be driven entirely by the immediacies of the infant's behavior but to have partial roots in parental history (Lyons-Ruth, 1992; Lyons-Ruth & Block, 1996; Lyons-Ruth, Zoll, Connell & Grunebaum, 1989). The infant's distress and disorganized behavior also may be influenced by other intrinsic or extrinsic factors not addressed here, however, and are likely to introduce additional difficulties into the parent's attempts to regulate the interaction between them. Perhaps not surprisingly, then, mutual cycles of coercion (Greenberg et al., 1991; Main et al., 1985) and mutual rejection of the other's overtures (Hann et al., 1991) appear to characterize the subsequent developmental pathways of a subset of disorganized infants and their parents.

The behaviorally detailed nature of the coding protocol and the lack of coder familiarity with the complex coding procedures for classifying infant disorganized attachment behavior also work against the possibility that coders assigned a high rating to a parent based on their judgment of the infant's attachment status. The high correlation between the frequency count for maternal atypical behaviors and the rating for level of disrupted communication, $r = .83$, indicates that the more qualitative coding judgments were closely tied to specific maternal behaviors.

Maternal Atypical Communication and Infant Gender

The pattern of gender effects in the data is open to two interpretations—male infants may be more likely than females to display overt conflict behaviors when caregiving is inadequate or, alternatively, male infants may exhibit some excess reactivity, displaying disorganized behavior even when maternal caretaking is adequate. The data indicated that 78% of male infants displayed disorganized behavior when their mothers were classified disrupted, compared to only 42% of females. Eight male infants, however, also were classified disorganized while their mothers were classified not disrupted, compared to only three females. Because we have multiple converging sources of data on the families in the current sample, we find the first interpretation more consistent with the data as a whole, namely, that male disorganized attachment behavior more accurately reflected the quality of caregiving than female disorganized attachment behavior. In seven of the eight male cases where the child's behavior was classified D while the mother's was not, we have reason to believe that the mother's atypical behaviors were not captured in our coding system. Of the eight male infants, five were in the DS group in which maternal behavior was more withdrawing and we misclassified these mothers as a group as not D. Of the three remaining boys, all in the DI group, AAI protocols of two of these mothers were designated *cannot classify* because of their unusual characteristics. Only in the eighth case was the male infant's D behavior not readily accounted for. In addition, among the nine maltreating mothers in the sample, four of five male infants displayed D behavior while only one of four female infants did so. Therefore, we are inclined to see male infants as more likely to display conflict behavior related to caregiving inadequacies while female infants appear equally likely to display forms of avoidant behavior as to display overt D behaviors even when maternal behavior is judged by observers as maltreating or disrupted.

Future Directions for Work on Atypical Attachments

The results reported here indicate that a fearful and withdrawing maternal stance may result in a lower overall frequency of atypical maternal behaviors (see also Schuengel et al., in press, for partially converging data). Therefore, fearful and withdrawing behavior needs to be weighted more heavily in frequency counts than it was in this study, perhaps by recoding withdrawal at intervals if it persists. Greater weight also needs to be given to fearful and withdrawing behaviors in rating and classifying maternal disrupted communication, and coding protocols are currently being revised with this in mind. Greater weighting of the serious interactive errors displayed in Table 14 also appears to improve the concordance between maternal and infant classification in the DS subgroup as revealed by comparison between Tables 11 and 14. Using only serious interactive errors to classify maternal behaviors improved the concordance rate in the DS subgroup from 30% to 50%, which was unanticipated. Thus, weighting fewer salient behaviors more heavily seems likely to improve the discrimination between mothers of DS infants and mothers of organized infants. Additional statistical and descriptive analyses of maternal behavior patterns in the DS subgroup are reported in Lyons-Ruth, Bronfman, and Atwood (in press).

Results of the study also support Main and Hesse's (1990) hypothesis that frightened or frightening maternal behaviors are associated with the disorganization of infant attachment strategies. Results further indicate that differential patterning of maternal FR behavior results in differential patterning of infant attachment behavior within the disorganized spectrum. Predominant mild maternal fearfulness was associated with DS infant attachment behavior, infant behavior that in our sample also often appeared hesitant, fearful, or helpless. In contrast, as maternal behavior became extremely frightened or predominantly frightening, or included disoriented or role-reversed behavior, the infant was more likely to display disorganized conflict behaviors that included marked avoidant or resistant behavior. The current results also indicate that maternal affective communication errors constitute part of the broader context in which maternal FR behavior occurs and that these affective communication errors also should be included in protocols for scoring maternal behavior. Because infant attachment behavior is observable in the Strange Situation, it will be important in future work to evaluate whether parental behavior in settings other than the Strange Situation is equally predictive of infant disorganized attachment status. Future work should include coding of maternal interactive behavior at home with the current protocol and evaluation of the link between disrupted maternal communication and maternal AAI classification. Both studies are currently underway in our laboratory.

Theoretical Integration

The two profiles of atypical behavior that characterized mothers of disorganized infants in this study converge with findings of other studies to offer an emerging overall typology of subgroups within the larger D classification. Integrating recent studies of controlling 6-year-olds by George and Solomon (1996) and Solomon, George, and DeJong (1995) with the body of prior work on infant disorganization, two subgroups emerge within the disorganized/controlling spectrum: a helpless, fearful subgroup and a hostile, punitive subgroup. These two subgroups appear to have different manifestations in infant attachment behavior, in maternal caregiving behavior, in preschool attachment behavior, and in preschool symbolic play, while they also share certain core features central to the conceptualization of the disorganized classification.

In the present study sample the DI subgroup has been best delineated, with DI infants showing an atypical mix of attachment behaviors, often including distress at separation combined with avoidance and resistance, and other conflict behaviors at reunion. Mothers of DI infants also appear to display a "mixed" caregiving strategy in which behavioral tendencies usually viewed as characteristic of different organized attachment patterns are combined. Their behaviors toward the infant included a correlated mix of role-reversing and negative-intrusive behaviors. Milder forms of these stances are thought to characterize distinct organized strategies, with the tendency to turn the child's attention *toward* attachment issues, including the needs of the parent, thought to constitute a core feature of the preoccupied parental stance (Cassidy & Berlin, 1994), whereas the tendency to discourage the child's seeking of close emotional contact through subtle negative cues, including intrusive behavior (Belsky, Rovine, & Taylor, 1984) and suppressed anger (Main, Tomasini, & Tolan, 1979), has been found to characterize avoidant dyads. Thus, the mother's mixed caregiving strategy, in which attachment cues are both heightened and rejected, appears to complement the infant's inability to adopt a single strategy in relation to the attachment figure. In contrast, mothers of DS infants were more fearful and withdrawing in relation to their infants without displaying active rejecting behaviors. Their infants continued to approach them for contact, but also displayed signs of conflict, apprehension, uncertainty, helplessness, or dysphoria.

We speculate further that these two infant dyadic groupings correspond to the two stances observed among controlling children at age 6 by Solomon, George, and DeJong (1995). They described one group of controlling 6-year-olds as extremely inhibited in play while the other group played out frightening and chaotic scenes with no positive resolution. In their reunion behavior with parents, controlling children also have displayed two identifiable strategies, a solicitous, caregiving stance or a coercive, punitive stance (Main et al., 1985). In addition, Solomon et al. (1995) found that children inhibited in play were more likely to be classified as caregiving, while children with more chaotic play scenarios were more often classified as punitive. Longitudinal data to evaluate these postulated links between the two D subgroups in infancy and the two controlling subgroups during the preschool period are still lacking, however. Along with Main et al. (1985) and Solomon et al. (1995), we view these two stances as different behavioral strategies for responding to similar core representational and affective themes, namely a disruption in the regulatory function of the caregiving system that exposes the child to inadequately modulated fear.

As noted, Main and Hesse (1990) have related the child's fearful affect to the parent's own unresolved fear. Empirical support for this conception has come from the repeated finding that disorganized/controlling child behavior is related to indices of parental unresolved loss or trauma on the AAI (van IJzendoorn, 1995). Main and Hesse (1990) further speculated that maternal frightened or frightening behavior toward the infant might mediate the link between unresolved maternal trauma or loss and infant disorganization. Lyons-Ruth and Block (1996) have broadened Main and Hesse's conceptualization of frightened or frightening maternal behavior to include the disruptions in maternal affective communication documented here that leave the infant little effective influence over the caregiver's behavior. In support of this conception, Lyons-Ruth and Block (1996) demonstrated an association between violence or abuse in the parent's past and an increased tendency for infant insecure attachment behaviors to take disorganized rather than avoidant or ambivalent forms. In addition, Lyons-Ruth and Block (1996) demonstrated that violence or abuse in mother's childhood was associated with two somewhat different patterns of maternal interaction with the infant at home. Violence or harsh punishment in mother's childhood was associated with more hostile and intrusive behaviors toward her infant, while the overall severity of trauma, including sexual abuse, was related to increased withdrawing behaviors. The data reported here further relate withdrawing or hostile-intrusive caregiving behaviors to infant disorganization and emphasize the common link of both caregiving patterns to a basic disruption in affective communication processes between mother and infant.

In agreement with Main and Hesse (1990), we see this disruption in mother-infant affective discourse as one manifestation of the mother's attempt to maintain coexisting but unintegrated representations of her childhood experiences (see Lyons-Ruth & Block, 1996). The maintenance of unintegrated representations of past experiences, in turn, interferes with the development of a flexible internal working model for relating the range of human emotions to their sources in experience, or, in the terminology of Fonagy, Steele, Steele, Moran & Higgitt (1991), interferes with the gradual development of a psychologically sophisticated theory of mind.

V. MALTREATMENT, NEGATIVE EXPRESSIVITY, AND THE DEVELOPMENT OF TYPE D ATTACHMENTS FROM 12 TO 24 MONTHS OF AGE

Douglas Barnett, Jody Ganiban, and Dante Cicchetti

In this longitudinal follow-up study of maltreated and demographically comparable nonmaltreated children, the issue of whether child negative expressivity was related to the formation of an Insecure-Disorganized/Disoriented, Type D, attachment pattern was examined. In addition, the stability of the Type D pattern and its influence on children's negative expressivity over time was investigated.

Developing a secure attachment predisposes children toward social and emotional well-being (Ainsworth & Bowlby, 1991; Carlson & Sroufe, 1995). Central to attachment theory is the idea that secure attachments result from infants receiving consistent, sensitive, responsive, and contingent care from their attachment figures, and not as a result of a constitutionally based child predisposition toward security (Ainsworth & Bowlby, 1991; Sroufe, 1985). Indeed, sensitive, empathic parenting repeatedly has been found to predict the development of secure attachments among infants (e.g., Ainsworth, Blehar, Waters, & Wall, 1978; Belsky & Isabella, 1988; De Wolff & van IJzendoorn, 1997). Research also has supported the notion that infant temperament variables such as difficulty and distress proneness have not consistently been found to exert a direct influence on the development of secure attachments (Goldsmith & Alansky, 1987; Sroufe, 1985).

Temperament and Attachment

Although temperament does not appear to determine whether or not a child will be securely attached, the temperament dimension of negative expressivity has been found to predict the manner in which secure and insecure attachments are expressed (Belsky & Rovine, 1987; Fox, Kimmerly, & Schafer, 1991). Children classified with either the Insecure-Type A or the B1 or B2 subtype of the Secure pattern have been found to demonstrate low levels of negative expressivity during the Strange Situation attachment assessment paradigm. This low negative expressivity appears as an absence of or blunted separation cries and fussing (Braungart & Stifter, 1991; Frodi & Thompson, 1985; Ganiban, Barnett, & Cicchetti, in press; Thompson & Lamb, 1984). In contrast, infants classified into either the Insecure-Type C, or the B3 or B4 subtypes of the Secure pattern have been found to demonstrate high negative expressivity styles, particularly in response to separations from their attachment figure in a laboratory context. The splitting of attachment patterns into low (A-B2) and high (B3-C) negative expressivity is referred to as molar grouping (Belsky & Rovine, 1987). The breakdown of subtype of attachment, negative expressivity, and attachment security is presented in Figure 2.

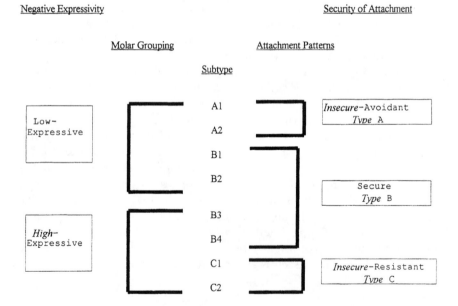

FIGURE 2. The correspondence between negative emotional expressivity temperamental molar groupings and traditional pattern of attachment.

Based on prospective research, children who exhibit high separation distress in the Strange Situation at 12 months have been rated earlier in their 1st year to be higher in proneness to distress and negative expressivity than children who exhibit low separation distress in the Strange Situation (Belsky & Rovine, 1987; Vaughn, Lefever, Seifer, & Barglow, 1989). Children who exhibit high separation distress also have been found to be rated by their mothers to be high on negative temperament and to be observed in other settings over time to exhibit more negative affectivity (Belsky, Hsieh, & Crnic, 1996). This relation between early precursors of negative expressivity and 12 months separation distress, however, has not always been replicated (Mangelsdorf, Gunnar, Kestenbaum, Lang, & Andreas, 1990; Seifer, Schiller, Sameroff, Resnick, & Riordan, 1996). Nonetheless, infants also have been found to demonstrate significant concordance between separation distress exhibited with their mothers and their fathers (Belsky et al., 1996; Belsky & Rovine, 1987; Bridges, Connell, & Belsky, 1988; Fox et al., 1991). Taken as a whole, the data indicate that separation distress is a relatively stable characteristic of the child and it is typically not associated with socialization or the parent-child relationship. In contrast, the distinction between secure and insecure attachment appears to reflect the history of the parent-infant relationship and not directly child temperament.

Examination of child temperament contributors and parenting history is necessary to validate and understand all patterns of attachment. Although convergent evidence has been accumulating supporting the role experience plays in the development of atypical attachment patterns, comparatively fewer studies have examined the relation between child factors such as temperament and the development of atypical patterns of attachment (van IJzendoorn, Goldberg, Kroonenberg, & Frenkel, 1992). In regard to familial contributions, atypical patterns of attachment consistently have been linked to having a caregiver with severe parenting problems, psychopathology, or personal difficulties. For example, parents with histories of perpetrating child abuse and neglect have been shown to be significantly more likely than matched comparisons to have infants and preschoolers with Type A/C, Type D, and Unstable Avoidant Patterns of attachment (Carlson, Cicchetti, Braunwald, & Barnett, 1989a; Cicchetti & Barnett, 1991; Crittenden, 1988; Lyons-Ruth, Connell, Zoll, & Stahl, 1987). Atypical patterns of attachment also have been found to be associated with having a caregiver with depression or a history of substance abuse (O'Connor, Sigman, & Brill, 1987; Radke-Yarrow, Cummings, Kuczynski, & Chapman, 1985; Spieker & Booth, 1988; Teti, Gelfand, Messinger, & Isabella, 1995). Finally, children with Type D attachments have been found to be more likely than children with other patterns of attachment to have caregivers with unresolved loss or trauma stemming from parents' own childhood attachments (Ainsworth & Eichberg, 1991; Lyons-Ruth, Repacholi, McLeod, & Silva, 1991; Main & Hesse, 1990).

Type D attachments are theorized to be an important link between environmental casualty and the development of emotional and behavioral regulatory problems (Cicchetti, Ganiban, & Barnett, 1991), an idea that has been supported by subsequent research. For example, infants and toddlers with Type D attachments have been found to exhibit indices of greater physiological stress such as increased heart rate and salivary cortisol responses to the Strange Situation compared to infants with secure attachments (Hertsgaard, Gunnar, Erickson, & Nachmias, 1995; Spangler & Grossmann, 1993). Toddlers with Type D attachments also have been found to be at increased risk for conduct problems such as aggression toward peers at age 5 (Lyons-Ruth, 1996; Lyons-Ruth, Alpern, & Repacholi, 1993). These studies have been viewed as providing support for the idea that youngsters with Type D attachments experience greater stress and dysregulation as a result of their failure to develop organized and effective coping strategies. The possibility remains, however, that high negative expressivity contributes to infants forming Type D attachments. The current study was designed to shed light on these alternate hypotheses. The issue of whether children with Type D attachments were more likely to demonstrate high levels of separation distress when compared to children without Type D attachments was examined. Longitudinal analyses also were conducted to examine whether vocal distress predicted the formation of a Type D pattern, or whether having a Type D pattern predicted changes in negative expressivity over time.

Longitudinal Stability

Continuity of functioning is another question addressed by attachment research. Attachment patterns are thought to reflect a process through which early experiences with caregivers influence general social and emotional well-being across the lifespan (Ainsworth & Bowlby, 1991; Sroufe, 1979; Sroufe, Carlson, & Shulman, 1993). Although infant attachment security has been shown to be an important predictor of social and emotional functioning during the preschool years and beyond, as a rule, attachment patterns are susceptible to change (Lamb, Thompson, Gardner, & Charnov, 1985; Teti, Sakin, Kucera, Corns, & Eiden, 1996). Changes in quality of attachment and the corresponding caregiving environment have been shown to have important implications for predicting children's adjustment at later ages (Sroufe, Egeland, & Kreutzer, 1990).

Stability of attachment patterns has been shown to reflect the relative consistency in the caregiving environment. Under conditions reflecting relative stability of parenting, such as in low-risk middle-class samples, general continuity in children's attachment patterns was found across periods from 6 months (Waters, 1978) to 5 years (Main, Kaplan, & Cassidy, 1985; Wartner,

Grossmann, Fremmer-Bombik, & Suess, 1994). Although subsequent investigators have not found attachment stability across 6-month periods to be greater than chance (Belsky, Campbell, Cohn, & Moore, 1996), instability in attachment patterns is generally thought to be associated with greater ecological risk. For the most part, researchers have been successful at predicting stability and change of attachment patterns prospectively. Movement from secure to insecure patterns over time has been associated with changes in family relationships and other stressors including parental job loss, poverty, spousal separations, shifts in caregiving arrangements, and the birth of a sibling (Egeland & Farber, 1984; Teti et al., 1996; Thompson, Lamb, & Estes, 1982; Vaughn, Waters, Egeland, & Sroufe, 1979; Vondra, Hommerding, & Shaw, this volume).

Based on a subsample of the data presented herein, Schneider-Rosen, Braunwald, Carlson, and Cicchetti (1985) found significant instability of attachment patterns among the maltreated infants. Children were classified using only the traditional tripartite attachment scoring system. Consequently, atypical patterns of attachment were not coded. Across both 12 to 18 months and 18 to 24 months, fewer than half of the maltreated children received the same attachment classification. In contrast, nonmaltreated children were found to demonstrate stability of attachment organization greater than could be expected by chance (Schneider-Rosen et al., 1985). These data were interpreted to suggest that under conditions of extreme ecological risk, such as in cases of child maltreatment, attachment patterns are likely to be unstable over time. Subsequent to the identification of the Type D pattern by Main and Solomon (1990), the majority of the maltreated children have been shown to exhibit this atypical pattern of attachment (Carlson et al., 1989a). In Carlson et al. (1989a), two hypotheses concerning the stability of attachment among maltreated children were raised: The first was that the Type D attachment pattern reflected a transitional state as children shifted across the traditional Type A, B, and C patterns. This possibility was supported by the fact that ecological risk had been associated with both placement in the Type D category, as well as with relative instability of attachment organization over time. The second possibility raised was that the attachment patterns of high-risk children were in fact more stable than had previously been estimated. With the advent of the Type D pattern, the possibility that high-risk children did in fact exhibit continuity in quality of attachment organization over time was proposed (Carlson et al., 1989a). This continuity, however, was thought to involve the maintenance of the Type D pattern. In the present analyses, the issue of attachment stability was reexamined by including the Type D pattern. Because Main and Solomon's system was recommended for classifying the behavior of children less than 24 months of age, the applicability of their system for children 24 months of age also was of interest.

METHOD

Subjects

The sample consisted of 44 12-month-olds (M = 12.9 months, SD = 1.1), who participated in the Harvard Child Maltreatment Project (Cicchetti & Manly, 1990; Cicchetti & Rizley, 1981). Of the 44 infants, 23 were girls. Data on 12-month-old attachment organization of 43 of these infants were presented in a previous publication (Carlson et al., 1989a). The present study focused on attachment and negative expressivity of the children across three assessment points over a 1-year period.

Longitudinal Follow-Up Assessments. Of the original 44 infants (22 maltreated and 22 comparison), 39 (19 girls) were assessed again at 18 months (M = 18.8 months, SD = 0.9). At 18 months there were 18 maltreated and 21 comparison toddlers. At the third assessment, 36 children (16 girls) were assessed at 24 months (M = 25.1 months, SD = 1.3). At 24 months there were 16 maltreated and 20 comparison youngsters. The maltreated and comparison groups were similar on child age and gender, and therefore, did not differ significantly on these characteristics at 12, 18, or 24 months of age.

Because the majority of maltreating families live in economic poverty (Barnett, 1997; Cicchetti & Rizley, 1981), a sample of nonmaltreated children from families of low socioeconomic status (SES) was selected as a comparison group to help control for the effects of living in a low SES environment. No child in the study had any physical handicaps or identifiable brain damage. All children were residing at home with their primary caregiver at the time of the study. As demonstrated in Table 16, the two groups were comparable on numerous demographic characteristics. The maltreating families, however, did have significantly more children residing in their homes, and had a smaller number of adults per children in their homes than did nonmaltreating families.

Maltreatment Group. All of the families of the maltreated children were being monitored by either the Department of Social Services (DSS) of the Commonwealth of Massachusetts or the Massachusetts Society for the Prevention of Cruelty to Children, and met state legal criteria for protective services due to maternal abuse and/or neglect of their children. Each family's Child Protective Service (CPS) worker was interviewed using Giovannoni and Becerra's (1979) checklist of maltreatment. According to CPS, two infants had been physically abused by someone other than the child's mother. Thirteen infants (59%) had been neglected by their mothers, and six (27%) had been emotionally maltreated by mother. Four infants (18%) experienced neglect and emotional maltreatment. Seven infants (31.8%) from the

TABLE 16

SAMPLE DEMOGRAPHICS AT INFANT AGE 12 MONTHS

	Comparison (Nonmaltreated) N = 21	Maltreated N = 22	
% Child Girls	52%	50%	ns
Child Mean Age in Months	12.6	12.9	ns
% Caucasian	95%	82%	ns
% African American	5%	9%	ns
Number of Adults in Home	2.05 (.65)	1.67 (.80)	ns
Number of Children in Home	1.73 (1.1)	3.05 (1.56)	$t = 1.71$**
Adult to Child Ratio	1.53 (.86)	0.69 (.42)	$t = 4.1$***
Male Partner in Home	55%	36%	ns
Mother's Highest Grade	11.05 (2.4)	11.0 (2.2)	ns
Household Prestige Score (SES)	47.97 (4.2)	47.04 (3.9)	ns
Currently Receiving AFDC	82%	86%	ns
Total Household Income	7.36K (3.8)	6.52K (3.4)	ns

Note. Standard deviations are presented in parentheses.
*$p < .05$, **$p < .01$, ***$p < .001$.

maltreatment group had no specific items checked by their CPS worker. We decided to include these infants in the maltreatment group for several reasons. In every case, the mother had maltreated the infant's older sibling. In this regard the infants were at extremely high risk for maltreatment. Legally documented cases of maltreatment generally underestimate the true number of maltreated children. This trend is exacerbated because it is more difficult to substantiate the presence of several of the major types of maltreatment (e.g., emotional maltreatment, sexual abuse) among infants than among school-aged children (Barnett, 1997). Consequently, we felt it was highly likely that these seven infants had in fact been maltreated. To provide a further indication of these mothers' caregiving practices, it is worth noting that when combining CPS maltreatment reports of all offspring, five (22.7%) had physically injured a child, 18 (81.8%) had neglected a child, and 15 (68.2%) had emotionally mistreated a child. In maltreating families, it is common for abuse and neglect and their various subtypes to co-occur (Cicchetti & Rizley, 1981). In this regard, the number of total cases of different maltreatment types of this study tallies more than 100%.

Comparison Group. The 22 mother-infant dyads were recruited through posters and leaflets placed in welfare offices, in housing projects, and in the neighborhoods of the maltreatment sample. The nonmaltreating status of these families was verified through parent interview regarding absence of CPS involvement or concern. Dyads in both groups were provided transportation to the laboratory to complete the study, and were paid $15 for their participation.

Measures

Attachment Classifications. Two raters (i.e., Barnett and Cicchetti), un-aware of the children's maltreatment status, coded the Strange Situation videotapes using Main and Solomon's (1990) instructions for the Type D category in addition to the traditional criteria developed by Ainsworth et al. (1978) for identifying Type A, B, and C attachments. To help prevent bias, Strange Situations from each age group were coded between 9 to 15 months apart. The coders believed the delay between coding each age group was effective in making them blind to prior classifications at the subsequent coding. It also should be noted that the coders classified more than 100 Strange Situation tapes from a variety of samples during the periods between coding the current sample. Under those conditions it is very diffi-cult to recognize a child who has aged and has not been viewed in 9 or more months. Moreover, it is not likely that details relevant to making a classi-fication would be remembered. Across the three age groups, interrater reliability was 88% ($\kappa = .81$), 85% ($\kappa = .77$), and 91% ($\kappa = .85$), at 12, 18, and 24 months respectively. All disagreements were resolved by discussion. Seventeen tapes from the 12-month assessment representing a variety of A, B, C, and D classifications were coded by Mary Main. Agreement between Main's codings and that of coders for this study was 94% ($\kappa = .90$). As a further examination of coder reliability, 10 tapes from the 18-month assess-ment and 10 tapes from the 24-month assessment were randomly selected and classified by two independent student coders. Reliability with these coders was 90% ($\kappa = .85$) and 80% ($\kappa = .74$) at the 18- and 24-month sessions respectively.

Negative Expressivity Molar Grouping. In addition to attachment classifi-cations, each child was assigned to either the low-reactive molar grouping (i.e., A1–B2), or the high-reactive molar grouping (i.e., B3–C2). Molar groupings are based on both the pattern of emotional expression as well as the behavioral pattern exhibited toward the caregiver (Ainsworth et al., 1978; Thomson & Lamb, 1984). Across the three ages, interrater reliability for molar grouping assignment ranged from 91% to 92%. All disagree-ments were resolved through discussion.

Vocal Distress Ratings. At each age, negative expressivity was assessed through Thompson and Lamb's (1984) affect coding system. This system fa-cilitates rating infant distress on a continuous scale through observations of child vocalizations during 15 s intervals. This scale includes 14 categories of distress vocalizations that are collapsed into a 6-point scale reflecting distress intensity: "1" = positive vocalization, "2" = neutral vocalization, "3" = mild distress (e.g., very brief frustration sounds, distress gasps), "4" = moderate distress (e.g., whining, continuous fussing), "5" =high distress (e.g., continuous and rhythmic crying, protest cries, screams), and "6" = extreme distress (e.g., panic cries, hyperventilation cries). If the child did not vocalize during a time interval, then the interval was scored as "2," neutral. Separate groups of rater pairs, blind to other information on the children's functioning, completed the coding at each age. Based on 75% of the tapes at each age, exact interrater agreement averaged 84%, ranging from 66% to 96% per Strange Situation. Differences were resolved through consensus.

Two negative expressivity summary scores were utilized for each separation (i.e., episodes 3, 5, and 6) and reunion (i.e., episodes 4 and 7) episode of the Strange Situation: *Peak Distress* was the highest level of negative vocalization the child exhibited during the episode. *Distress Duration* was the percentage of the episode the child was distressed. Since only two children exhibited vocal distress during the first reunion at 24 months, and five during the second reunion at 24 months, only vocal distress variables for the Strange Situation separation episodes were examined at 24 months. Within each age, Peak Distress and Distress Duration were moderately to highly correlated within and across episodes (mean rs = .62, .72, and .71 at 12, 18, and 24 months, respectively). Because of the relative consistency among these negative expressivity variables, they were standardized and summed to create a single vocal distress variable at each age. These scores appear to assess a general disposition toward intense, lengthy vocalizations of distress in response to the Strange Situation episodes. The internal consistencies for this index were .93, .95, and .91 at 12, 18, and 24 months, respectively.

RESULTS

Maltreatment and Attachment Organization at 12, 18, and 24 Months

Children's attachment classification at each assessment was examined in relation to maltreatment and demographic influences. Table 17 presents the number and percentage of infants in each of the four attachment groupings by maltreatment status, as well as the chi-square test for effects of maltreatment on attachment organization. Because of the small cell sizes for Type A and C attachments, effects of maltreatment were examined at the level of attachment security (i.e., Type B vs. all others), and attachment disorganization (i.e., Type D vs. all others). At each age, maltreated children were significantly less likely to be securely attached and significantly more likely to be classified as Disorganized/Disoriented.

There also was a significant effect for child gender on attachment security at 12 months (see Carlson et al., 1989a, for a full presentation of these findings). Boys were significantly more likely to be insecurely attached than

TABLE 17

Attachment Classifications at 12, 18, and 24 Months of Age

12 Months	Type A	Secure	Type C	Type D	TOTALS
Maltreated	0	3 (13.6%)	0	19 (86.36%)	22
Comparison	3 (13.6%)	10 (45.45%)	3 (13.6%)	6 (27.27%)	22
TOTALS	3 (6.8%)	13 (29.5%)	3 (6.8%)	25 (56.8%)	44

Maltreatment × Security, χ^2 (1) = 5.31, p = .02; Maltreatment × Type D, $\chi^2(1)$ = 15.66, p < .001.

18 Months	Type A	Secure	Type C	Type D	TOTALS
Maltreated	1 (4.8%)	4 (22.2%)	2 (11.1%)	11 (61.1%)	18
Comparison	1 (4.8%)	11 (52.4%)	3 (14.3%)	6 (28.6%)	21
TOTALS	2 (5.1%)	15 (38.5%)	5 (12.8%)	17 (43.6%)	39

Maltreatment × Security, χ^2 (1) = 3.73, p = .05; Maltreatment × Type D, $\chi^2(1)$ = 4.17, p = .04.

24 Months	Type A	Secure	Type C	Type D	TOTALS
Maltreated	1 (6.3%)	2 (12.5%)	1 (6.3%)	12 (75.0%)	16
Comparison	1 (5.0%)	11 (55.0%)	2 (10.0%)	6 (30.0%)	20
TOTALS	2 (5.6%)	13 (36.1%)	3 (8.3%)	18 (50.0%)	36

Maltreatment × Security, χ^2 (1) = 6.96, p = .008; Maltreatment × Type D, $\chi^2(1)$ = 7.20, p = .007.

girls (85.7% vs. 56.5%, respectively), χ^2 = (1, N = 44) = 4.49, p = .03. There was no significant effect for child gender at 18 or 24 months. There were no significant child sex by maltreatment interactions on attachment at any age. Follow-up logistic regression analyses predicting attachment security (secure vs. insecure) or disorganization (Type D vs. Non–Type D) at each of the three age periods revealed that the effects for maltreatment status remained significant at each age, controlling for the effects of child gender, number of children in the home, and adult to child ratio. The results of the logistic regression indicated that no variable other than maltreatment status contributed unique variance to the prediction of attachment security or disorganized attachment at 12, 18, or 24 months. For example, the effect for gender was not significant over and above the effect for child maltreatment.

Negative Expressivity at 12, 18, and 24 Months

At 12 months, 23 infants (52.3%) were classified in the low-reactive molar grouping and 21 (47.3%) were classified in the high-reactive molar grouping. At 18 months, 17 (43.6%) were classified in the low-reactive molar grouping and 22 (56.4%) were classified in the high-reactive grouping. At 24 months, 23 children (63.9%) were placed in the low-reactive molar grouping and 13 (36.1%) were classified in the high-reactive molar grouping. Molar grouping was not significantly related to age, $\chi^2(2, N = 119)$

= 3.04, p > .20. At the three age periods (i.e., 12, 18, and 24 months), children were about equally likely to be in either molar grouping.

Attachment Organization by Molar Grouping

Next we examined whether children with Type B or Type D attachments were more likely to be placed in either the high- or low-reactive molar grouping. Chi-squares examining Type B by Molar Grouping and Type D by Molar Grouping were computed at each age. Children with either secure or disorganized/disoriented attachments were about equally likely to be placed in either the low- or high-reactive molar grouping as demonstrated by the fact that there were no significant chi-squares at any age. There also was no significant relation between child gender and molar grouping or maltreatment and molar grouping at any age. Importantly, there was no significant relation between the child temperament grouping and the Type D classification or maltreatment status.

Predicting Emotional Distress

As noted, there was no significant relation between either Type B or Type D attachment and molar grouping at any age. We next examined whether having a Type D attachment was related to vocal distress at any age. A strong effect for molar grouping was expected as this dimension has been shown to reflect a temperamental predisposition toward intense displays of vocal distress (Belsky & Rovine, 1987; Thompson & Lamb, 1984). A 2 (Type D) × 2 (Molar Grouping) analysis of variance (ANOVA) was computed predicting the summary negative expressivity variable at the three age assessments. As expected, there was *no* main effect for Type D attachment at any age, suggesting that Type D attachment was unrelated to a tendency to exhibit intense displays of vocal distress, $F(1, 42) = 0.3$, *ns*; $F(1, 37) = 0.2$, *ns*; $F(1, 34) = 0.1$, *ns*; at 12, 18, or 24 months, respectively. Also as expected, there *was* a significant main effect for the molar groups at each of the three age periods, $F(1, 42) = 55.2, p < .0001$; $F(1, 37) = 55.9, p < .0001$; $F(1, 34) = 26.6, p < .0001$; at 12, 18, and 24 months, respectively. Comparison of mean vocal distress at each age indicated that children in the B3–C2 molar grouping compared to those in the A1–B2 molar grouping emitted significantly more intense vocal distress at each age period. At 12 months, a significant Type D by molar grouping interaction effect also emerged, $F(3, 40) = 12.3, p < .002$. Follow-up, post hoc tests indicated the significant Type D by molar grouping interaction effect was due to a significant difference between children with and without Type D attachments among the high-reactive molar group, $t(20) = 4.2, p < .0001$.

Children with Type D attachments in the high-reactive molar grouping had significantly lower vocal distress than children without Type D attachments in the high-reactive molar grouping. This interaction effect is presented graphically in Figure 3. Differences by gender, maltreatment status, and attachment security on vocal distress at each age period were examined in follow-up analyses. Only an effect for gender emerged. At 18 months, boys ($M = 2.3$, $SD = 5.7$) displayed significantly more vocal distress than girls ($M = -2.3$, $SD = 7.3$), $t(38) = 2.2$, $p < .04$. The effect for molar grouping remained unchanged when the effect for gender was controlled at 18 months. The absence of findings for maltreatment and attachment security suggests there is no relation between vocal distress and maltreatment or attachment security.

Stability of Attachment

The distribution of patterns of attachment across the longitudinal assessments is presented separately by maltreatment status for 12 to 18 months in Table 18, 18 to 24 months in Table 19, and 12 to 24 months in Table 20. Of the 39 children seen in the Strange Situation at 12 and 18 months, 25 (64.1%) received the same classification at both ages ($\kappa = .43$, $p <$

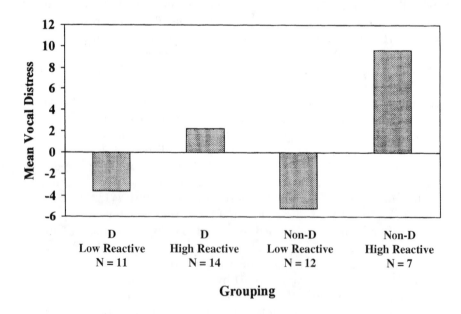

FIGURE 3. Mean vocal distress z-score as a function of molar grouping and attachment disorganization at 12 months of age.

TABLE 18

STABILITY OF ATTACHMENT CLASSIFICATIONS FROM 12 TO 18 MONTHS OF AGE

12-Month Classifications		18-Month Classifications			
		A	B	C	D
Comparison Children (N = 21)	A	0	3	0	0
	B	1	7	0	1
	C	0	0	2	1
	D	0	1	1	4
Maltreated Children (N = 18)	A	0	0	0	0
	B	0	2	0	1
	C	0	0	0	0
	D	1	2	2	10

TABLE 19

STABILITY OF ATTACHMENT CLASSIFICATIONS FROM 18 TO 24 MONTHS OF AGE

18-Month Classifications		24-Month Classifications			
		A	B	C	D
Comparison Children (N = 20)	A	1	0	0	0
	B	0	8	1	1
	C	0	1	1	1
	D	0	2	0	4
Maltreated Children (N = 16)	A	0	0	0	1
	B	1	1	0	1
	C	0	0	1	1
	D	0	1	0	9

TABLE 20

STABILITY OF ATTACHMENT CLASSIFICATIONS FROM 12 TO 24 MONTHS OF AGE

12-Month Classifications		24-Month Classifications			
		A	B	C	D
Comparison Children (N = 20)	A	0	2	0	1
	B	1	6	1	0
	C	0	1	1	1
	D	0	2	0	4
Maltreated Children (N = 16)	A	0	0	0	0
	B	0	2	0	0
	C	0	0	0	0
	D	1	0	1	12

.001). Continuity of attachment was similar for comparison and maltreated children (62% and 66%, respectively). Of the two most common patterns, 14 of 21 (66.7%) children were classified as Type D at both 12 and 18 months, and 9 of 12 (75%) were classified as Type B at both ages. Maltreated infants were significantly more likely than nonmaltreated infants to be classified as Type D at both ages (56% vs. 19% for maltreated and comparison infants, respectively: $\chi^2 = 5.61$, $p = .02$).

Of the 36 children seen in the Strange Situation at 18 and 24 months, 25 (69.4%) received the same classification at both ages ($\kappa = .52$, $p < .001$). Continuity of attachment was similar for comparison and maltreated children (70% and 68.8%, respectively). Of the two most common patterns, 13 of 16 (81.3%) children classified as Type D at 18 months received the same classification at 24 months, and 9 of 13 (69.3%) classified as Type B at 18 months were so classified at 24 months. Nonmaltreated infants were significantly more likely than maltreated infants to be classified as secure at both ages (40% vs. 6% for comparison and maltreated infants, respectively: $\chi^2 = 5.40$, $p = .02$). Maltreated infants were significantly more likely than nonmaltreated infants to be classified as Type D at both ages (56% vs. 20% for maltreated and comparison infants, respectively: $\chi^2 = 5.06$, $p = .02$). There was, however, not a statistically significant difference between nonmaltreated and maltreated infants on stability of secure attachments from 12 to 18 months (33% vs. 11% for comparison and maltreated infants, respectively, $\chi^2 = 2.70$, $p = .10$).

Of the 36 children seen in the Strange Situation at 12 and 24 months, 25 (69.4%) received the same classification at both ages ($\kappa = .53$, $p < .001$). Continuity of attachment was higher for maltreated than comparison children (87.5% and 55%, respectively: $\chi^2 = 4.43$, $p = .03$). Of the two most common patterns, 16 of 20 (80%) children classified as Type D at 12 months received the same classification at 24 months, and 8 of 10 (80%) children classified as Type B at 12 months received the same classification at 24 months. Maltreated infants were significantly more likely than nonmaltreated infants to be classified as Type D at 12 and 24 months (75% vs. 20% for maltreated and comparison infants, respectively: $\chi^2 = 10.89$, $p = .001$). There was not, however, a significant difference between nonmaltreated and maltreated infants on stability of secure attachments from 12 to 24 months (30% vs. 13% for nonmaltreated and maltreated children, respectively).

Stability of Molar Groupings and Negative Expressivity

Of the 39 children seen in the Strange Situation at 12 and 18 months, 28 (71.8%) were placed in the same molar grouping at both ages ($\kappa = .44$, $p < .01$). Seven children (18%) changed from low to high molar grouping

110

from 12 to 18 months, and four changed from high reactive to low reactive. Of the 36 children seen in the Strange Situation at 18 and 24 months, 24 (66.7%) were placed in the same molar grouping at both ages (κ = .36, p < .05). Two children (6%) changed from low to high molar grouping from 18 to 24 months, and 10 (28%) changed from high reactive to low reactive. Of the 36 children seen in the Strange Situation at 12 and 24 months, 22 (61%) were placed in the same molar grouping at both ages (κ = .21, p = ns). Five children (14%) changed from low to high molar grouping from 12 to 24 months, and nine (25%) changed from high reactive to low reactive. Generally, molar groupings were stable across 6-month time periods, but not significantly stable above chance across the 12-month period. The greatest shift was the move from high- to low-reactive molar grouping from 18 to 24 months.

Vocal distress ratings of negative expressivity were moderately stable across age periods (r = .60 from 12 to 18 months; r = .41 from 12 to 24 months; r = .40 from 18 to 24 months, p < .02 in all cases). Stability of attachment did not moderate the stability of vocal distress.

Change in Negative Expressivity and Attachment Disorganization

Examined next was whether negative expressivity in the form of vocal distress or molar grouping at a prior age was related to having or forming a Type D attachment at a subsequent age. Logistic regressions were conducted predicting dichotomous variables reflecting either having or forming a Type D attachment at 18 or 24 months of age. In each case, vocal distress or molar grouping from the prior age assessment was entered as an independent variable. In all cases, no single or cumulative indices of negative expressivity significantly predicted having or forming a Type D attachment at a subsequent age.

Change in Negative Expressivity Across Age

Change in vocal distress was examined by conducting a 2 (Type D) × 2 (Molar Grouping) repeated measures ANOVA predicting the 12- and 18-month summary vocal distress scores. Attachment and molar grouping classifications from the 12-month assessments were the independent variables. Of interest here are the main and interaction effects with time. Only a significant Time by Type D interaction effect emerged, $F(1, 35)$ = 4.62, p < .04. Examination of the means indicated that children with Type D attachments demonstrated an increase in vocal distress from 12 to 18 months, in comparison to a decrease for children without Type D attachments. Follow-up analyses indicated that the significant change for children with Type D attachments could not be attributed to gender, maltreatment, or security of attachment. Mean changes in vocal distress by Type D Attachment Organization are graphically presented in Figure 4.

Repeated measures ANOVAs were conducted to examine change in vocal negative expressivity from 18 to 24 months and from 12 to 24 months of age. In order to be compatible with the 24-month score, only summary scores for separation reactions were utilized for the 12- and 18-month indices. No significant main or interaction effects were found for Time for change from 18 to 24 months, or for change from 12 to 24 months.

Type of Maltreatment

To examine the effects of different subtypes of maltreatment (i.e., physical abuse, neglect, emotional maltreatment) on children's patterns of attachment and negative expressivity, the number of documented occurrences of each of the three maltreatment subtypes as well as the total number of occurrences of all subtypes were correlated with dichotomous scores for each of the four attachment groupings (e.g., Type A, not–Type A; Type B, not–Type B; etc.) at 12, 18, and 24 months, the vocalization ratings at each age, and the change scores in negative expressivity. Few significant

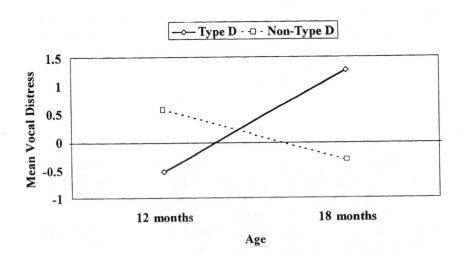

FIGURE 4. Change in mean vocal distress z-score between 12 and 18 months of age as a function of attachment disorganization.

differences emerged between maltreatment types and attachment or negative expressivity variables. Given the number of tests that were carried out we view these results as chance occurrences. Of the seven infants in the maltreatment group without documented maltreatment experiences, only one was classified as securely attached. This infant was judged as securely attached at 12 and 18 months, but did not participate in the study at 24 months. None of the remaining six were classified as secure at any age.

DISCUSSION

The results of this study indicate that experiencing child maltreatment in infancy is associated with having a Type D attachment through at least the toddler years and suggest that the Type D pattern is not transitory, but is likely to persist during this period. The findings reported herein also provide important discriminant validity by showing that having or forming a Type D attachment is not a function of children's negative expressivity. Furthermore, this study furnishes new information on how the Type D pattern may contribute to the development of emotional and behavioral regulatory problems. Each of these findings are elaborated upon below.

At each of the three ages, the majority of maltreated children were classified as Type D (i.e., 86%, 61%, 75% for 12, 18, and 24 months, respectively). In contrast, the children from demographically comparable nonmaltreating families were most commonly classified as securely attached (i.e., 45%, 52%, and 55%, at each age). The fluctuations in rates of security and disorganization across the three ages were not significant. Because this is a longitudinal study, children assessed at 12, 18, and 24 months cannot be treated as independent samples, and, therefore, as independent estimates of the distribution of attachment among maltreatment and low-income samples. Nonetheless, these rates are consistent with trends found across studies indicating that as the types of parenting problems examined increase in severity, rates of atypical patterns of attachment increase and rates of security decrease (Lyons-Ruth et al., 1991; Spieker & Booth, 1988; van IJzendoorn et al., 1992).

Type D Attachments During the Toddler and Preschool Years

In slightly older samples, markedly diminished rates of atypical attachment patterns (36%–28%) for maltreatment samples at 30, 36, and 48 months were found (Cicchetti & Barnett, 1991). The smaller percentages of maltreated children demonstrating atypical patterns of attachment at older ages may be attributable to differences in the scoring criteria for identifying atypicality during the preschool years. Currently, the recognized systems of identifying manifestations of atypical attachments beyond toddlerhood include (a) applying Main and Solomon's (1990) criteria to older children, (b) the controlling patterns identified in the MacArthur system for preschool attachment (Cassidy & Marvin, 1991), or (c) Crittenden's (1994) Preschool Attachment Assessment that includes the A/C pattern. Cicchetti and Barnett (1991) utilized Cassidy and Marvin's (1991) system to examine attachment in 30- to 48-month-olds. In the current study, 50% of the 24-month-olds demonstrated evidence of a Type D attachment using Main and Solomon's (1990) classification system. Child maltreatment is thought to be traumatically frightening, and therefore, according to Main and Hesse (1990), should be specifically associated with attachment disorganization. The utility of Main and Solomon's system at 24 months was supported by the fact that it effectively discriminated maltreated from comparison children (75% vs. 30%, respectively) on attachment disorganization. Further research on attachment atypicality during the preschool years is necessary before concluding that there is a "true" drop in rates of atypical attachments among maltreated children during the preschool period. On the other hand, children may be more likely to form traditional (i.e., A, B, and C attachments) as they mature. Future research should examine the extent to which cognitive factors and other emerging capacities play in influencing how children organize their representational models of attachment (cf. Crittenden, this volume; Lynch & Cicchetti, 1991).

Longitudinally, the data indicated general stability of the Type D pattern over time. Two other studies examined the continuity of the Type D pattern from 12 to 18 months. Vondra and colleagues (this volume) found the same rate for Type D stability as reported herein, 67%. Lyons-Ruth et al.'s (1991) rate was considerably lower, 30%, which might be related to the fact it was obtained in an intervention study. Within each study, the stability rates for the Type D pattern were highly comparable to the corresponding rates for each sample's Type B pattern. In other words, disorganized attachments have been found to be as stable as secure attachments.

Vondra et al. (this volume) and Lyons-Ruth et al. (1991) both found slight increases in the rates of disorganization from 12 to 18 months. In contrast, a higher percentage of Type Ds at the 12-month assessment than at the 18- or 24-month follow-ups were found in this investigation. This difference may be due to the high number of maltreated children in the current sample compared to these other studies. Maltreated children were significantly more likely than comparison children to exhibit stable Type D attachments across each of the age periods, with 75% of the maltreated children compared to 20% of the nonmaltreated children being classified as Type D at both 12 and 24 months. Prospectively, 80% of children classified as Type D at 12 months received the same classification at 24 months.

Retrospectively, 86% of maltreated children classified as Type D at 12 months were classified as Type D at a previous age. These data are interpreted as strong evidence against the idea that Type D attachments are classifications in transition and suggest that atypical patterns are established early and are then likely to persist over time.

Two studies examined the stability of attachment among maltreated children before Main and Solomon (1990) developed the Type D classification scheme. In both studies (Egeland & Sroufe, 1981a, 1981b; Schneider-Rosen et al., 1985), maltreated infants were found to demonstrate instability of attachment over 6-month periods, in contrast to comparison children who were found to demonstrate significant rates of continuity in attachment pattern. The current study obtained similar rates of stability in both the maltreated and comparison group. The form of stability exhibited by maltreated and comparison children often differed, however, with nonmaltreated children being more likely to demonstrate stable secure patterns and maltreated children being more likely to demonstrate stability in attachment disorganization. The fact that the inclusion of the D category improved the prediction of children's functioning—particularly among the maltreated youngsters—further supports the utility of the Type D pattern for increasing our understanding of the development of children at high risk for psychopathology.

Negative Expressivity and Attachment Disorganization

A tendency to express distress does not predispose children to form Type D attachments. This contention was supported by the absence of a significant association between attachment disorganization and either molar grouping or vocal distress at each of the assessment points. It also was supported by the absence of a significant relation between prior negative expressivity style and subsequent attachment. Associations between indices of negative expressivity and child maltreatment status also were not found. High negative expressivity is a central component of the difficult temperament construct (Bates, 1980). Consequently, these findings can be added to previous data indicating that infant difficulty does not predispose children to being maltreated (Crittenden, 1985; Egeland & Sroufe, 1981a, 1981b). Nonetheless, limitations of the study must be taken into consideration. These include the fact that child temperament was not assessed prior to 12 months, independent assessments of negative expressivity were not made outside of the Strange Situation, and data on the reoccurrence of maltreatment were not gathered. It also must be recognized that the small sample size precluded the identification of small effect sizes. Future research on the relations among child temperament, maltreatment, and attachment should be conducted prospectively, utilizing a large sample size and repeated assessments of these factors across the early years of life.

Although temperament was not related to maltreatment status or attachment disorganization, it certainly is a variable parents need to consider in providing care to their offspring. How parents respond to the particular style and cues of their infants is an important component of maternal sensitivity (Seifer et al., 1996). In this regard, sensitive caregivers of distress prone babies are those who modify their responses to soothe and redirect a highly distressed infant. Under these conditions, babies with high negative expressivity should develop secure B3 or B4 attachment patterns. In contrast, the sensitive caregivers of low reactive children must read subtle cues of distress or overstimulation in their efforts to parent and support their child's regulation. Sensitive parenting in such a dyad should result in secure B1 or B2 attachments.

This implicit link between parental sensitivity and infant style may explain why in low-risk samples, parents of avoidantly attached babies have been found to be overstimulating (e.g., Belsky, Rovine, & Taylor, 1984; Smith & Pederson, 1988). These parents may be thought of as "sensitive" in that they are responding to their child's signals. Perhaps such parents appear overstimulating, in part, because they misinterpret their low reactive infants' subtle cues of arousal to mean they are understimulated. For instance, parents have been found to react to nonirritable in contrast to irritable newborns with greater physical and visual involvement (van den Boom & Hoeksma, 1994).

In contrast, parents of ambivalently attached infants have been found to be inconsistently available and understimulating (e.g., Isabella, 1993; Vondra, Shaw, & Kevenides, 1995). There is some evidence that irritability or other forms of child vulnerability may predispose children toward resistant behavior or Type C attachments in the Strange Situation (Goldsmith & Alansky, 1987; Vondra et al., this volume). Perhaps under conditions of low-risk, parental insensitivity with highly reactive children takes the form of fatigue or lower involvement after repeatedly responding to an emotionally demanding child (van den Boom & Hoeksma, 1994). These types of influences would be consistent with a transactional model of infant and parent influences and help to integrate the data that have emerged in the literature on temperament, parenting, and attachment in low-risk samples. Although models examining statistical interactions between parent functioning and child temperament have successfully predicted child attachment security (Crockenberg, 1981; Mangelsdorf et al., 1990), there have been no empirical examinations of a transactional model of parent and child reciprocal effects on the formation of infants' attachment organization.

Within a transactional framework, mothers in the middle range of parental sensitivity and children in the moderate range of the molar groupings influence one another in complementary ways, forming one of the three typical patterns of attachment. Such a model would be consistent with data indicating parents are the primary influence on attachment security, whereas child negative expressivity may influence the manner in which (in)security is expressed. Conditions such as cultural styles and ecological risk can alter the relation between caregiving patterns and child temperament. For instance, an intervention study conducted in the Netherlands found irritable infants to be predisposed toward the Type A rather than the Type C attachment pattern (van den Boom, 1994). Perhaps this difference is due to cultural influences or the at-risk nature of the sample. Nonetheless, most of the infants in the Dutch sample who did not receive intervention formed an organized pattern. In cases of extreme insensitivity and unresponsiveness, caregivers drift far from the actual cues and styles of the children receiving care. In cases of severe maltreatment, children may be forced to modify their styles and responses to adapt to extreme and inconsistent parenting styles. Accordingly, children with low-reactive temperament styles may be driven to adopt Type C strategies, and those with high-reactive dispositions have to adopt Type A strategies. Through these processes, children of extremely insensitive parents may be forced to develop strategies contrary, and, therefore, poorly suited to their emotional predisposition. As a result, they may appear to have a disorganized attachment strategy as behaviors consistent with their temperamental predisposition "leak out" in the context of behaviors adapted to cope with their anticipations of their parents' behavior. At 12 months, a significant interaction between molar grouping and Type D attachment status was found whereby children in the high-reactive grouping emitted low vocal distress if they had a Type D attachment. This finding is consistent with the idea that children with Type D attachments are behaving in a fashion inconsistent with their temperamental dispositions.

In the transactional model of attachment, child cues would not only influence parenting behavior, but also parenting behavior, particularly in extreme cases, would affect children's style of negative expressivity. The longitudinal findings reported herein support this perspective. Specifically, children with Type D attachments exhibited significant increases in vocal distress from 12 to 18 months of age. No other factor examined (i.e., maltreatment status, attachment security, molar grouping, child sex, or stability of attachment) accounted for the change in vocal distress over this time period. In addition, negative expressivity did not predict having or forming a Type D attachment.

Attachment disorganization explained not only the degree of vocal distress change, but also the direction of change. Children with organized attachment patterns demonstrated decreases in vocal distress as they matured in the first half of their 2nd year. In contrast, children with disorganized attachments exhibited significant increases in their vocal distress as they got older. These data suggest that attachment disorganization interferes with the development of emotional regulatory systems, a finding consistent with prior research on attachment disorganization. Infants with atypical attachments have been found to exhibit high levels of physiological distress based on their heart rate and cortisol responses during and after the Strange Situation (Hertsgaard et al., 1995; Spangler & Grossmann, 1993). Longitudinal studies of infants have found that Type D attachments in infancy predict conduct problems during the early school years (Lyons-Ruth, 1996). Assessments of attachment among clinically referred preschoolers also suggest that atypical patterns of attachment in particular may contribute to the development of psychopathology (Greenberg, Speltz, DeKlyen, & Endriga, 1991; Lyons-Ruth, 1996; Speltz, Greenberg, & DeKlyen, 1990). The significant increment in vocal distress evidenced by infants with Type D attachments during our study suggests that these children's regulatory problems may begin in infancy and accrue over time unless children's attachment relationship moves toward security in the interim.

The increase in vocalized negative expressivity among children with Type D attachments, however, did not extend during the period from 18 to 24 months. Evidence for an increase in emotional vocal expressivity also was not found when change was examined from 12 to 24 months. These findings could be taken to suggest that the increments in distress from 12 to 18 months either were not reliable findings or were effects children "outgrew" during the subsequent 6-month period. We favor an alternative explanation; namely, children with disorganized attachments do continue to experience negative changes in their negative expressivity and regulatory capacities, but these difficulties are not captured by the vocal distress measure. Vocal distress may not be as sensitive a measure of negative expressivity after 18 months of age. As children mature during infancy and toddlerhood, they develop increasingly sophisticated strategies of emotional expression and regulation (Cicchetti et al., 1991). Perhaps if a second measure of negative expressivity such as coding of facial expressions or psychophysiological indices had been included in this investigation, evidence for continued increases in negative expressivity at the 24-month follow-up would have been obtained. Nonetheless, these data provide evidence of how atypical attachments are not based in temperamental differences, yet can result in problems with distress regulation over time. These findings suggest new conceptualizations regarding how child and parental factors may transact over time to influence the development of maladaptation or psychopathology.

VI. STABILITY AND CHANGE IN INFANT ATTACHMENT IN A LOW-INCOME SAMPLE

Joan I. Vondra, Katherine Dowdell Hommerding, and Daniel S. Shaw

Research on attachment across infancy suggests, on the one hand, that there can be stability of attachment both within infancy (Owen, Easterbrooks, Chase-Lansdale, & Goldberg, 1984; Rauh, Ziegenhain, Muller, & Wijnroks, in press; Waters, 1978) and from infancy to early childhood (Howes & Hamilton, 1992; Main & Cassidy, 1988; Wartner, Grossmann, Fremmer-Bombik, & Suess, 1994). But it also suggests that *in*stability of attachment, which appears to be more common than originally documented (Belsky, Campbell, Cohn, & Moore, 1996; Goldberg et al., under review), may be "lawful" and predictable (Egeland & Farber, 1984; Rauh et al., in press; Thompson, Lamb, & Estes, 1982; Vaughn, Egeland, Waters, & Sroufe, 1979). Change in attachment patterns is associated with changes in caregiving and with maternal and ecological risk factors that themselves can predict caregiving, though usually not in synchrony with changes in attachment (Spieker & Booth, 1988). Understanding not only what individual, family, and even community circumstances are associated with change in attachment, but also how they appear to operate, is critical for understanding the ecology of parenting, parent-child relations, and child development.

The purpose of this investigation was to study the power of various individual and ecological factors (maternal characteristics and behavior, perceptions of social support, and infant characteristics) to differentiate early trajectories toward security (B), organized insecurity (A or C), and disorganization (D) among a sample of socioeconomically disadvantaged families. It also was designed to test the relative stability of attachment in a low-income sample and the relation between these various ecological factors and the level of disorganization or atypicality observed in each attachment. Thus, there is a focus on both traditional patterns of attachment as well as level of disorganization in attachment behavior, and the relation of each to a variety of maternal, child, and contextual factors.

Maternal behavior and maternal and ecological risk factors have already been found to explain higher rates of insecure infant-mother attachment at one point in time. Theoretically important categories of variables that Belsky (1984; Vondra & Belsky, 1993) proposed should influence the quality of parenting have, in fact, been associated with infant attachment security. The vast majority of these studies have been conducted with White, middle-class families, and have used the traditional A, B, C attachment classification system (Ainsworth, Blehar, Waters, & Wall, 1978). Research on high risk or dysfunctional parents, however, has replicated and extended these findings. Summarizing results from seven programs of research involving attachment studies of high-risk, mentally ill, and/or maltreating families, Spieker and Booth (1988) concluded that adolescent parenting, low educational attainment, perceptions of low social support, maternal defensiveness and/or depressive symptomatology, and "insensitive" maternal behavior (whether hostile, unavailable, or intrusive/controlling) all are associated with insecure attachment. To some extent, these also are factors that explain changes toward insecurity *over time*, usually assessed between infancy (12–14 months) and toddlerhood (18–22 months).

Although much of the research supporting hypotheses about stability (and occasionally change) in attachment security has been based on samples of low-risk, middle-class mother-child dyads, a handful of studies have investigated stability of attachment across infancy among low-income and/or high-risk populations. These studies suggest, first, that changes in attachment security—particularly increases in disorganized or atypical ("Unstable A" or "A/C" or "Unclassifiable") attachments—are more characteristic of disadvantaged, high-risk, and/or maltreating populations than they are of low-risk, middle-class populations (Egeland & Sroufe, 1981b; Lyons-Ruth, Repacholi, McLeod, & Silva, 1991; Spieker & Booth, 1988; Vaughn et al., 1979). They also indicate that among the most consistent correlates of the emergence of insecure patterns by 18 months are maternal negative affectivity and psychologically unavailable or hostile/controlling behavior.

Studies involving only classification into the traditional (organized) A, B, and C categories reveal that negative affect or unavailability on the part of mothers is associated with stable insecurity or movement toward insecurity by the 2nd year of life. In most cases, the predominant insecure pattern is avoidance (resistant attachments occur with less frequency, and usually cannot be analyzed separately). Negative affect has been assessed in terms of depressive symptomatology (Egeland & Sroufe, 1981a, 1981b) and a combination of self-reported aggressiveness, suspiciousness, and low social desirability (Egeland & Farber, 1984). Both maternal unavailability (Egeland & Erickson, 1987) and punitive attitudes or controlling behavior (Frodi, Grolnick, & Bridges, 1985) have been studied. Each of these indices of maternal functioning was assessed in the present investigation. Using the D classification, both Egeland and Sroufe (1981b) and Lyons-Ruth and her colleagues (1991) found that psychologically dysfunctional mothers (i.e., those with psychiatric hospitalizations or evidence of child maltreatment) had infants who moved to an atypical classification (usually force-classified as insecure) by 18 months. Barnett, Ganiban, and Cicchetti (this volume) report a high percentage of D classifications beginning at 12 months among a sample of maltreated toddlers and relatively greater stability of classification, perhaps due to the high percentage of type D attachments at every age. A small number of families in the present study were reported for child maltreatment, either of the index child ($n = 6$) or a sibling ($n = 2$), permitting some anecdotal information regarding maltreatment and disorganized attachment.

In terms of infant characteristics, studies show higher physiological reactivity among infants with D attachments in the Strange Situation (Hertsgaard, Gunnar, Erickson, & Nachmias, 1995; Spangler & Grossmann, 1993), although their observed distress isn't significantly different from that of infants with other attachments (Barnett et al., this volume). Prospective studies on observed or mother-rated temperament of infants with atypical attachments are rare (Carlson, 1998). The extant literature suggests that these infants are not necessarily more negative in affect during early infancy, but become easily aroused and/or less able to return to baseline arousal—at least in a separation context—over the course of their early experiences. Their observed distress in the Strange Situation subsequently increases over the 2nd year (Barnett et al., this volume). Whether this increase in distress occurs outside a separation context is unknown. Both observer ratings of fussiness in the lab and maternal ratings of temperamental difficultness were gathered on repeat occasions in the present investigation, allowing examination of these questions.

Given the greater frequency of insecure and disorganized or atypical attachment patterns in at-risk samples, longitudinal studies of attachment in children from disadvantaged and/or troubled families have two distinct, but related, issues to address. First, are there unique correlates of attachment trajectories that move *toward* versus *away from* security? Second, are there unique correlates of trajectories that move *toward* versus *away from* disorganized attachment patterns? In most cases, sample sizes have not been sufficient to examine these two issues simultaneously. Specifically, there are almost no data available adequate for analyses to distinguish infant-mother relationships that show increased avoidance, resistance, or disorganization, versus security. Since many infants from at-risk samples who are classified as atypical or disorganized show modest to moderate avoidance (and are force classified avoidant), it would be particularly useful to distinguish between infants showing movement over time toward organized avoidance versus disorganization. This would begin to build a bridge between older research using the traditional A, B, C scheme versus more recent work incorporating a disorganized or atypical category. An important question that has not yet been addressed empirically is whether a different set of ecological correlates distinguish attachments according to the A, B, C scheme versus attachments varying along a dimension of atypicality. The current study provides an opportunity to address this need, given the availability of longitudinal data on both organized and disorganized attachments for a sample of 90 mother-infant dyads from low-income, socioeconomically disadvantaged families.

METHODS

Sample

Mother-infant dyads for this study were drawn from a sample of 103 urban, low-income mothers and their 1-year-old infants participating in a longitudinal investigation of vulnerability and resilience in early childhood. Mothers with infants between the ages of 5 and 11 months were recruited for the larger investigation from the Women, Infant, and Children (WIC) Supplemental Nutrition Program administered by the County Health Department. Inclusion in the WIC Program requires low income (e.g., less than $22,385 for a family of four, less than $14,837 for a single mother and child in 1989, the 1st year of study recruitment). Women contacted through the WIC office who completed brief background questionnaires and took part in an initial lab assessment with their infant at 12 months were included in the longitudinal investigation. Seventy-two percent of the women approached at WIC came to the University for the first research visit. Only 5% of those contacted at WIC refused to participate, and an additional 23% never appeared. Because screening data were collected at WIC on mothers in the first cohort who agreed to participate, it was possible to test for differences between mothers who did or did not appear for their first visit, or completed only two of four infant assessments. No differences emerged on maternal age, education, race, marital status, or number of children, on self-reported personality, or on perceptions of infant difficultness. Of the 103 mother-infant dyads who appeared for a laboratory visit, 90 had attachment data at both the initial 12-month visit and a follow-up, 18-month visit. These 90 dyads comprise the sample for the present investigation.

At the first laboratory visit (12 months), 41% of mothers reported being married or living with a partner, 14% reported being separated or divorced, and 45% reported being single. Three quarters of the women (75%) reported having a high school education or less at the time of recruitment (19% had no high school degree), 89% reported having a family income of less than $1,500 per month, 40% were of minority race (1 Hispanic, 35 African American), and 17% were teenagers at the time of their first child's birth. Mothers were asked about child maltreatment occuring in their home and six mothers either reported that the target child had been a victim of maltreatment or subsequently had their child removed from the home by Child Protective Services. Two additional mothers reported maltreatment of the child's sibling. Maternal age at the time of recruitment ranged from 16 to 37, with a mean of 25. Of the 90 infants, 40% (36) are female, 47% (42) are firstborn, and 12% (11) were born more than 2 weeks prematurely. The date of the assessments was corrected for infant gestational age.

Procedures

Mothers were paid for completion of the recruitment instruments at the WIC office and for completion of two laboratory visits at the university and one home visit (at 15 months). Each laboratory assessment (12 and 18 months) began with a free play period for the infant (when mothers worked on questionnaires with the Examiner), followed by a series of interactive activities (Examiner absent from the room), a rest/snack period in another room, and the Strange Situation. Mothers then completed questionnaires with the Examiner while a staff member entertained the infant. The laboratory visits took approximately 2 hours to complete and were videotaped through a one-way mirror. The home visit was conducted when infants were approximately 15 months old, and consisted of an infant developmental assessment, an infant free play period (when mothers completed questionnaires with the Examiner), and an interview/observation period during which the quality of the home environment as a context for child development was assessed.

Measures

The purpose of the present investigation was to examine attachment stability and change—and factors associated with each—from 12 to 18 months of age. A primary goal was to distinguish infants moving *toward* versus away from attachment security (i.e., on trajectories toward socioemotional competence or vulnerability) and moving *toward* versus away from organized attachment strategies (i.e., showing any *dis*organization across infancy). Measure selection was guided, in part, by the work of Egeland and his colleagues (Brunnquell, Crichton, & Egeland, 1981; Egeland & Farber, 1984) on attachment among a large sample of infants from disadvantaged backgrounds, and attachment coding strategies were guided by the growing body of work on attachment disorganization and atypicality among infants at risk for developmental psychopathology.

The measures used for this study are summarized in Tables 21 and 22. In some instances, data were combined across two or three assessments to capture a broader index of individual or family circumstances over time. Whenever possible, repeated measures also were examined in terms of change scores from 12 to 18 months.

Infant-Mother Attachment Classification. Attachment security was assessed using the Strange Situation paradigm (Ainsworth & Wittig, 1969). Three coders were trained to reliability (within this lab) and also were separately tested for interrater agreement (outside this lab) using two different sets of attachment assessments, one set from the lab of J. Belsky and a second set from the lab of A. Sroufe. The principal coder, J. Vondra, was trained in the A, B, C system (Ainsworth, Blehar, Waters, & Wall, 1978) by Mary Jo Ward and Brian Vaughn, and in the D system (Main & Solomon, 1990) by Dante Cicchetti; the two additional coders were trained by Vondra. The

TABLE 21

STUDY DESIGN

WIC Screening	Lab 1 Visit	Home Visit	Lab 2 Visit
(5–11 months)	(12 months)	(15 months)	(18 months)
Maternal Interview:	**Maternal Interview:**	**Maternal Interview:**	**Maternal Interview:**
1. Infant Difficult Temperament	1. Infant Difficult Temperament	1. Maternal Anger Control	1. Infant Difficult Temperament
2. Maternal Personality Risk	2. Family Demographic Risk	2. Negative Life Events	2. Maternal IQ and Personality Risk
	3. Relationship Satisfaction		3. Family Demographic Risk
	4. Family Effects		4. Relationship Satisfaction
	5. Maternal Depression		5. Family Effects
			6. Maternal Depression
	Mother-Infant Observation:	**Mother-Infant Observation:**	**Mother-Infant Observation:**
	1. Attachment	1. Quality of Home Environment	1. Attachment
	2. Infant Difficult Temperament		2. Infant Difficult Temperament
	3. Maternal Caregiving		

124

TABLE 22

Constructs and Measures

Maternal Variables	
1. Demographic Risk (Interview Questions) (Scored 0/1 and summed)	Teen at time of first birth High school dropout Racial minority status
2. Intelligence	Estimated IQ (two subscales of WAIS)
3. Personality Risk (Personality Research Form)	High Aggression score with High Defendence score with Low Social Desirability score (Screening + 18 months)
4. Anger Control (State/Trait Anger Inventory)	Anger Control—Anger Expression Difference score (15 months)
5. Relationship Satisfaction (Marital Adjustment Test)	Total score (12 + 18 months) Change score (12 – 18 months)
6. Depressive Symptomatology (Beck Depression Inventory)	Total score unless no feeling state items endorsed (scored 0) (12 + 18 months)
7. Disruptive Events/Influences (Life Events Scale, Interview Questions)	High life events score (15 months) Child care changes > 2 (12–18 months) Neg/No family influences (12, 18 months) More than two moves (12–24 months) Birth of a sibling before 18 months
Infant Variables	
8. Reported Infant Difficultness (Infant Characteristics Questionnaire)	Total score (Screening + 12 + 18 months) Difference score (S – 12 – 18 months)
9. Observed Infant Difficultness (Behavioral Observations)	Sum of Fussing in free play (12, 18 months) and Demanding in high chair (12 months) Difference in free play Fussing (12 – 18 months)
Care Variables	
10. Sensitive Care (Behavioral Observations)	Sensitivity and Cooperation ratings Frequency of Appropriate responses (12 months)
11. Negative Behavior (Behavioral Observations)	Frequency of Intrusive Responses Instances of Negative Affect directed at the infant (12 months)
12. Unresponsive Behavior (Behavioral Observations)	Frequency of Insufficient Responses (12 months)
13. Quality of Home Environment (The HOME Inventory)	Total score (15 months)

principal coder scored 84 (all but six) attachments at 12 months and 30 attachments at 18 months (generally attachments where there was disagreement between coders). All other tapes were scored by one or both additional coders. Of the 28 tapes given a final rating by the principal coder at both 12 and 18 months (with scoring always separated by one to two years), stability of classification was somewhat less (36%) than overall study stability (50%), with stability similarly concentrated among Type B and Type D attachments. Mean interrater reliability (in this lab) on major classifications was

125

80% for all combinations of the three raters using a random set of 10 assessments (representing all four major classifications) from the current study. External agreement on A, B, and C classifications ranged from 80% to 100%, with a mean of 86%, across the three raters for the test assessments.

Because D training took place before publication of the D system, when the D-scale had not yet been developed (a seven-step decision process was outlined), coding of disorganized attachment was conducted conservatively in this investigation, as described below. Raters looked for two sets of features: (a) behavioral indices of disorganization or depressed affect as described by Main and Solomon (1990)—for example, covert swipes at mother, backward or sideways approaches to mother, backing up when mother approaches, simultaneously moving toward and away from mother—and (b) disorganized behavioral sequences across the Strange Situation episodes—for example, marked distress and search for mother in the stranger's presence, followed by immediate avoidance of mother at reunion; intense avoidance in the first reunion with mild or marked resistance but no avoidance in the second reunion. An attachment was classified as disorganized only when (a) there was an overwhelming number of behavioral indices of disorganization or depressed affect in the *absence* of disorganized behavioral sequences (i.e., an organized classification could be identified, but multiple behavioral indices of disorganization were observed simultaneously) or (b) there were at least some behavioral indices of disorganization, but there also was disorganization of behavioral *sequences* so that a traditional classification could not be readily identified (A/C), or each reunion had a distinct—and opposing—classification (usually A then B4, or A then C, with a drop of 4 or more points in avoidance, the Unstable A designation). In contrast to the Main and Solomon (1990) criteria, no single behaviors were considered sufficient—in and of themselves—for inclusion in the disorganized category. The presence, however, of a small number of indices of disorganization in the absence of disorganization in the behavioral sequences was noted by use of the designation, "D-signs." This would be roughly comparable to a 3 to 5 on the 9-point D-scale (Main & Solomon, 1990). The D classification would be roughly comparable to a score of 6 to 9 on the D-scale. Infants were designated as stable in having a disorganized attachment when they were classified as disorganized in at least one assessment, but also showed some behavioral indices of disorganization at the second assessment, whether or not they were formally classified as "disorganized." Of the 12 cases designated as stable D, five were classified D at both assessments, four were coded as having D-signs at both assessments, and three showed D-signs at 12 months and were classified D at 18 months.

Demographic Risk. A summary risk score for each mother was computed on the basis of demographic information collected during the initial recruitment session. Contributing factors (scored as zero or one, and summed) were teen parenthood at first birth, failure to complete high school, and racial minority status. Each of these indices of demographic status is associated with socioeconomic hardship and lower social status in the United States, important risk factors for individual and family functioning.

Maternal IQ. Maternal IQ was estimated from two subscales of the WAIS-R, administered when infants were 24 months old. The composite score from these two subscales, Vocabulary and Block Design, has a high correlation with the full-scale IQ (Sattler, 1988).

Personality Risk. Based on Egeland and Farber's (1984) work, a personality risk score was created from subscales of a personality inventory (the *Personality Research Form*, Jackson, 1989) administered both at recruitment (5–11 months) and at the 18-month laboratory visit. The three scales each include 16 true-false items, with internal consistency ranging from .72 to .87 (Stumpf, Wieck, & Jackson, 1976), and test-retest reliability ranging from .84 to .87 (Jackson & Morf, 1973). Mothers scoring above the sample mean on both aggressiveness and defendence, and below the sample mean on social desirability, were considered at risk of fostering an insecure attachment relationship with their infant. Risk scores (0 or 1) were summed across the two assessments in an effort to create a more reliable measure by capturing more enduring personality dispositions. Final scores therefore ranged from 0 (never fit the personality profile) to 2 (fit the personality profile at both assessments).

Anger Control. Maternal self-reported anger control versus anger expression was obtained during the home visit at 15 months. This variable was computed as the difference between anger control and anger expression scores on the Anger Expression Scale of the *State-Trait Anger Expression Inventory* (Spielberger, 1991). Mothers scoring higher on this measure endorse items indicating ability to control anger ("I keep my cool"), but not items indicating behavioral expressions of anger ("I argue with others").

Depressive Symptomatology. Self-reported maternal depressive symptomatology was assessed at 12 and 18 months using the short form of the Beck *Depression Inventory* (Beck & Beamesderfer, 1974). Scores were both subtracted (12 – 18 months), to create a measure of change in depressive symptoms, and summed (12 + 18 months), to capture average level of depressive symptomatology over the six-month study period.

Relationship Satisfaction. Maternal perceptions of the quality of her relationship with a partner were assessed using the short form of the *Marital Adjustment Test* (Locke & Wallace, 1959). This measure has proven successful

127

in discriminating harmonious and disturbed/conflicted marriages (Gottman, Markman, & Notarius, 1977; Hershorn & Rosenbaum, 1983; Rosenbaum & O'Leary, 1981), and also predicts children's behavior problems (Emery & O'Leary, 1982). Scores on the measure correlate with self-reported relationship violence and with children's distress reaction to expressed adult anger (Cummings, Pellegrini, Notarius, & Cummings, 1989). Because a number of mothers reported that a person other than a husband or boyfriend served as their significant other (16% mother, 9% other relative or friend, 11% no significant other at 12 months), the measure's wording was modified ("relationship" vs. "marriage") for use with whatever partner (mother, sister, girlfriend) might be identified. Scores at the 12- and 18-month laboratory visits were once again combined in two ways: (a) difference scores were computed to measure change in level of satisfaction, and (b) sums were computed to capture the average quality of partner relationship over the period of study.

Disruptive Events and Influences. Other contextual influences of importance were examined through a summary score of events and influences that mothers reported during the period from 12 to 18 months. This score was the sum of five measures, each scored present or absent: (a) negative life events reported at the 15-month visit above the sample mean (using the *Life Experiences Survey*, Sarason, Johnson, & Siegel, 1978), (b) more than two changes in childcare arrangements reported between 12 and 18 months (e.g., from maternal care to grandmother care to babysitter), (c) mother's report of *only* negative family influences on her child or her denial of *any* family influence during this same period (it was assumed that denial of family influence is an indication that mothers will fail to see a need to protect their child from problematic family events or circumstances), (d) the birth of a sibling before the target child turned 18 months, and (e) two or more moves in the child's 2nd year of life. Total scores reflect disruptive, stressful events occurring before the children turned 2.

Infant Difficultness. Two kinds of assessments for infant difficultness were obtained to distinguish between observed infant behavior and maternal perceptions of difficultness. Behavioral measures consisted of (a) the *sum* at 12 and 18 months of the number of seconds infants fussed during the 15-min free play, and at 12 months, the number of seconds infants demanded maternal attention during a brief period sitting in a high chair (most typically by fussing) and (b) the *difference* in amount (seconds) of fussing at the 12- versus 18-month free play. The perceptual measures were (a) the *sum* of ratings of difficultness mothers made at the screening, the 12-month, and 18-month visits, using items constituting the "difficultness" factor for each age on the *Infant Characteristics Questionnaire* (ICQ; Bates, Freeland, & Lounsbury, 1979), and (b) the *change* in ratings from the screening to the 12- and 18-month visits (S – 12 – 18 difference score). Interrater reliability for infant demandingness was calculated on 14 cases selected at random from the sample as the mean percentage agreement among three coders who were blind to attachment classification of incidences of each behavioral code for 3-s scoring intervals. Mean agreement was 93%. Interrater reliability for fussiness during play was calculated on 60 cases at 12 months and 20 cases at 18 months. Percent agreement between raters about the occurrence of any fussing across the entire play session was 85% and 75%, respectively. Among children with any coded fussing, agreement about the amount of fussing (in seconds) was computed by correlation. Correlations were .98 at both time points.

Small correlations (around .20, $p < .10$) were found between the three observed indices of fussing/demanding, moderate to strong correlations (.51 to .70, $p < .001$) correlations were found between the three maternal reports of difficultness, but *no* correlations were found between observed fussing and reported difficultness. The authors of the ICQ reported moderate correlations between mothers' and observers' ratings on the ICQ, $r(98) = .34$, $p < .001$, and acceptable test-retest stability ($r = .59$) between observations (2–10 day intervals).

Quality of Maternal Care. Measures of maternal care included both behavioral ratings (Ainsworth et al., 1978) and behavioral frequencies (Martin, 1981; Smith & Pederson, 1988) assigned to mothers by trained raters blind to attachment classification during three different interactive tasks during the laboratory visit at 12 months. In the first, infants were seated in a high chair for 3 min while mothers worked on questionnaires nearby; in the second, infants were removed from the high chair but given no toys to play with for an additional 3 min while mothers continued completing questionnaires; and in the third, mothers were asked to get their child to complete a series of challenging tasks (e.g., putting away toys, working an activity box, completing a puzzle) for a total of 12 min. Independent raters coded each of the three tasks. These caregiving tasks and scores are described in more detail elsewhere (Vondra, Shaw, & Kevenides, 1995), demonstrated adequate interrater reliability and, when used to create composite indices, discriminated among mothers of infants with avoidant, resistant, and secure attachment classifications at 12 months.

Quality of the Home Environment. Ratings of the quality of the home as a supportive context for child development were completed by observers at the 15-month home visit using the *Home Observation for Measurement of the Environment (HOME) Inventory* (Caldwell & Bradley, 1984). The infant version consists of a 45-item checklist arranged in six subscales, including "Emotional and Verbal Responsivity of Parent," "Acceptance of Child Behavior," and

"Provision of Appropriate Play Materials." Information needed to score Inventory items is obtained through a combination of observation and interview (with the mother). The total score was used in analyses.

RESULTS AND DISCUSSION

Attachment Stability

Table 23 provides data on stability and change in attachment classification from 12 to 18 months. At 12 months, 50% of the sample was scored secure, 30% organized insecure, and 20% disorganized. By 18 months, only 42% was scored secure, 29% organized insecure, and 29% disorganized. The number of secure attachments decreased and number of disorganized attachments increased across infancy. Stability in this sample, like that in Barnett's (this volume) maltreated sample, was concentrated among children with either secure or disorganized attachments. Twenty-nine percent of the 90 children were coded as having secure attachments at both 12 and 18 months; 13% were coded as showing disorganization in their attachment at both 12 and 18 months. Only 8% of the sample showed a stable pattern of organized *in*security (either avoidance or resistance). This represents a 50% rate of classification stability, a very modest but—with a sample of 90—statistically significant pattern ($\kappa = .28$, $p < .05$). There was as much change in classification as there was stability over a 6-month interval.

Table 24 provides a comparison of these results with four other investigations of infant-mother attachment among disadvantaged populations. Egeland and Farber (1984) reported only stability data within the A, B, C classification scheme. Both Lyons-Ruth et al. (1991) and Barnett, Ganniban, and Cicchetti (this volume) had smaller samples, about half of which consist

TABLE 23

STABILITY OF ATTACHMENT CLASSIFICATIONS

12-Month Attachment Classification	18-Month Attachment Classification				
	(B) Secure	(C) Resistant	(A) Avoidant	(D) Disorganized	TOTAL
Secure	26	3	9	7	45
Resistant	4	2	5	3	14
Avoidant	4	0	5	4	13
Disorganized	4	1	1	12	18
TOTAL	38	6	20	26	90

Stable Secure (B) = 58% of Bs, 29% of sample
Stable Resistant (C) = 14% of Cs, 2% of sample
Stable Avoidant (A) = 38% of As, 6% of sample
Stable Disorganized (D) = 67% of Ds, 13% of sample
Overall Stability = 50% ($\kappa = .28$, p < .05)

TABLE 24

Stability Comparisons Across Samples

	N	ABC Scheme	ABCD Scheme	% D 12/13 months	% D 18/20 months	Stable D
Egeland & Farber, 1984 (disadvantaged)	189	60%	—	—	—	—
Current Investigation (disadvantaged)	90	54%	50%	20%	29%	67%
Maslin-Cole & Spieker, 1990 (disadvantaged)	75	—	—	29%	33%	—
Lyons-Ruth et al., 1991 (half maltreated)	46	60%	30%	22%	41%	30%
Barnett et al., this volume (half maltreated)	39	54%	64%	54%	46%	67%

of cases of child maltreatment. Maslin-Cole and Spieker (1990) did not provide overall stability figures. In terms of forced classifications, the four relevant investigations are quite comparable, with stability of classification ranging from 54 to 60%. There is great variability in terms of stability, however, when disorganization is identified and distinguished from organized classifications (30–67%). The only figure in any way comparable across all three investigations, in that case, is the percentage of disorganization noted at 18 months (29–46%), which is higher than that van IJzendoorn, Schuengel, & Bakersman-Kranenburg (1999) reported (24%) in their metanalysis of low-socioeconomic-status samples. Although rates of disorganization were lowest in the current investigation (no doubt reflecting both the maltreatment sampling in other studies and the conservative scoring strategy adopted in the present study), they were comparable to two of the three other investigations. These data suggest sample variability, certainly, but also probable variation in scoring criteria for disorganization. Although there is reasonable agreement, based on the work of Main and Solomon, about the various behavioral indices indicative of disorganization, there is potential for disagreement about the number and severity of indices that must exist before a child's attachment is deemed "disorganized." This is captured in the broadly delineated "D scale" by Main and Solomon (1990), and by the distinction between no D signs, some D signs, or the D classification in the present study.

Attachment Disorganization

Among the 24 children whose attachment showed at least some signs of disorganization at 12 months, 13 were designated as having D-signs, five showed the A/C mix, five showed unstable avoidance, and one appeared depressed. Of these subsets of children, the A/C group was least likely to be force-classified as secure or *to become secure* at 18 months. Among the 35 children whose attachment showed at least some signs of disorganization at 18 months, 14 were designated as having D-signs, seven showed the A/C mix, six showed unstable avoidance, and eight appeared depressed. Of these subsets of children, the A/C group was again the least likely to be force-classified secure or *to have been secure* at 12 months. Disorganized attachments designated as A/C were somewhat less likely to be associated with security and more likely to be associated with disorganization than were those designated as Unstable A, probably due to the coding requirements of each (e.g., the Unstable A pattern requires a marked decrease in avoidance). Attachment history and force-classification of attachments showing some disorganization are summarized in Table 25.

Group Differences

In this section, data are summarized with respect to attachment group differences on each of the indices summarized in Table 22. Six attachment subgroups were identified for study that reflect two methodological objectives: (a) maintaining distinctions between different patterns of attachment across time, and (b) ensuring adequate subsample size and internal consistency within groups. The six attachment subgroups designated in Table 26 seemed to provide the best balance between these two priorities. It should be noted, however, that the relatively large number of subgroups (six) and the small group sizes (6 to 26 dyads) limit the power of the statistical tests. These

TABLE 25

ATTACHMENT HISTORY AND FORCED CLASSIFICATION IN CASES WITH DISORGANIZATION

		12-Month Attachment		
	D-Signs	Unstable A	A/C	Depressed
N	13	5	5	1
Percentage Forced Secure	38%	20%	0	100%
Percentage Secure at 18 Months	31%	60%	20%	0
Percentage With Some Disorganization at 18 Months	54%	20%	60%	100%
		18-Month Attachment		
	D-Signs	Unstable A	A/C	Depressed
N	14	6	7	8
Percentage Forced Secure	36%	83%	0	12%
Percentage Secure at 12 Months	29%	50%	29%	25%
Percentage With Some Disorganization at 12 Months	36%	33%	57%	12%

TABLE 26

ATTACHMENT TRAJECTORY SUBSAMPLES

12–18 Month Attachment Subsample	n	Percentage of 12-Month Group	Percentage of Total Sample	Percentage with D-Signs at any Time
Stable B	26	58% (of Bs)	29%	19% (5)
A,C,D → B	12	27% (of A,C,D)	13%	17% (2)
A,B,C,D → C	6	7% (of A,B,C,D) (3 from Bs)	7%	17% (1)
A,B,C,D → A	20	22% (of A,B,C,D) (9 from Bs)	22%	40% (8)
A,B,C → D	14	19% (of A,B,C) (7 from Bs)	16%	0% (0)*
Stable D	12	67% (of Ds)	13%	67% (8)*
FULL SAMPLE	90			27% (24)

* By definition, any 12-month-old with D-signs classified as having D-signs or being D at 18 months was considered a stable D.

consisted of univariate ANOVAs for each independent variable and Bonferoni tests for post hoc comparisons of differences that emerged.

Given the relative stability of the secure and disorganized groups from 12 to 18 months, we distinguished between those infants who were consistent over time in their security ("Stable B") or their disorganization ("Stable D") and those who moved *toward* security ("A,C,D → B") or disorganization ("A,B,C → D"). On the other hand, the relative instability of avoidant and resistant strategies forced us to combine infants into groups based on their movement *toward* organized avoidance ("A,B,C,D → A") or organized resistance ("A,B,C,D → C") in their attachment. As can be seen from the group difference results, summarized in Tables 27 and 28, this scheme proved fairly successful in providing some insights into individual, relational, and

TABLE 27

SUBSAMPLE DIFFERENCES: MATERNAL VARIABLES

12–18 Attachment Subsample	n	Demographic Risk Sum	Personality Risk Sum	Anger Control Score	Relationship Satisfaction Sum	Depressive Symptoms (Sum)	Disruptive Events
Stable B	23–26	.50	.15[a]	6.72	211.88[a]	12.42	.72[a]
A,C,D → B	10–12	1.00	.17[a]	9.45	221.45[a]	16.82	.55[a]
A,B,C,D → C	6	.00	.17	7.33	141.17[b]	21.00	.67
A,B,C,D → A	18–20	.90	.35	2.39[b]	201.60	17.45	1.06
A,B,C → D	13–14	.93	.21[a]	10.62[a]	15.00[a]	13.43	1.69[b]
Stable D	12	.85	.83[b]	5.08	230.50[a]	18.42	.83
		$F(5, 84)$ = 3.65**	$F(5, 84)$ = 3.00*	$F(5, 79)$ = 3.32**	$F(5, 82)$ = 1.96	$F(5, 83)$ = ns	$F(5, 79)$ = 2.90*

*$p < .05$
**$p < .01$
[a, b] Column means with different superscripts are significantly different from each other at $p < .05$.

TABLE 28

Subsample Differences: Infant Variables

12–18 Month Attachment Subsample	n	Summed Reported Infant Difficultness	Change in Reported Infant Difficultness	Summed Observed Infant Difficultness	Change in Observed Infant Difficultness
Stable B	23–26	−.26	.53	−.55[a]	.85[a]
A,C,D → B	10–12	.87	−.32	.19	−3.25[a]
A,B,C,D → C	6	.23	.59	2.47[b]	43.33[b]
A,B,C,D → A	18–20	.57	−.36	−.29[a]	9.33[a]
A,B,C → D	13–14	−.53	.36	.31	3.57[a]
Stable D	12	.44	−.79	−.79[a]	0.00[a]
		$F(5, 82)$ $= ns$	$F(5, 82)$ $= 2.61*$	$F(5, 76)$ $= 3.10*$	$F(5, 82)$ $= 3.93*$

* $p < .05$
** $p < .01$
[a, b] Column means with different superscripts are significantly different from each other at $p < .05$.

circumstantial differences between the mother-infant dyads we studied. Overall effects are summarized here, and differences between attachment subgroups are described subsequently.

Maternal Variables. Of the maternal variables, demographic and personality risk, self-reported anger control, and reported disruptive events and influences each showed an overall (sample-wide) effect of attachment subgroup. Summed maternal relationship satisfaction showed a trend toward significance, due to differences related to one of the smaller subgroups. Only maternal depressive symptomatology showed no relation to subgroup membership. It is not the case, however, that depressive symptomatology was unrelated to changes in attachment. Separate analyses (Hommerding, Shaw, & Vondra, 1993) showed that mothers reporting greater symptomatology had infants who were more likely to move from a secure to *any* insecure pattern by 18 months, particularly girls. Self-reported depressive symptoms did not, however, distinguish among the trajectories toward the *specific* patterns of insecurity examined in the present study.

Finally, change scores based on both 12- and 18-month data, computed for partner satisfaction and depressive symptomatology, did not distinguish among the attachment subgroups. The failure of the change scores to explain changes in attachment security may reflect methodological issues more than substantive ones. Summing 12- and 18-month scores may improve the reliability of the measures significantly over change scores. Alternatively, *changes* in mothers' relationship perceptions and self-ratings may be relatively insignificant in the face of broad individual differences *between* mothers in these perceptions, and/or may not be apparent in terms of mother-infant relationship quality until some later point in time. It is worth noting, however, that five of the six (individual or summed) maternal variables under investigation showed some effect of infant-mother attachment trajectory in this analysis.

Infant Variables. Group effects were also found using the infant temperament variables, particularly observed behavior. Decreases in high observed infant fussiness from the first to the second year (12 months–18 months) helped distinguish the "C" attachment subgroup. Greater overall (summed) observed fussiness also showed this group difference, but mothers' summed rating of infant difficultness (screening + 12 months + 18 months) did not. Decreased difficultness of the group of children who became "C" by 18 months resulted from extremely high difficultness scores at 12 months, due to a subset of unusually fussy infants, and scores that were still high, but more consistent with the rest of the sample, by 18 months. Likewise, mothers in the "C" group reported the highest infant difficultness at screening (when infants were 6 to 12 months old), but lower difficultness at 12 and 18 months. Less sensitive care and insecure attachment have both been associated with greater behavioral and emotional "difficultness" across infancy (Engfer, 1986; Fish, Stifter, & Belsky, 1991; Matheny, 1986). Whether a baby with "difficult" temperamental characteristics elicits less sensitive care, or a parent who sees his or her infant in a negative light provides less sensitive care, there is certainly a basis for expecting some association between infant fussy, demanding behavior and both parental caregiving and infant-parent attachment security. At the same time, fussy, demanding infants may be somewhat more prone to developing anxious-resistant attachments (Calkins & Fox, 1992; Crockenberg, 1981; Grossmann et al., 1985), or at least insecure attachments (Type A, van den Boom, 1989), as some data suggest. In this sample, assessed difficultness among the children whose attachments moved to C at 18 months seemed more exclusively an issue in the 1st year of life.

Care Variables. Only the indices of care were consistent in showing no effect of attachment trajectory. Across all groups, measures of maternal care and the quality of the home environment, surprisingly, did not show any pattern of systematic covariance with attachment classification over time. Although 12-month measures were associated with contemporaneous, 12-month forced classifications (Vondra et al., 1995), there was no predictive association with attachment at 18 months using 12-month indices of sensitive care, negative behavior, or unresponsive behavior. In most cases, the variability within groups was quite large, easily overpowering variability between groups. The only consistent observable pattern was a tendency for the small number of mothers of infants who were classified as resistant by

135

18 months to look consistently *best* on 12-month care measures and the 15-month measure of home environment, similar to a finding reported by Egeland and Farber (1984). It should be noted, however, that none of these measures attempts to capture covert hostility (also termed affective communication errors), a contradictory blend of positive affect and hostile behavior, disorientation, or role reversal, which Lyons-Ruth and her colleagues (1991, this volume) found useful in distinguishing infants with disorganized attachments. On the other hand, both withdrawal and negative, intrusive behavior were assessed, and proved unsuccessful in differentiating attachment change groups. In the six cases of known child maltreatment involving the target child, however, all but one involved a "D" classification at 12 or 18 months, and the single exception was designated as stable D, because D-signs were noted at both 12 and 18 months. One of the two sibling abuse cases was classified as D at 12 months (both moved to "A" at 18 months).

In the next section, these overall effects are examined in greater detail in terms of their ability to discriminate among the attachment subgroups. Rather than present the findings in piecemeal fashion, variable by variable, the findings are summarized for each subgroup. The point in doing this is to create a more integrated picture of the nature of and differences between mother-infant dyads comprising the six attachment trajectory groups. The relevant data appear in Tables 26 to 28.

Attachment Subgroups

Stable Security. Almost 60% of the infants who were secure in their attachment relationship at 12 months also were secure at 18 months. This group of mothers and infants was most remarkable for never scoring high on any risk factors. In this sample, the stable secure dyads stand out for what they *lack* by way of risk. In fact, this group was usually among the lowest on all mean risk indices, although there was enough subgroup variation across the whole sample that this difference was only occasionally significant. Relatively few mothers reported aggressive and suspicious feelings without a need to look socially desirable (significant), clinically significant depressive symptoms, either notably angry feelings or high anger control, or dissatisfaction with intimate relationships. They also reported fewer disruptive family events or influences (significant).

Trajectory Toward Security. About one quarter of the infants insecurely attached at 12 months appeared secure by 18 months. Avoidant, resistant, and disorganized attachments at 12 months were equally represented (*n* = 4 of each) in this group. In 75% of the cases, this was a first child, and there was some indication that these were more likely to be teen mothers, high school dropouts, and/or of minority race. They were also the least likely to have a spouse or cohabiting partner at both 12 and 18 months (only one third had one). But these mothers scored relatively *low* on the aggressive/suspicious personality risk complex that Egeland and Farber (1984) identified, high on mean relationship satisfaction (with partner, friend, or mother), and low on disruptive events and influences on their infants in the 1st year. These may be women who became mothers before they were psychologically prepared for the role, but who were able—in the absence of too many personal or circumstantial stressors—to grow with the role across infancy.

Trajectory Toward Organized Resistance. This was the smallest subgroup of the study, only 7% (*n* = 6, two of whom showed stable resistance) of the sample, so differences associated with this group are most tenuous. Still, they provided the clearest replication of results Egeland and Farber (1984) reported for their low-income sample; namely, what appears to be a group of hard-to-care-for infants with mothers who grow increasingly anxious and depressed across infancy.

In the current sample, these infants were more often firstborn and male, with the highest sample mean on total observed difficultness, but also the greatest decline in fussing from 12 to 18 months. This was the only subgroup scoring high across all three measures of observed temperamental difficultness (two at 12 months, one at 18 months). Mothers did not, however, report that their infants were noticeably difficult, except at the initial screening when infants were between 6 and 12 months old. None of these women were at demographic risk due to age, education, or minority status, but instead were all White and had intimate, cohabiting partners both at 12 and 18 months. They were noticeably negative, however, about their marital relationship. This group may represent the problematic combination of a struggling marriage and a baby who is, at least initially, more difficult in temperament.

Trajectory Toward Organized Avoidance. By 18 months, 19% (*n* = 20, five of whom showed stable avoidance) of the infants were classified as avoidant. These children were more often laterborn. Mothers in this group were *least* likely to have someone they could call a partner or significant other at 12 months, and half had no husband or cohabiting boyfriend at both points in time, a finding that echoes the pattern of not living with a partner discerned by Egeland and Farber (1984) in their "Stable Avoidant" group. This may be an important reflection of discontinuity of relationships among women in this group, who not only had had a partner a year or two earlier, but also tended to have older children as well.

The only other distinguishing characteristic noted for women in this group is their self-reported anger. On average, these mothers reported the most anger expression and the least anger control in our sample. Both at 12 and at 18 months, however, these mothers were among the least likely to *show* anger toward their infants during the teaching tasks. The negative affectivity that both Belsky (Belsky & Nezworski, 1988) and Spieker (Spieker & Booth, 1988) have discussed in relation to attachment insecurity was expressed quite differently in the various subgroups of mothers of insecurely attached infants. Whereas the mothers of infants who moved toward resistance expressed feelings of sadness and of dissatisfaction with their close relationships, the mothers of infants who moved toward avoidance reported feelings of anger. A third pattern of negative affectivity emerged for the mothers of infants demonstrating a disorganized attachment, relating to personality factors and disruptive family events and influences.

Stable Disorganization and Trajectory Toward Disorganization. Twenty-nine percent of the sample was classified as disorganized in attachment by 18 months of age, with half of that group showing either disorganized signs or patterns at 12 months as well. As Lyons-Ruth and her colleagues found (this volume) there may be an overrepresentation of boys in these subgroups (67–71% male, vs. 40% male for the sample as a whole). Mothers scored highest on the personality risk complex that Egeland and Farber (1984) identified: high on aggressiveness, high on defendence or suspiciousness, and low on social desirability. A question worth raising is how many of the children in the "B"-to-"A" group in Egeland's sample, whose mothers scored high on this complex, would actually have been classified as disorganized at one or both assessments, using current standards.

Mothers of the 15% of children who moved *out* of an organized attachment strategy at 12 months to a disorganized attachment classification at 18 months reported the most disruptive family events and influences across the 1st year. These same mothers, however, reported having the *least* expressed anger and the *most* anger control at the home visit, although they showed no less anger toward their infants during teaching tasks at 12 and 18 months than did other mothers. At 12 months, their infants' attachments had largely reflected the sample distribution (50% "B," 21% "C," and 29% "A"). They described negative events and changes, talked about entirely negative or no family influences whatsoever on their infant, but also described themselves as people who do not get angry.

In sum, both groups of mothers whose infants were classified as disorganized in their attachment by 18 months seemed different on several personality indices. It is not, however, simply a case of their being higher on overall negative affectivity. Mothers whose infants began showing signs of disorganization only at 18 months tended to report many disruptive events or circumstances, but not the affective experiences one might expect to accompany them, neither depression, anger, nor dissatisfaction with their intimate relationship. Mothers whose infants were consistently disorganized were more likely to describe themselves and others as hostile, yet were satisfied in their relationship with a significant other (whether husband, friend, or mother). It is possible that this is another reflection of the kind of affective inconsistency Lyons-Ruth and her colleagues (1991, this volume) have captured behaviorally in mothers of infants with D attachments.

Analyses Within the Disorganized Group

Two kinds of subgroup analyses were run using only children with disorganized attachments by 18 months, but *no* consistent differences were found on any of the variables from Table 22. These analyses distinguished between (a) infants who were force-classified as secure versus insecure and, separately, (b) infants who demonstrated a pattern of mixed avoidance and resistance in each reunion (A/C) versus high avoidance in the first reunion and no avoidance (but often resistance) in the second reunion (Unstable A). Means were so similar in *both* comparisons that sample size restrictions (and consequent lack of statistical power) did not appear to be an explanation. Thus, the distinction Lyons-Ruth and her colleagues (1991, this volume) found useful between infants with signs of disorganization who fit a "secure" versus insecure pattern did not prove effective here in distinguishing mothers on a variety of demographic and self-report measures. Similarly, mothers of children whose attachments combined avoidance and resistance in each reunion (A/C) or changed dramatically across reunions from avoidance to proximity-seeking with or without resistance (Unstable A) did not differ in describing themselves, their children, or their circumstances.

As noted earlier, however, the A/C combination was somewhat less likely to be associated with security and more likely to be associated with disorganization within and over time. Of the six child maltreatment cases, all of which showed some disorganization, one was designated as D-signs at both 12 and 18 months, one each showed the A/C or Unstable A pattern at 12 months, and three appeared depressed at 18 months. Three of the children were classified or force-classified B at some point. Again, the distinction among different subgroups of disorganized attachments did not appear especially revealing. Indeed, analyses described in the next section indicate that on some measures, the mothers of children whose attachments were considered only borderline disorganized ("D-signs") appeared most problematic.

Classification Scheme Versus Disorganization Level

The final set of analyses, partly redundant with the ANOVAs already conducted, demonstrated the importance of taking into account both (a) the *style* of the attachment pattern over time (forced classification) and (b) the amount of *disorganization* present, particularly by 18 months. These two pieces of data accounted for unique variance in data on the children, mothers, and family circumstances across the infancy period. The nonoverlapping nature of their contributions is evident in analyses using forced classifications (A, B, C) versus level of disorganization (none, D-signs, D classification) at 12 months and 18 months as independent variables (along with their interaction) in separate analyses of variance to account for variation in maternal and infant data. Results appear in Table 29. With the exception of the demographic risk score, maternal reported anger control, and change in reported infant difficultness, either forced classifications or disorganization resulted in a significant model. There was no factor, however, for which *both* schemes demonstrated significant effects. When one scheme demonstrated a pattern of group differences, the other did not.

Thus, *forced classifications* at one or both ages explained differences on scores for maternal depressive symptoms ("Cs" highest), anger control at 18 months only ("As" lowest), relationship satisfaction ("As" highest, "Cs" lowest), and observed infant difficultness ("Cs" highest). In previous analyses of caregiving (Vondra, Shaw, & Kevenides, 1995), mothers of infants with resistant (force-classified) attachments at 12 months scored highest on a composite score of unresponsiveness to their infants' signals at the same assessment. Those having avoidant relationships with their infants scored highest on a composite of controlling behavior, and those having secure relationships scored highest on sensitive care. Level of *disorganization*, in contrast, explained differences on scores for hostile, suspicious personality ("D-Signs" highest) and for disruptive events and influences ("Ds" highest). In the few instances where differences in 12-month maternal interactive behavior exist, it is the mothers of infants with only a moderate level of disorganization ("D-Signs") who looked worst on individual indices of care. Again, disorganization also was related to child maltreatment in the small number of known cases in this sample. Obviously, there is an association between relationship insecurity and maternal negative affectivity in general, but the form and expression differed considerably across the different patterns and quality of insecurity. Because these analyses to some extent repeat the ANOVAs conducted on subgroups, there is likely some inflation of alpha in reporting results. The pattern, however, is striking and deserves both replication and consideration.

The fact that either one *or* the other scheme provided significant discriminative power supports the original subgroup analysis, which in many ways represents an effort to capitalize both on the style *and* presence of attachment organization. By using both sets of information, we appear to have gained in our understanding of how individual and/or contextual factors can differ systematically with qualitative differences in the parent-infant relationship.

TABLE 29

Alternative Group Difference Models

	Forced Classification (A,B,C)	Degree of Disorganization (None, D-Signs, D)
Demographic Risk	model F = ns	model F = ns
Summed (S + 18 months) Personality Risk	model F = ns	model $F(8, 78)$ = 3.14** 18m F = ns 12m $F(2, 78)$ = 5.98** 12m × 18m = ns (at 12m: D-signs > None)
Anger Control (15 months)	model F = ns 18m $F(2, 71)$ = 5.12** 12m F = ns 12m × 18m = ns (at 18m: B > A)	model F = ns
Relationship Satisfaction (12 months + 18 months)	model $F(8, 75)$ = 3.76*** 18m $F(2, 75)$ = 6.12** 12m $F(2, 75)$ = 6.22** 12m × 18m = ns (at 12m: A > B,C) (at 18m: A,B > C)	model F = ns
Disruptive Events (12 months–18 months)	model F = ns	model $F(7, 68)$ = 2.18* 18m $F(2, 68)$ = 5.82** 12m = ns 12m × 18m = ns (at 18m: D > D-signs, None)
Depressive Symptomatology (12 months + 18 months)	model $F(8, 76)$ = 3.34** 18m $F(2, 76)$ = 7.79*** 12m F = ns 12m × 18m F = ns (at 18m: C > B)	model F = ns
Observed Infant Difficultness (12 months + 18 Months)	model $F(8, 70)$ = 4.58*** 18m F = ns 12m $F(2, 70)$ = 14.82*** 12m × 18m = ns (at 12m: C > A,B)	model F = ns
Reported Change in Difficultness (S – 12 months – 18 months)	model F = ns	model F = ns

* $p < .05$
** $p < .01$

SUMMARY AND CONCLUSIONS

Results of this investigation support the need to consider both traditional *patterns* of attachment (A, B, C) and level of *disorganization* or atypicality as each change over time. Change in patterns of attachment was at least as common as stability over a 6-month period for this sample of infants from socioeconomically disadvantaged families. On the one hand, a likely circumstance receiving little attention in the empirical literature is that attachment classification and change in classification may well reflect "error" variance associated, for example, with infant illness or fatigue and temporary disruptive family events, as well as coder unreliability. The somewhat low rate of stability in this and other disadvantaged samples could reflect greater coder unreliability in scoring infant adaptations to social class differences in parenting style, to stressful home experiences, and to changing social circumstances. The higher rate of stress and mental health problems in lower-income families, however, also could explain "lawful" discontinuities in attachment classification. Collaboration across laboratories in double-scoring of attachment videotapes is one strategy for studying these issues, as are social class comparisons of Strange Situation behavior conducted within a laboratory.

At the same time, attachment instability appears to be more common than originally thought, even among White, middle-class samples (Belsky, Campbell, et al., 1996). It seems clear from this and other research on attachment stability and change across infancy that there is a systematic component to change that covaries with individual maternal and infant factors, as well as with family circumstances. This systematic component involves meaningful variation both in the type of organized pattern discerned *and* in the degree of disorganization apparent over time, each of which have unique contextual correlates.

Organized insecurity was associated with maternal reported depressive symptoms, relationship dissatisfaction, and observed infant difficultness. Disorganized patterns and indices were associated with maternal reported aggressiveness and suspiciousness, with disruptions in or instability of family life and, anecdotally, with child maltreatment. Within the group of disorganized attachments, distinctions between forced classifications (secure, not secure) and between subtypes (A/C, Unstable A), though limited by small numbers, were notably unrevealing. More important were the boundaries of what constituted a "disorganized" attachment. By studying those children whose attachments appeared borderline disorganized ("D-signs"), and by including in the disorganized classification children with the Unstable A pattern, patterns of association emerged with maternal report and observer ratings. The inconsistency between these findings and results reported by Lyons-Ruth (this volume) may reflect sampling fluctuation, since both are based on small samples. They also may point to differences across laboratories in criteria for D classification. Viewing disorganization along a continuum of severity seems a fruitful approach at the present time, while distinctions among children showing atypical attachment patterns receive further examination.

Results replicated earlier findings that insecurity by 18 months is associated with indicators of maternal negative affect, but not with earlier maternal behavior that was unresponsive to, controlling of, or angry in relation to the infant. Self-reported anger distinguished mothers of infants with avoidant attachments, relationship dissatisfaction, mothers of resistant infants, and perceived hostility in self and others, mothers of infants with stable, disorganized attachments. Mothers in the resistant attachment group were at noticeably lower demographic risk (none were teen mothers, high-school dropouts, of minority race, or without a male partner) than were mothers in all but the stable secure group, but their infants expressed the most negative affect of any group at 12 months and their intimate relationships caused these mothers the most dissatisfaction.

This study was unique in being able to compare circumstances and behavior of mothers whose infants *became* secure or disorganized by 18 months, versus those whose infants showed a stable pattern of security or disorganization from 12 to 18 months. Mothers of infants who became secure at 18 months may have been less prepared psychologically for childrearing than mothers in the stable secure group in that they were often young and usually dealing with a firstborn child. Mothers of infants who became disorganized at 18 months, like mothers in the secure groups, scored lower on the personality complex of aggressiveness and suspiciousness (perceived hostility) that characterized mothers of infants showing stable disorganization, but highest of all groups on intervening, disruptive life events that they often did not see as having an effect on their child. Both change groups rated themselves higher on anger control than did mothers in the avoidant group. Across maternal report measures, there was an inconsistency of negative experiences and negative affect in the disorganized group that brought to mind Lyons-Ruth et al.'s (this volume) affectively contradictory maternal behavior.

Future Research on Atypical Attachment

Just as different attachments, including different forms of atypical attachments, exist and either have proven or may prove developmentally informative (Crittenden, this volume; Lyons-Ruth et al., this volume), changes in attachment exist and appear to be ecologically informative. Work remains to be done, however, linking patterns of maternal reported negative affect and defendence to disorganized attachments in infancy (and to controlling, A/C, or AD attachments in the preschool period, see Crittenden, this volume; Solomon, George, & DeJong, 1995). Very little research tests the role of maternal interactive behavior as a possible mediator of maternal defendence and atypical attachment, although preliminary evidence indicates that a fruitful avenue is to examine frightened, frightening, and/or disorganizing behavior on the part of mothers (Lyons-Ruth, this volume; Schuengel et al., in press). But there is an important missing piece, which is the infant's experience in the home. Family violence (spouse abuse, sibling abuse), parental substance abuse, traumatic parent-child separations, frequent disruptions in caretaking arrangements, and other extreme experiences are rarely assessed directly and probably are captured only partly in measures of maternal interactive behavior. But it is these more extreme experiences that may distinguish homelife for mothers with unusual defendence against negative affect and for infants and children with atypical attachments.

Clearly, there is ecological significance both in the form of secure and insecure attachments and in the presence of behaviors indicative of disorganization. Both aspects of infant-mother attachment covaried with infant, maternal, and familial characteristics. Until more data become available that test these distintions, we can only offer hypotheses regarding the meaning of these two dimensions of early infant-mother attachment. It is consistent with the growing literature on adult attachment (e.g., Ainsworth & Eichberg, 1991; Cassidy & Kobak, 1988; Grossmann & Grossmann, 1991b) to suggest that parental styles of acknowledging and dealing with negative affect and infant temperamental styles distinguish early attachments according to traditional, or "forced," classifications, but that more serious indicators of parental pathology (clinical depression, personality problems, childhood experiences of parental loss or maltreatment) and of unstable, chaotic, abusive child experiences distinguish disorganized or atypical attachment behaviors or patterns in infancy. If one point seems clear at this stage, it is that atypical or disorganized attachment patterns in infancy and early childhood do appear to be an important link between variations in early experiences, behavior, and functioning that may be considered "normative," and are studied under the rubric of developmental psychology, and those that are more extreme or deviant and may be considered "nonnormative," more often studied under the rubric of developmental psychopathology. Whether atypical or disorganized attachment patterns will prove to be both an empirically and clinically useful prognostic indicator of emerging psychopathology remains to be seen.

VII. DANGER AND DEVELOPMENT:
THE ORGANIZATION OF SELF-PROTECTIVE STRATEGIES

Patricia McKinsey Crittenden

Attachment theory is a theory about protection from danger. This chapter is built on the base of Bowlby and Ainsworth's theory and addresses infants' and young children's strategies for coping with danger. It is proposed that perception of danger elicits mental and behavioral organization. Furthermore, it is proposed that the propensity to organize protective strategies is innate and evolved in humans' "environment of evolutionary adaptiveness." A critical feature of this environment is danger. Because humans have always been at risk from a variety of dangers, survival has depended upon organizing successful strategies for protection of self and progeny. Thus, in contrast to those who emphasize the role of security in fostering organization, it is proposed that *danger creates the need and occasion for humans' capacity to organize.*

An important component of this statement is the contribution of context to the development of strategies. Although attachment research has focused on caregivers' sensitivity to infants, danger in the environment constitutes an important influence. Caregivers not only must respond to infant signals, they must also prepare their children to be safe in their environment. An implication of this is that the secure strategy of open and direct communication of intentions and feelings, together with interpersonal negotiation of these, might not be adaptive in all contexts; indeed, one can imagine contexts where it could be endangering (Crittenden, 1997a). Instead of conceptualizing attachment as promoting security, it should promote safety, with the strategy that best does so being considered most adaptive. Thus, it is in samples of children in dangerous circumstances that attachment theory is best tested, because these children experience the sorts of danger that require parental protection. If children do not organize protective strategies *when there is a need for protection*, the basic assumptions of attachment theory are severely challenged. Furthermore, it is proposed that, as children mature, they become able to develop increasingly sophisticated, complex, and contextually adapted strategies for reducing the danger of the specific environments in which they find themselves. Again, in contrast to the emphasis on continuity of pattern[1] of attachment and on attachment as a state, I emphasize the dynamic process of adaptation of humans to their environments. Change in pattern of attachment should be expected as a function of both change in circumstances and also individual maturation. Change will be reflected in shifts among major patterns and from infant subpatterns to reorganized and more sophisticated, but later developing, childhood, adolescent, and adulthood patterns. When organization is conceptualized as being motivated by threatening circumstances, the greatest change in pattern of attachment should occur in complex and/or threatening environments, because these environments require complexity of response to promote the probability of safety. Specifically, children who experience danger are expected to develop strategies that reduce the sorts of danger that they have experienced. When the danger is lack of parental response, adaptive strategies will elicit parental attention, even if this involves angry or risk-taking behavior; when the danger is parent hostility, adaptive strategies will reduce it.

This perspective is explored first through a brief consideration of how humans transform sensory stimuli into information with implications for the organization of behavior. A "dynamic-maturational" model of the development of strategies for predicting, preventing, and responding to dangerous circumstances is then delineated. These two sections use empirical findings to generate an integrated theory; the hypotheses drawn from the theory, however, are speculative and require empirical testing. A particular contribution of this expansion of attachment theory is differentiation of subgroups within Types A and C whose risk is different in different contexts. The utility of this model is explored by applying it to issues raised elsewhere in this volume, specifically issues of (a) what is normal versus atypical, (b) complex organization versus disorganization, and (c) neurological disorders and temperament. Based on this dynamic-maturational perspective, issues of assessment of pattern of attachment and analysis of attachment data are considered. This chapter concludes with a discussion of security and adaptation in which it is argued that full adaptation cannot be achieved until

---

[1] The term "pattern" of attachment is used throughout, in preference to "quality" of attachment, to reduce the implication of evaluative differences among the patterns.

adulthood, does not imply stability of behavior or a particular behavioral strategy, for example, Type B, and is not synonymous with feelings of security or happiness (Crittenden, in press b). To the contrary, adaptation requires flexibility of strategy in the face of changing life contexts.

TRANSFORMATIONS OF INFORMATION AND PATTERNS OF ATTACHMENT

Because behavior can be no more adaptive than information is accurate, this chapter begins with a discussion of information processing. The central nervous system is exquisitely adapted to identify and respond to danger. Put another way, safety does not exert selective pressure on species. Danger does and those species that survive tend to be those that best detect and respond adaptively to potential danger. Three issues seem relevant: detection of stimulation, attribution of meaning, and behavioral response. The first and third are the classic features of temperament, that is, threshold of sensitivity to stimuli and intensity of response. Their relevance to patterns of attachment is discussed toward the end of this chapter. Of interest here is the attribution of meaning to sensory stimuli. Two basic transformations, cognition and affect, and five modifications of each are used to construct the dynamic-maturational model of patterns of attachment. It is proposed that, with this array of 10 sorts of information, adult humans are prepared to identify and protect themselves from a very wide range of dangers (Crittenden, 1997a, 1997b).

Cognitive Transformations. Incoming sensory stimulation is meaningless; it must be transformed into self-relevant information before it can be used to organize behavior. One way this occurs is temporal and involves sensorimotor recognition of patterns of temporally ordered events. When temporal associations are made, behavior becomes organized as though prior events "caused" successive events.

Because temporal order is insufficient to establish causation, there is a potential for superstitious learning and erroneous attributions of causation. Usually these are corrected when repetitions of the event are not followed by repetitions of the outcome. When outcomes are dangerous, however, a single trial may produce inhibition of initiating events, thus eliminating opportunity to correct error. Furthermore, in species capable of expectation, protective qualities may be attributed to behavior that precedes expected danger that doesn't occur. When adversity is expected frequently, compelled behavior may be displayed. Such behavior can include anything that precedes expected danger: fidgeting, appeasing smiles, anxiety induced stumbling that becomes intentional self-injury, obedience. If the attribution is accurate (i.e., true), inhibited and compelled behaviors are adaptive; if it is erroneous,

147

they can be maladaptive. These transformations are self-relevant; they tell *when* in the flow of one's behavior danger may be expected. They also have implications for disorders of inhibition and compulsion (Tracy, Ghose, Strecher, McFall, & Steinmetz, 1999), that is, behavior associated with Type A attachment. Later developing transformations include (a) distortions, in which a true causal relation is perceived in an exaggerated or minimized form, for example, relations that obtain sometimes are treated as being universally present or absent; (b) omissions, in which there is so little expectation of temporal predictability that the information is discarded in the organization of behavior; and (c) falsification, in which the apparent temporal relation is the opposite of the actual relation.

Affect and Attribution of Meaning to Contextual Information. A second sort of meaning that is attributed to sensory stimuli is "affective." Feelings of anxiety and comfort are elicited, without prior experience or learning, by certain contextual stimuli. Extremes of intensity are associated with danger: darkness/brilliant light, open spaces/entrapping conditions, loud noises/silence, harsh touch/light, hair-raising touch, and crowds/being alone, whereas comfort is elicited by moderate stimuli: rhythmic rocking, soft sound and touch, and being with people. Nevertheless, these conditions are not themselves dangerous or safe. As a consequence, feelings of anxiety can be accurately predictive or not.

Affect serves an organizing function. Displayed as anger, it motivates a fight response and may elicit compliance from others; displayed as fear, it motivates flight and may elicit caregiving from others. When distorted by exaggeration, affect can clarify one's own intention and motivate others' responses. These responses increase the probability of safety and of having access to protective attachment figures. When, however, in the past, affect has had no implications for subsequent events, it may be omitted from processing, and when it has elicited attack from others, it may be falsified. Information about experienced dangerous contexts identifies contexts *where* danger may be expected. Excessive dependance on affect, through distortion of display of feelings, erroneous association of feelings with outcomes, and omission of cognitive information, reflects aspects of the Type C pattern and may be associated with anxiety disorders. For example, Barkley's (1997) account of Attention Deficit Hyperactivity Disorder closely fits the description of both Type C information processing and behavior. On the other hand, omission or falsification of affect reflect aspects of the Type A pattern and may be associated with a different set of disorders.

Integration of Information. Humans have two ways to predict danger. Although each can be inaccurate, the errors result from different processes and are unlikely to co-occur. When affect and cognition provide similar predictions, action decisions are simple, quick, and efficient. When the predictions differ, mental activity must either construct a higher level of understanding that produces concordance or accept one source of information in preference to the other. It is proposed here that, beginning in infancy, humans learn to integrate information and whether to trust or distrust each source of information. These operations become, in themselves, mental procedural schemata that operate rapidly, efficiently, and often out of awareness.

Although some researchers, Bowlby included, conceptualize working memory as playing an "executive" role, more current thinking is structured in terms of self-organizing, interactive, parallel distributed networks. Using this model, sensory stimuli initiate a cascade of concurrent processing pathways. Each processes information differently and yields, in Damasio's terms, a disposition to action (Damasio, 1994). Each dispositional representation combines information and associations from the past with information about the present to create a unique, never-to-be-repeated representation of a possible response of self to current circumstances. At any given moment and until action is taken, multiple such representations exist. Because the range of possible representations increases with maturation, the range of possible behavioral responses would be expected to change as well.

When the action potentials of various representations differ, "decisions" must be made. The first is whether to continue processing or to take immediate protective action. When "danger predicting" thresholds of intensity are exceeded, behavior is initiated and further processing is suspended. This phenomenon may be the basis for "impulsive" behavior in individuals with innately or recalibrated low perceptual thresholds. Processing continues among multiple representations until a threshold, an integration, or the ceiling of maturational capability is reached. This implies that full processing will occur more often under safe than dangerous conditions and in older individuals.

A DYNAMIC-MATURATIONAL PERSPECTIVE ON INDIVIDUAL DIFFERENCES IN FUNCTIONING

The outcome of the interaction of mental functioning, maturation, and experience can be described in terms of three major patterns of learned mental and behavioral adaptation, each concatenated through successive periods of neurological maturation (Ainsworth, 1979; Bowlby, 1980; Crittenden, 1994). Elsewhere, a developmental process whereby infants' potential to transform and organize sensory input interacts with experienced environmental contingencies to yield Ainsworth's three patterns of attachment has been delineated (Crittenden, 1995, 1997a). Framed this way, the patterns of attachment are both patterns of behavior and also patterns

149

of mentally processing information. Here the dynamic and adaptive aspects of this process are emphasized.

Infancy

Information and the ABC patterns of Attachment. Human neonates express (without intention) states of discomfort by fussing and crying. Caregivers can respond to infants' signals in only three ways:

(a) *With behavior that predictably transforms infants' distress to comfort*: Such infants are on a schedule of predictable positive reinforcement of their negative affect. In attachment notation, they are classified as Type B (see Figure 5, B1–4).

(b) *With behavior that predictably increases infants' distress*: Such caregivers are predictably rejecting of, or unresponsive to, their infants' distress. In addition, some use false affective signals that mislead their infants; that is, they display false positive affect when they feel angry (Crittenden, 1981, 1985; Crittenden & DiLalla, 1988; Grossmann & Grossmann, 1991a; Lyons-Ruth, Connell, Grunebaum, & Botein, 1990; Main & Cassidy, 1988). Their infants learn to inhibit displays of negative affect so as to prevent punitive outcomes. Thus, infants classified as Type A use true cognitive information and discard affective information (see Figure 5, A1–2). When experience of danger has foreclosed other behavioral alternatives, such infants may have increased risk for disorders of inhibition.

(c) *With unpredictably and inconsistently sensitive behavior*: A third group of infants has inconsistent caregivers whose comfort is delivered on a schedule of unpredictable, intermittent positive reinforcement of negative affect. These infants become very distressed, but cannot organize their behavior on the basis of either affect or cognition. Instead they learn to express feelings at increasingly low thresholds of arousal and with great intensity. Especially when ambiguous stimuli and inconsistent outcomes are combined with danger, this condition may result in many competing dispositions to action, that is, to attack, to flee, and to seek comfort. This has implications for children classified as Type C (see Figure 5, C1–2).

The patterns of attachment are dyadic patterns that reflect an interaction of child, parent, and contextual variables. By 2 years of age, infants use several transformations of sensory stimulation, including true, erroneous, discarded, and false affect and true and erroneous cognition; the particular array transforms an infant with a potential for any strategy into one with a strategy tied specifically to his or her developmental context. In the context of danger, the transformations reduce maximally the possibility of underestimating danger, but the cost may be inability to recognize safe circumstances. Thus, those Type A and C infants who have experienced danger

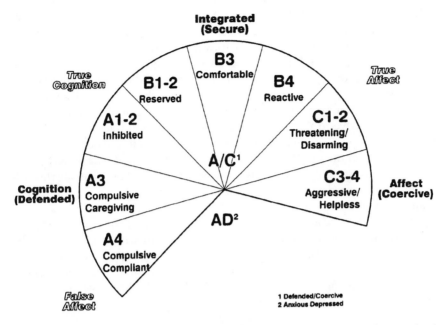

FIGURE 5. Dynamic-maturational array of patterns of attachment in the preschool years. From "Attachment and Psychopathology," by P. M. Crittenden, in S. Goldberg, R. Muir, & J. Kerr (Eds.), *John Bowlby's Attachment Theory: Historical, Clinical, and Social Significance*, 1995, New York: The Analytic Press. Copyright 1995 by The Analytic Press. Adapted with permission.

may be at current and subsequent risk, *under conditions of safety*, for developmental problems that are associated with the A and C strategies, for example, inhibitions, compulsions, anxiety, and so on.

Preschool Years

Following the period of rapid neurological change at the end of the 2nd year of life, infants gain new mental capabilities. The focus here is on changes in affective behavior and the influence of children's mental maturity on their organization of self-protective strategies and on their attachment relationships. The outcome is an expanding set of increasingly context-specific strategies for dealing ever more effectively with a wider range of dyadic circumstances.[2] The alternative perspective is a model of continuity that extends the infant classificatory system, with only minor

[2] Beginning in the school years and continuing thereafter, the process becomes one of individuals' increasing variability of strategy across contexts and relationships.

151

adjustments, throughout the lifespan. Such models tend to find at-risk children, of all sorts, to be disorganized (Capps, Sigman, & Mundy, 1994; Carlson, Cicchetti, Barnett, & Brunwald, 1989b; Erickson, Sroufe, & Egeland, 1985; Lyons-Ruth & Block, 1996; Vaughn et al., 1994; Vondra, Hommerding, & Shaw, this volume). The dynamic-maturation model suggests that there are important subgroups within the so-called disorganized category and that many of these reflect children's use of organized and contextually adaptive strategies that offer protection from specific sorts of risk.

This perspective is in contrast with studies that find greater disorganization in risk infants at 18 months than at 12 months (Egeland & Sroufe, 1981b; Lyons-Ruth, Repacholi, McLeod, & Silva, 1991; Vondra et al., this volume). With regard to this finding, it seems more likely that 18-month-old toddlers in interpersonally complex and threatening environments are in the early stages of constructing *more* complex and self-protective patterns of behavior (patterns that were beyond their mental capacity as 12-month-olds) than that their increasing maturity leads to decreasing ability to organize. The sections below describe an increasing array of complex patterning and its possible function in adapting toddlers' behavior to the constraints of dangerous environments.

Coercion: Intuitive Cognition and Coy Affect. In the preschool years, children gain intuitive logic and coy affect. Coy behavior can be described as sets of signals that terminate aggression (e.g., baring the neck and belly) and elicit nurturance (e.g., opening the mouth with covered teeth, glancing eye contact; Eibl-Eibesfeldt, 1979; Marvin, 1977). These signals enable children to regulate dominance hierarchies and disputes. With coy behavior, preschool children construct a new strategy for regulating parental behavior. Specifically, children split the display of anger, fear, and desire for comfort into displays of (a) threateningly angry aggression and (b) disarming fearfulness and desire for nurturance. One display is shown in exaggerated form, while the opposite display is inhibited; then the displays are alternated contingent on parental placating or threatening behavior. This strategy reduces the dangers of parental inattention and parental anger.

Although the coercive strategy is discovered by all children, it becomes characteristic of children of inconsistent caregivers because it increases the predictability of caregiver behavior. Behaviorally, affect is *distorted* to achieve cognitive predictability. Moreover, the greater the danger of parental unresponsiveness, the greater the distortion, such that "threatening" behavior escalates to "aggressive" and "disarming" behavior escalates to "feigned helpless." Ironically, as children escalate their display, some parents habituate to the intense displays. Their attitude becomes one of resignation: "Just let him cry; he'll get over it." Children of such parents may further escalate their behavior to angry provocativeness, that is, doing exactly what they were told not to do, and, if necessary, to risk-taking that puts the issue to protection directly before the parent (see Figure 5, C3–4). In all cases, however, the coercive strategy requires that the caregiver observe the affective display; this may explain, in part, coercive children's desire to maintain access to attachment figures.

The coercive strategy transforms parental unpredictability into child unpredictability. This leaves parents feeling trapped. To escape the coercive "trap," many parents use bribes or threats, but, after the child has acquiesced, they fail to fulfill the prediction. Such parents deceive children with regard to temporal contingencies. False predictions (whether intentional or not) constitute false cognitive information. Type C coercive children learn to discard (some or all) cognitive information because it leaves them unprotected. Instead they engage in affectively intense, peerlike struggles with parents.

The coercive strategy is ideally suited to caregiver inconsistency and unpredictability. Given their limited linguistic abilities and their exposure to new dangers through locomotion, the majority of toddlers are expected to feel anxious and to use intense affective communication to regulate parental protective behavior. This is expected to be displayed as an increase in the proportion of children classified as Type C as compared to infancy. When speech becomes more functional, the proportion of coercive children would be expected to drop, but still to exceed the proportion in infancy. The children of the most and least sensitive mothers would be expected to retain their Type B or A strategy. These hypotheses are supported by longitudinal studies using the Preschool Assessment of Attachment (PAA; Fagot & Pears, 1996; Rauh, Ziegenhain, Müller, & Wijnroks, in press; Teti, Gelfand, Messinger, & Isabella, 1995) as well as by Vondra et al.'s (this volume) finding that Type C 18 month olds were "middling" with respect to most maternal and familial variables. Thus, both change and continuity are expected in the dynamic-maturation model. Moreover, maturation is thought to be an important factor in children's ability to organize self-protective strategies.

Defended Children and False Affect. Because, in the preschool years, avoidance is interpreted by caregivers as rude behavior, it elicits intrusive and punitive responses from caregivers. Type A children, however, desire to prevent exactly that sort of response. Consequently, preschool-aged Type A children learn to use sophisticated strategies that involve substituting distorted and false positive affect for inhibited true negative affect. Safe Type A children use neutral or exaggerated (distorted) overbright affect to elicit adult approval and closeness.

Type A children who have experienced self-threatening danger use strategies with compelled behaviors (for example, bright smiles when fear is felt, compliance when resistance is felt, giving care when care is desired) to increase their safety. With withdrawn and unresponsive caregivers, Type A children use false positive affect to elicit attention. A more extreme form of the same pattern involves role reversing, compulsive caregiving (see Figure 5, A3; Bowlby, 1980). Although the boundary between parent and child roles is maintained, child and parent switch roles (therefore, this is different from peerlike role confusion). It appears that children construct a compulsive caregiving organization when nonhostile caregivers fail to function protectively, regardless of whether the parent is withdrawn (Type A) or childishly incompetent (Type C). This is consistent with both the findings of Lyons-Ruth, Bronfman, and Parsons (this volume) that mothers who sought caregiving from their children tended to be negative/intrusive and also Vondra et al.'s (this volume) finding that some children classified as "disorganized" at 18 months had mothers with high scores for depressive symptoms.

Other Type A children use compulsive compliance to prevent aggression from abusive caregivers (see Figure 1, A4; Crittenden & DiLalla, 1988). They are vigilantly wary of caregivers (i.e., their threshold for novelty and intensity are lowered) and attend to discerning what parents want and are likely to do, in order to take protective action before the parents become dangerous. Such children seem similar to Vondra's group with "high levels of disorganization" and mothers with high scores for hostile, suspicious personality, disruptive life experiences, and the least expressed anger and most anger control. The findings regarding anger, in particular, are reminiscent of findings regarding abusive mothers' covert expression of hostility (Crittenden, 1981).

Differentiation Versus Continuity of the Infant Classificatory System. The longitudinal studies by Rauh et al. (in press) and Teti et al. (1995) comparing outcomes using both the infant and the PAA classificatory systems at 21 months provide clear evidence that the more differentiated PAA patterns better fit both longitudinal and concurrent validating variables. Similar patterns of age-related shifts in behavior have been reported for maltreated children with the particularly important finding that children had different patterns of change depending upon the nature of experienced danger (Crittenden, 1992b). The Barnett, Lyons-Ruth, and Vondra studies in this volume suggest that the process of reorganization to more highly differentiated and environmentally adaptive strategies may already be underway at 18 months. The Barnett et al. study that includes a measure of emotionality provides the most detailed data from which to reconstruct the developmental process. At 12 months, they found that high reactive maltreated children classified as disorganized displayed little crying, whereas, at 18 months, they cried a lot and, at 24 months, there was so little crying on reunion that it was not rated. No examined factor (i.e., maltreatment status, attachment security, molar group-ing, gender, or stability of attachment) explained this, leading to the conclusion that "children with Type D attachments are behaving in a fashion inconsistent with their temperamental dispositions" (Barnett et al., this volume).

It is possible that an interaction of maturation and context can explain these findings in a way that reflects the "increasingly sophisticated strategies of emotional expression and regulation" (Barnett et al., this volume) pro-posed by Cicchetti & Barnett (1991). Specifically, at 12 months, infants are able to inhibit display of distress, when their mothers have previously reacted punitively to negative affect, by perceptually avoiding the mother. By 18 months, however, mothers respond punitively to avoidance as "rude" behavior; thus, when satisfying the mothers' demand for a (polite) greeting, toddlers' true affect is elicited and they cry. In addition, however, maturation permits relational integration of information, such that toddlers are able to inhibit crying when the punitive caregiver departs while displaying their true feelings of extreme distress when the caregiver is absent and cannot perceive or punish the display. By 24 months, children are able to inhibit, without perceptual avoidance, the behavioral expression of experienced feelings leading to the near absence of crying on reunion by both nonmal-treated children who no longer experience high distress and also highly distressed maltreated children who inhibit the display when the mother is present. Underlying this interpretation, there is both the hypothesis of an interaction of maturation with context, and also the presumption that displayed affect may not always reflect internal feelings. As Barnett and his colleagues point out, physiological measures of arousal could address this issue. Given the absence of that data, however, it would be interesting to examine crying during the departures of mothers at 12, 18, and 24 months. It would be consistent with a maturational hypothesis for maltreated 18 and 24 month olds' crying during separations to begin only *after* the mother was out of the room, that is, when the children presumed that mothers could no longer perceive their distress.

The notion of regulation of *display* of affect as distinct from regulation of affect is central to the dynamic-maturational perspective. Its relevance to in-hibition was just discussed. False positive displays when true feelings were negative are worthy of note because they may have led to (mis)classification of some maltreated children as securely attached or, in the Lyons-Ruth sample, as disorganized/secure. In both cases, the argument is that children become capable of regulating displayed affect in ways that are discordant with their feelings, but concordant with both caregivers' desires and children's protec-tion. More than other children, endangered children may need to exercise this potential. If so, it would be indicative of highly sophisticated and adaptive organization around a specific and dangerous developmental context. With "disregulated" Type C children, the notion is that distorted affect is used

155

strategically to elicit attention from inconsistently responsive caregivers. Reclassification of the Barnett, Lyons-Ruth, and Vondra samples using the PAA could test these hypotheses. They are important because the developmental implications of presuming that maturing children are *less* able to cope effectively, that is, more often become disorganized, than younger children are hard to understand and bode poorly for the developmental process.

Three studies in this volume find risk toddlers to be "disorganized" (Barnett et al.; Lyons-Ruth et al.; Vondra et al.). It is proposed that these children may be in the process of reorganizing to the more adaptive and protective coercive, compulsive caregiving or compulsive compliant patterns. Attention to the nature of the danger experienced by "disorganized" children and the potential of their behavior to reduce that danger should be explored.

The observation that "disorganized-forced secure" toddlers tended to have withdrawn and nonhostile mothers (Lyons-Ruth et al., this volume) suggests a misinterpretation of false positive affect combined with approach to a nonthreatening, withdrawn caregiver. Such behavior is shown by both compulsive caregiving and anxious depressed preschoolers. (Teti et al. [1995] initially classified many children of depressed mothers as secure when, after reclassification with the PAA, they were more often classified as coercive, anxious depressed, or compulsive caregiving.) The anxious depressed pattern of nonstrategic interpersonal behavior combined with intense affective displays of sadness and strategic self-comforting behavior (rocking, sucking, periods of zoning, etc.) reflects the inability of the child to construct a dyadic strategy with an unwilling partner and the attempt to comfort the self. It is an *intra*personal strategy that achieves some success during periods of safety, but is not helpful when protection from an unresponsive caregiver is needed. This is a reminder that groups of children in similar circumstances need to be studied carefully with an eye to pattern and organization if we want to understand more fully the ways in which differences in experience shape adaptation. The clustering together of many sorts of atypicality does not as easily yield evidence of organization.

An important aspect of the model offered here is that the A and C strategies are conceptualized as opposites, in that they protect children from different sorts of danger, involve opposite mental and behavioral processes, and incur different developmental risks. One implication of this is that the data from Type A and Type C children should not be analyzed together. Indeed, one of the advantages of using an expanded developmental model of attachment strategies is that information can be captured regarding both type and severity of distortion.

ISSUES REGARDING THE DEVELOPMENT OF AT-RISK CHILDREN

What Is Normal?

Developmental research, including attachment research, has typically been conducted using middle-class, two-parent, "Western" subjects. Such subjects are described as "normal." Other samples are usually treated as atypical. Nevertheless, there is reason to question whether our evolution functioned to maximize our preparation for this sort of "advantaged" environment. Indeed, even now the overwhelming majority of humans live in poverty, face real threats of disease, famine, and natural disasters, suffer under totalitarian and dangerous governments, and struggle to survive during recurrent wars. In addition, for most people, the loss of a parent or child is a normative event. Furthermore, violence within homes and between family members still accounts for the great majority of human suffering. There is no reason to believe that it was different in the past; danger and instability have been and are a universal part of human experience. The point is that research has tended to study atypical and highly advantaged populations, leading to the inaccurate perception that risk is an unusual condition with which humans are not prepared to cope.

This is not to say that children from risk environments are not in fact at risk. They are and their lot is not a happy one. Nevertheless, they are probably more typical of our species than children from middle income families. This suggests that coping with threats and danger is likely to have been a pervasive problem across the evolution that led to homo sapiens. Therefore, it seems more reasonable to ask how we have evolved to cope with danger than how danger incapacitates us.

This is part of the rationale underlying this chapter. Children are viewed as robust organisms with innate systems that facilitate identifying and responding protectively to many of the threats and dangers to which they are exposed. Rather than presuming that danger overwhelms children and then searching for corroborating evidence by comparing risk children to advantaged children, it is presumed that children are prepared for danger, that they actively construct self-protective strategies, and that, with maturation, they become able to construct more protective strategies that also free them to attend to other aspects of life. It is important to understand how children accomplish this.

Organization and Disorganization

The designation of disorganization depends upon the presence of a specified set of behaviors. This implies that the presence of certain behaviors is disorganization. Moreover, the association of these with more troubled relationships has been treated as proof of disorganization. A major thrust of this chapter has been to show that this is not a logically necessary conclusion. Two points are central. First, is there a contingent relation between display of the critical behavior(s) and the interpersonal context? Second, does the contingent relation increase the safety or comfort of the child, given the parent's behavior? If the answer to the first question is affirmative, the behavior is organized; if the second answer is also affirmative, the organization is adaptive.

This is where work with large, differentiated samples of endangered children can be helpful. If the patterns are organized, rates of maltreatment should drop when children acquire the compulsive strategies, that is, A3 and A4. On the other hand, if the behaviors mark disorganization, rates of abuse and neglect should increase because disorganized children would be unable to influence caregivers in self-protective ways and also unable to regulate themselves. Testing this hypothesis requires longitudinal data of a particular sort on well differentiated samples of maltreated children. Using cross-sectional data, patterns of age-related and adaptive change in different groups of maltreated children's behavior have been demonstrated (Crittenden, 1992b). This serves as an empirical basis for longitudinal replication.

Another approach is to identify codable organizations of behavior and analyze whether the presumed strategy affects caregiver behavior in ways that benefit the child. For example, if "inhibited" (A1–2) preschool-aged children are strategic, their use of overbright affect (i.e., exaggerated expression of true positive affect) should function to slow the intimate approach of caregivers and to maintain more neutral forms of involvement, for example, reading a book or doing a puzzle. Furthermore, if the behavior is strategic, the parent-child relationship should improve over time in terms of dyadic synchrony and expressed perceptions of satisfaction. Compulsive caregiving (A3) children would be expected to elicit more parental involvement, including the intrusive behavior associated with nonwithdrawn Type A mothers. Easterbooks, Lyons-Ruth, Biesecker, and Carper's (1996) finding that mothers of 7-year-old children who were classified as disorganized/secure in infancy were not underinvolved is consistent with a strategic interpretation of their children's behavior. Among compulsively compliant (A4) children, the use of false positive affect, perceptual vigilance, and rapid compliance should correlate with reduced evidence of maternal covert hostility, demands for child behavior, and rejection of child initiatives. Evidence of this sort is available for the A/C pattern and its association with extreme variability in children's homes, specifically abuse-and-neglect and bipolar depression (Crittenden, 1985; Radke-Yarrow, Cummings, Kuczynski, & Chapman, 1985). In each of these cases, strategic response to danger is expected to reduce the danger; furthermore, by less often triggering action-initiating thresholds of stimulation, the strategy might lead to more complete cortical processing of information, observed as forms of resilience. Finally, in the more immediate setting in which the behavior occurs, it might be fruitful to consider the temporal consequences of the indicators of "disorganization." For example, stilling might be a particularly appropriate behavior when a highly variable and potentially angry mother first enters the room. Because the infant knows the mother is variable, the best strategy may be to do nothing until her current state can be ascertained.

It also would be helpful if developmental pathways were elaborated that could be seen to emerge in infancy and become more differentiated, better organized, and more effective as children gained experience and maturity. If new organizations emerge among children who experience substantial threats, then analyses using these differentiated organizations should account for more variance than analyses placing all the children in one disorganized category. Moreover, the amount of variance accounted for should increase as development enables children to organize increasingly more finely tuned variants of strategies. In particular, there should be differences in kind between As and Cs and differences of severity between less and more endangered subgroups within A and C. A review of infant Strange Situation tapes, carried out with Mary Ainsworth after the creation of the preschool A3 and A4 patterns, suggested that the forerunners of the compulsive caregiving and compliant patterns were discernable among infant "D-forced A" infants. Finding such pathways would both fit Bowlby's notion of attachment serving a protective function and also be consistent with Sroufe's elaboration of attachment as an organizational theory. In addition, it would recast attachment theory in a developmental framework based on the notion of evolving pathways rather than in a static framework based on the notion of enduring states that were established in infancy.

This said, a word about the Barnett et al. (this volume) finding of high stability of pattern across time is relevant. Because Types B and D reflect the extremes of the distributions of maternal sensitivity and contextual safety, they would be less likely to show categorical change than the A and C patterns nearer the middle of the distribution. Even so, the findings of stability are not informative about the impact of early relationships on later functioning unless it can be shown that the environment changed and that the child's pattern did not also change. In the Barnett case, it is more likely that the environment did not change because maltreatment is both an event and an indicator of ongoing contextual influences that are likely to support the maintenance of self-protective organizations. Indeed, the only certain change in this study is maturation. Unfortunately, the effects of maturation are obscured by a checklist approach to identifying disorganized attachment.

The presumption that many indices of "disorganization" are aspects of organized patterns does not preclude acceptance of the notion of disorganization, especially in cases where the complexity and dangerousness of the threat are beyond children's capacity for response. Disorganization, however, would not be defined by the specific behaviors. Instead, it would reflect the functional inability of children to reduce the danger of their circumstances. It seems almost certain that such disorganized states do exist in some children although it is proposed here that they are found in many fewer children than are now labeled "disorganized." Furthermore, it often happens that, over time, previously anomalous observations come to be understood better and, often, can be seen to reflect previously unidentified strategies or transitions into more complex levels of functioning. Thus, it might be that "disorganization" should be considered a provisional category reflecting either children's disorganization or investigators' inability to discern organization at the time of coding.

Neurological Issues

The relation between innate aspects of individual functioning, that is, genetic or neurological aspects, and pattern of attachment has been discussed for some time without resolution. A central concern to those outside of attachment is that these innate conditions may account for the patterns that attachment researchers attribute to insensitive parenting (Pipp-Siegel, Siegel, & Dean, this volume). It seems essential to differentiate among conditions in order to clarify the range of possible relations. Because of the information processing and behavioral organization approach to attachment that is used here, the focus is on sensory deficits (because these affect the information available to the infant as well as communications from the infant), intellectual deficits (because these affect both cortical integration and maturational processes), neurological deficits (because these affect the presence and absence of some behaviors as well as organizational capacity), temperamental differences (because these affect the probabilities of specific behaviors or types of behavior), and, finally, disorders of unknown etiology (because these fascinate us and draw forth some of the most intensely held beliefs). Needless to say, the literature in these areas cannot be reviewed; instead, the focus is on defining areas of logical error in our thinking about physiology and behavior.

Sensory Deficits. Infants with clear sensory deficits provide an especially auspicious opportunity for considering the relation between attachment theory and physiology. Such infants have indisputable physiological limitations to the information they can send and receive; this is relevant to both infant organization and caregivers' response. In addition, such infants need greater protection than do unimpaired infants; the need for protection is central to attachment issues. Possibly because the issues are so clear, there is relatively little dispute: parents find it difficult to accept and know how to respond to their impaired infants, especially when physical attractiveness or communication are involved (Ammernan, Lubetsky, Hersen, & Van Hasselt, 1988; Koester, 1995; Langois, Ritter, Casey, & Sawin, 1995; Meadow-Orlans & Steinberg, 1993; Preisler, 1990; Robinshaw & Evans, 1995). Nevertheless, when they learn how their infants communicate and how to communicate with them, the relationship becomes organized using the available behavioral repertoire. Put another way, humans appear to be quite flexible with regard to which behaviors are used to fulfill a function and sensory impaired infants are entirely able to participate in organized relationships that fulfill the protective function. The relationships exhibit the full range of types and patterning of relationships in unimpaired infants (Cicchetti, Beeghley, Carlson, & Toth, 1990). The central issue, then, is being certain that functional definitions of behavior are used to assess pattern of attachment. The risk is how sensory impaired infants will organize when caregivers are less than normally protective, that is, how much of the responsibility for the organization can the infant manage?

Intellectual Deficits. Intellectual deficits have provided greater problems in part because not all deficits are innate and in part because they are often combined with other deficits. Studies of Down syndrome demonstrate that low IQ infants do form specific attachments that reflect the patterns described by Ainsworth (Atkinson et al., this volume; Cicchetti, Beeghly, et al., 1990; Vaughn et al., 1994). Nevertheless, there are higher frequencies of indicators of "disorganization" than in intellectually normal samples. Several issues warrant further study. First, do infants displaying "disorganization" elicit greater protection from their parents, that is, are they organized adaptively? Second, does IQ covary with organization, when organization is defined functionally? Third, does it become more difficult for lower IQ children to reorganize to more sophisticated organizations as they mature? If so, do low intelligence children maintain an organization typical of younger children or do they become disorganized in an ultimately incomplete transition to more mature functioning? Finally, do low IQ children of less sensitively responsive mothers have more difficulty organizing functional strategies than do normally intelligent infants with similar mothers? Atkinson et al.'s study confirms the importance of these issues. That speed and breadth of cortical processing would be relevant to construction of self-protective strategies seems certain; similarly, maternal responsiveness constitutes an essential component of the strategy. A question that remains is whether any of Atkinson's disorganized/unclassifiable children show organization and/or adaptive organization when these are defined functionally.

Neurological Deficits and Insults. Children with neurological disorders and insults, for example, cerebral palsy, provide another interesting population. There are, however, three potential problems. First, clear evidence of neurological abnormality is not always available. Second, single diagnoses often group heterogeneous children (Pipp-Siegel et al., this volume). Third, outcome variables do not always differentiate among functionally different outcomes; assessment of attachment in risk samples often reflects this problem with risk children being classified simply as "disorganized" (O'Connor, Sigman, & Kasari, 1992; Rodning, Beckwith, & Howard, 1989, 1991; Rogers, Ozonoff, & Maslin-Cole, 1991). Careful studies could explore the interpersonal meaning (if any) of behavioral indicators of "disorganization" in infants and children with neurological disorders. Evidence of atypical behavior should be sought in the neonatal period and then observed, in an interactional context, across the 1st year of life. With such a behavioral record, one could replicate Ainsworth's study in which the pattern of parental responses to neonates' reflexive behavior ultimately shaped the behavior into flexible and intentional dyadic signal systems. In the case of neurologically impaired children, there would probably be some substitutions of "abnormal" for "normal" behaviors as well as some uncontrolled "noise" behavior, but it should be possible to assess the process of organization, that is, whether caregiver and infant behaviors come to be under operant control of the other's behavior. Of course, such observations must be analyzed individually rather than with predetermined patterns or lists of behaviors.

Temperament. Temperament is a troublingly murky concept. Of course, it exists, but what is it and when can it be measured without measuring environmental influences as well? Certainly after as little as a week of life, contingencies between mothers and infants are forming, such that temperament can no longer be measured with purity. Possibly, it would help to differentiate universal and essential neurological processes, such as the transformation of incoming sensory stimuli to affective and cognitive information and the cortical integration of these, from nonessential individual differences in thresholds of perception and response intensities, that is, temperament. The transformations themselves are integral to human survival (Tooby & Cosmides, 1990). Similarly, caregivers' responses to infants can be conceptualized in a universal form as reinforcement patterns. Put in more abstract terms, the mental processing of information is universal to humans, as is caregiver behavior; these interact to create the three patterns of attachment.

Temperament, on the other hand, represents unique, nonessential variation. The data on temperament converge on the notions of (a) innate differences in threshold for detection of change in stimuli (i.e., sensitivity to novelty and intensity) and (b) intensity of response, both of which are responsive to environmental input (Weinberger, 1993). Other unique characteristics also may contribute to differences in temperament. In either case, the interaction of pattern of attachment with temperament can be conceptualized as a second level interaction that yields "personality." Thus, there are an infinite number of possible expressions of each strategy, one for each uniquely different person. Conceptualized this way, attachment and temperament are not competing explanations. Instead, they both contribute to the construct of personality.

Furthermore, just as the current evaluative stance of attachment theory in favor of the Type B pattern may distort our understanding of the strategies, the evaluative stance of the temperament literature may create distortion. Terms such as "difficult" describe children with low detection thresholds and high response intensities; this may both overlook the value to the individual and our species of such behavior and also misinterpret the behavior of parents. For example, highly reactive individuals may more consistently and quickly identify potential danger than individuals with higher thresholds. Although this will lead to many false positive attributions and, in extreme cases, possibly to anxiety disorders among the reactive individuals, it also reduces the proportion of false negative attributions. Put more directly, these individuals are the least likely to overlook real danger and the most likely to warn others quickly of potential danger. This characteristic has value to both individuals and species. Interpersonally, parents may revel in the sensitivity and robust responses of their infant or they may be dismayed by these same characteristics. The child's strategy is not, however, determined by the threshold of detection or intensity of response. To the contrary, the strategy reflects experienced contingencies associated with the cognitive and affective transformations of information.

Similarly, the "slow to warm" child may have the advantage of more processing time (with which to evaluate the validity of the reactive individual's warning) and may please some parents while frustrating others. That is, the characteristic itself does not determine parental evaluation. On the other hand, parental attributions may greatly affect how the characteristic affects the child's functioning. Parents who assist a child in transforming a characteristic into the child's unique asset promote the child's development whereas parents who devalue and try to diminish the child's "liability" may limit and distort the child's potential. The meaning of temperamental differences is in the eye of the beholder and it does take all kinds to maintain a successful species in the face of changing and variable threats to survival.

Disorders of Unknown Etiology. There are a number of disorders of childhood with unknown etiology. Childhood autism and attention deficit disorder with or without hyperactivity are among these. In both cases, the prevailing opinion is that they reflect neurological disorder. Nevertheless, evidence of innate neurological dysfunction has not been offered for either diagnosis. Moreover, it is possible that diagnoses like autism in fact cluster several conditions that may be unrelated in etiology. Until we have a clearer understanding of these conditions, it seems futile to dispute the relative contributions of pattern of attachment and neurology to the display of particular behaviors. More useful would be whether the behavior can be brought under operant control in the relationship. With this information, one can consider how the behavior is used and how one might want to intervene.

In summary, it would be best to keep in mind that all behavior is neurologically based whether "normal" or not. The issue is whether it can be influenced by operant conditions; most behavior regardless of its origin can be shaped, that is, it has interpersonal meaning. The meaning, however, does not reside in the morphology of the behavior, nor is it the same for every dyad. For attachment researchers, the critical meanings have to do with protection of the child.

ASSESSING AND ANALYZING PATTERN OF ATTACHMENT

The perspective offered here highlights some issues in the assessment of pattern of attachment and analysis of attachment data.

Assessment. The assessment issue turns on whether attachment can be *measured* (by the presence, absence, frequency, variety, or intensity of specified behaviors) or whether it is best *assessed* in terms of the functional patterning of classes of behavior in which an open-ended set of behaviors fulfills specific functions. The first approach is exemplified by the rating of specific behaviors to determine disorganization in the Strange Situation (Main & Solomon, 1990) and by the rating scales applied to the AAI (Main & Goldwyn, in preparation). In both cases, the trend over time is toward increasingly complete and specific delineation of the morphology of the behavior and toward more explicit rules for rating them. The second approach, in which functions are specified as the central criterion, is used in the CARE-Index for infants and the PAA (Crittenden, 1981, 1988, and Crittenden, 1990–1995, respectively). In these procedures, dyadic behavior is considered in the process of interpreting individuals' behavior. Furthermore, although example behaviors are provided, it is deemed impossible to construct a complete set of qualifying behaviors, both because a specific behavior can serve multiple functions and because varied behaviors can fulfill a single function. The trend in these assessments has been away from delineation of behavioral specificity and toward elaboration of the functional organization of the pattern for the dyad, that is, toward the psychology of interpersonal behavior.

Because the Ainsworth Strange Situation classificatory procedure forms the model for both approaches, it is worth exploring that methodology. Ainsworth created rating scales with behaviorally defined points to assess infant pattern of attachment in the Strange Situation. Although this suggests a morphological approach, nevertheless, numerical ratings do not determine classification. To the contrary, classification requires evaluation of both the rated behaviors and the pattern of ratings. This, in turn, hinges on comparisons of infants' behavior before and after stress, behavior directed to the mother versus the stranger, and behavior at the moment of reunion versus a minute or two later. Such comparisons evaluate patterning. Finally, close examination of the scales indicates that they are dyadic in nature, that is, they describe dyadic contingencies. Moreover, for most scale points, several dyadic organizations fulfill the requirement. From this perspective, it can be seen that the Ainsworth procedure is inherently dyadic and variable with regard to specific behaviors. It is the organization of behavior between two people and across time that determines classification (Sroufe, 1990).

Ainsworth's method works well, but only up to a point. Particularly when samples included endangered children, the unmodified Ainsworth classificatory method generated a substantial number of anomalous classifications in which maltreated children were (mis)classified as secure. This was true both for infant data and for extensions of the infant system to older children (Carlson et al., 1989b; Cicchetti & Barnett, 1991). Review of these "false secure" cases in one sample demonstrated that there are important arrays of behavior, including the A/C pattern, that were not apparent in Ainsworth's Baltimore sample (Crittenden, 1985). Without re-entering the discussion of whether these are organized or disorganized, it is clear that we must expand the classificatory system to account for them.

Thus, it could be concluded that Ainsworth was fortunate in being able to adapt rating scales to her systemic and organizational perspective, but that her method of classification resolved ultimately into a series of functional comparisons of the organization of behavior across time and between interactants. In expanding her work, we should carefully evaluate the relative advantages of morphological definitions and deterministic assignment of meaning to behavior versus functional definitions of dyadic behavior and psychological assignment of meaning on a dyadic basis. It may be that only the latter can account for the flexibility and complexity of our species. If this is correct, then our assessment procedures must be open-ended, systemic tools that can be revised and updated whenever satisfactory evidence can be offered that a new construction makes meaningful distinctions. Furthermore, as Lyons-Ruth has noted (this volume), the coding of dyadic behavior is important because the meaning of children's behavior lies in the interactants' patterns of prior and subsequent behavior. Finally, even dyadic behavior must be compared as it changes across time, rather than viewed solely in reunion episodes (Pipp-Siegel et al., this volume).

Analysis. Most analyses of infants' attachment have reduced Ainsworth's three patterns to two by combining Types A and C. The outcome has been to focus discussion on the secure/anxious distinction and to reduce discussion of potentially different strategies for protection from different sorts of danger. With the addition of a disorganized category, the discussion has shifted to a comparison of secure, anxious, and disorganized groups. Again, potentially informative distinctions have been lost and the power of attachment variables to differentiate forms of person/context adaptation has been reduced. The empirical finding is that the disorganized category is associated with infants' past, current, and future risk status. The consistency of this finding is impressive, but not terribly informative. We knew these infants were at risk on the basis of other variables and, when they have come to the attention of child protection authorities, we know far more than that. The question becomes what we learn in addition from knowing that they are assigned to the disorganized category.

Although there are few Type C children in infancy, this is not true in toddlerhood and the preschool years. Regardless of what classificatory system one uses, almost everyone finds more Type C toddlers and children than infants (Rauh et al., in press; Speltz, Greenberg, & DeKlyen, 1990; Stevenson-Hinde & Shouldice, 1990, 1995; Teti et al., 1995; Vondra et al., this volume). At the same time, when disorganization is used, Type C tends to disappear (Atkinson et al.; Lyons-Ruth et al.; both this volume). This being the case, it seems unfortunate not to explore the meaning of these changes in distributions. If, as Ainsworth proposed, there are important distinctions between Types A and C in developmental history and functioning, exploring these could have considerable value, especially after infancy when the Type C pattern becomes a more prominent pattern. For example, knowing the differential risk for various types of disorder could be helpful to prevention programs. Moreover, determining that the neurological and psychological processes underlying the A and C organizations were opposites would suggest that different sorts of interventions would be needed (and might imply that applying techniques suited to one group to the opposite group could be counterproductive). In addition, differentiating the Ainsworth patterns from the patterns of children who have experienced danger could enable us to identify more precisely risk associated with attachment by eliminating from concern the unendangered As and Cs; this is consistent with Easterbrooks et al.'s (1996) finding of no differences between 7-year-old children classified in infancy as B1–4 and A1–2. Viewing children as actively constructing meaning from their experience and organizing self-protective strategies on the basis of their constructions suggests new ways to interpret and respond to their behavior. For example, from the perspective on the processing of information offered in this chapter and elsewhere (Crittenden, 1997a), psychological maltreatment might be defined as patterns of transformations of information (i.e., true, erroneous, discarded, distorted, and falsified affect and cognition). These could be assessed and their implications for children's potential to establish safe relationships and to feel comfortable during safe conditions could be explored empirically. Finally, the expansion of the subclassifications within Types A and C permits analysis of both type and severity of effect. This could augment clinical observation and contribute to the development of a theoretically meaningful diagnostic system as well as to more precise forms of prevention, intervention, and therapy.

Highly differentiated approaches require analyses that focus on important distinctions. Thus, because important information may be lost or "averaged out," it would not be recommended that the extreme As, Cs, and A/Cs be clustered together as "atypical" until there was evidence that there were no meaningful differences among the patterns. On the whole, it seems unfortunate to constrain more differentiated systems to the limitations of less differentiated systems. Even when subgroup sizes were too small for full group comparisons, a priori contrasts can be used to test theoretically derived hypotheses about subgroup differences. This, of course, presumes that the other variables assess relevant constructs, particularly interactive and dyadic constructs that are central to the notion of organization.

WHAT IS SECURITY?

This chapter has focused on alternative ways of conceptualizing pattern of attachment. Organizations of both mental processes and behavior have been considered in terms of their protective function. Critical to the perspective offered here has been the notion of individual change in mental and behavioral processes as essential to adaptation to uncertain and variable conditions. Emphasis has been placed on mental flexibility as underlying behavioral adaptation and on the power of danger to instigate mental activity. Although some of what is proposed can be considered in contrast to what others have proposed, there are points on which there is substantial agreement. In particular, when one views behavior very carefully, distinctions must be made that were not articulated in the original infant classificatory system developed by Ainsworth. Moreover, when these distinctions are made, there is always a reduction in the number of children classified as securely attached.

This leads to several questions. What is security of attachment conceptually? Why does it vary with classificatory method? Does it vary developmentally (with more infants than older humans being classified as secure)?

Is Type B the most adaptive pattern? In all circumstances? Does security foster organization and does increasing anxiety lead to disorganization?

Answering these questions empirically exceeds the domain of this chapter. Consequently, several conceptual issues are addressed. To do this, security, that is, open and direct communication of intentions and feelings with interpersonal negotiation, must be differentiated from adaptation, that is, promotion of safety (Crittenden, in press b). Does security require a supportive and nondangerous home environment during childhood? In infancy, it may, but data from the AAI suggest that, by adulthood, it does not. In this case, the change seems tied to the increasing ability of the maturing human mind to consider and modify its own functioning. Does danger threaten the ability to organize? The theory presented here, together with empirical findings based on highly differentiated classificatory systems, suggests that disorganization is not the predominant response to threatening conditions. Consideration of the severity or complexity of threatening conditions, however, covaried by child maturity, might indicate that, when complexity is sufficiently beyond the capability of children to comprehend, children either organize at a less complex and potentially maladaptive level or become disorganized. Exploration of this question requires far more differentiation within samples and assessment procedures than is usually found. It has be shown, however, that when distinctions are made among types and complexity of threats, many children can be seen to organize in meaningfully self-protective ways at very young ages (Crittenden, 1992b). Does security become less common with age or is it less frequent at some ages? Apparently so, at least until adulthood when internally directed change can be undertaken. This fits well with everyday knowledge of children's development. Particularly in the preschool years and adolescence, children often seem less sure of their parents, their own roles, and their competencies. Possibly, they are also less secure. Neurologically, it may be meaningful that the preoperational shift culminates a critical period of brain maturation and that puberty marks the next such period. Moreover, both preschoolers and adolescents become exposed to new sorts of danger. Does security at one age predict security at later ages? Sometimes, but it definitely does not ensure it.

Explaining these puzzling observations requires differentiation of organized environments from inner organization. Both safe environments and sensitive caregivers increase the probability of safety and thus promote security. But both do so from outside the individual; the individual feels secure and is safe, but not as a consequence of personal efforts or mental organization. Were conditions to deteriorate, the person might be neither secure, nor safe and might be unable to change this situation. Clearly, such dependence on external conditions is not adaptive.

Viewed from this perspective, infants' security would appear to be closely tied to their actual situation. Even by 1 year of age, however, safety is increased for some children when mental functioning is different from overt behavior, that is, when some behavior is inhibited. Thus, these infants become more safe without feeling more comfortable and without having sensitively responsive caregivers. Moreover, the mental process that results in increased safety depends upon distorting transformations of information in which affect is largely discarded and/or falsified. As long as the environment remains constant, this self-protective strategy functions, is adaptive, and promotes safety. Neither children nor environments remain constant, however. To resolve the problem of safety, the issue of change must be addressed.

With maturation, the mind becomes capable of making new distinctions, new integrations, and new organizations of behavior that may not be directly observable. Thus, a school-aged child can mislead others with regard to his intentions by hiding evidence of his mental functioning. Similarly, an adolescent can choose to hide feelings with one person and to act on them with another, that is, to select behavioral strategies on the basis of different conditions. This suggests that, with sophisticated transformations of information and the freeing of mental activity from behavioral enactment, humans may be able to behave in a manner that promotes self-protection under varied conditions. Because conditions change constantly and because probabilities are never certainties, protective accommodation of self to circumstances must be an ongoing process, one that, after the preschool years, enables humans to use an increasing range of behavioral strategies in contextually adaptive ways.

Put this way, adaptation becomes a *process* of (a) freeing behavior first from mental functioning and later from environmental constraints and (b) regulating mental and behavioral functioning to achieve, under conditions of uncertainty and ambiguity, a tolerable balance between the threat associated with exploration and the safety needed for survival. Maybe adaptation is best conceptualized as a process, a lifelong process, of discerning reality from appearance and of organizing one's behavior to promote a balance of risk to opportunity. In information-processing terms, adaptation may be a process in which not fully accurate dispositional representational models are constantly reorganized into less inaccurate dispositional representational models that permit flexible and appropriate use of all behavioral strategies without distorting the mental processing of information. Because ambiguity of information and change of conditions may be the only certainties, adaptation may be tied inextricably to tolerance of ambiguity and acceptance of change, whereas dysfunction may reflect the wish for certainty and invariance. Possibly as researchers, we can best understand the process of adaptation if we accept uncertainty in our models (reflected in probabilistic rather than deterministic modeling) and structure our work around expectation of change.

CONCLUSION

In concluding this discussion of young children's adaptation to conditions of risk, it should first be noted that there is no implication that the empirical findings presented in this volume and in many other studies of attachment are unsound. The concern is in the interpretation of them. Possibly we need to return to the roots of attachment theory. Specifically, we need to recall that *the organization of attachment behavior functions to promote protection under circumstances of danger.* Thus, organization of attachment under conditions of safety is less crucial for the substantiation of attachment theory than its application to risk populations. Effort needs to be exerted to understand *how children protect themselves when they have experienced danger.* This will require intensive, naturalistic observation of carefully selected children, followed by systematic research on large and well-differentiated samples of endangered children grouped in psychologically meaningful ways. It is ironic that our fascination with longitudinal designs has obscured recognition that we must first know the topology of each developmental period. Otherwise, we risk pooling dissimilar children and families, following them for long periods of time, and in the end, being able to offer little more than a description of their continuing risk. Studies of maltreatment and psychopathology, when they are subdivided in psychologically relevant ways, provide the possibility of understanding the interaction of self, caregiver, and context in precisely those situations where attachment can mean the difference between life and death.

Second, we need to think in developmental terms. Infants do not have the mental or behavioral breadth to define patterns of attachment throughout the lifespan (see Crittenden, in press a, for a fuller discussion). We should look carefully at the interaction of maturation with individual experience in the expectation that this will yield new organizations, organizations that by adulthood reflect the complexity that we experience daily among adult members of our species.

Third, we should carefully consider the Type C pattern. Ainsworth defined it in unique terms and, with the insight of truly great theorists, in terms that are even more meaningful beyond the range of her data in infancy than within it. Most humans are more or less inconsistent. How does that affect our behavior after the sensorimotor period? It is proposed that the coercive pattern of the preschool years becomes the dominant organizing strategy for most humans and over time will be shown to differentiate into more substrategies than the other patterns.

Fourth, we need to assess attachment in systemic terms. This means coding behavior at the dyadic level, if not at higher levels. Because interpersonal contingencies provide the most meaningful information about relationships, we should address them. There are a variety of ways of doing this, for example, rating scales that describe dyadic behavior, sequential analysis of behavior, coding of designated organizations of behavior. The critical feature is that we move beyond assignment of meaning to specific behaviors to consideration of the interpersonal function of behavior.

Finally, we need to differentiate happiness from adaptiveness. We are very lucky in most of the Western world. We live in peace and abundance. This has not always been our condition and it is not the condition of many humans now. Indeed, even in "safe" societies, it is estimated epidemiologically that one in five individuals needs mental heath treatment at any given point in time and one in three across a lifetime. Attachment functions to improve the survival of people experiencing the uncertain and variable risks associated with life. Attachment theory, on the other hand, has tended to idealize infant security to the point of creating an evaluative theory that overlooks the achievement of safety by threatened children. This near exclusive focus on the value of security may promote too narrow a view of human potential. Many Type A and C individuals live satisfying lives and make contributions of great value to human culture. In the light of this, we might benefit from greater emphasis on describing the dynamic interaction of person and context that yields adaptation. As Maslow (1970) pointed out, it is only after the basics of survival have been satisfied that attention can turn to higher functions. This is the contribution of inner security, achieved in adulthood, to human adaptation.

This chapter has raised questions about widely accepted constructs and procedures. In addition, it has offered an alternative, a dynamic-maturational model of attachment, that emphasizes a strengths approach to response to danger and focuses on processes rather than enduring states. There are not sufficient data to test most of the issues that have been raised nor to validate the hypotheses of this model. Nevertheless, it is hoped that a plausible rationale for reconsidering long accepted notions has been offered. Furthermore, it is hoped that this alternative perspective has been stated in a manner that makes it testable. Indeed, it may be possible to test aspects of it with recoding of existing longitudinal data sets. With a combination of a return to the basics of Bowlby's clinically rich development of theory and Ainsworth's empirically sound integration of naturalistic observation with systematic and empirical assessment, we can move attachment theory forward as a systemic theory, focused on processes that yield variations in organization, in a dynamic interaction of person, maturation, and context. Such a theory would be truly developmental and relevant to addressing the needs of people who have experienced threat. Because, over the course of every human life, there are critical times of threat and danger, studying the process by which we prepare to survive these is important to us all.

VIII. ATYPICAL PATTERNS OF EARLY ATTACHMENT: DISCUSSION AND FUTURE DIRECTIONS

Douglas Barnett, Christine M. Butler, and Joan I. Vondra

For more than 20 years, a growing body of work has documented the fact that a substantial proportion of infants from low (~15%) to moderate (~35%) to high risk samples (~85%) do not fit into one of the three categories of attachment first identified by Ainsworth's research group. Further examination of these exceptional cases has contributed significantly toward understanding psychologically healthy and pathological adaptation. This *Monograph* brings together four empirical and three theoretical chapters that illustrate current debates and findings concerning the role of atypical patterns of attachment in early development. These chapters support and extend what is known about parenting and child socioemotional development from an attachment perspective. In this final chapter, the ideas and data presented in this volume are synthesized, summarizing how the study of atypical infants and toddlers has contributed to what is known about human attachments and what requires further clarification and revision. The first part of this chapter includes a discussion of implications for attachment theory; the second half includes recommendations for further study.

ATYPICALITY AND THE REFINEMENT OF ATTACHMENT THEORY

Developmental psychology, like all sciences, is founded upon observation and description, as well as the explanations of those observations. Data and theory operate in a dynamic process of revision. Attachment theory was the context leading Ainsworth and her colleagues (Ainsworth, Blehar, Waters, &

Wall, 1978) to use a "Strange Situation" to capture qualitative differences in mother-infant relationships. The research following from their observations has led to substantial refinements of attachment theory regarding the role experience plays in shaping individual differences in attachment and regarding the degree to which attachments are stable across early childhood. For example, meta-analyses of intervention studies with parents and observational studies of parenting and attachment have provided convincing evidence that sensitive parenting significantly increases the chances that a child will be securely attached (De Wolff & van IJzendoorn, 1997; van IJzendoorn, 1995). Research also has found attachment security to be resilient and not directly affected by infants attending child care during their first year (NICHD Early Child Care Research Network, 1997). There also appears to be significant variability in children's patterns of attachment over time (Belsky, Campbell, Cohn, & Moore, 1996), with attachment patterns appearing to be loosely connected with changes in family environments (Egeland & Farber, 1984; Spieker & Booth, 1988; Vondra, Hommerding, & Shaw, this volume). Taken as a whole, data from the study of traditional patterns of attachment begin to map the parameters between conditions that promote security, and those that detract from it. On the one hand, the data from attachment research have supported Bowlby's hypotheses about maternal sensitivity. On the other hand, the largest percentage of the variance in attachment security is still unaccounted for by dimensions examined in developmental research (De Wolff & van IJzendoorn, 1997). The extent to which children have been shown to change attachment patterns over periods as brief as 6 months certainly does not support a sensitive period model of attachment security. Thus, although research on traditional patterns has confirmed some aspects of attachment theory, it has called others into question.

With the addition of substantial data on children who do not fit Ainsworth's original tripartite system, it is important both to examine potential explanations for the phenomenon in light of attachment theory and to consider the adequacy of current theory as it stands to account for variations in atypical attachment behavior. There are at least three ways in which the study of atypical patterns of attachment clarify the parameters of attachment theory. First they suggest that child factors such as developmental disorders and cognitive delays—though not necessarily physical disabilities—do influence the formation of attachment patterns (Atkinson et al., this volume; Pipp-Siegel et al., this volume; van IJzendoorn, Goldberg, Kroonenberg, & Frenkel, 1992). Although Bowlby emphasized the role of actual experience in determining attachment security, he de-emphasized the influence of child factors. The study of atypicality illuminates new ways in which investigation of child contributions can be understood. Second, the data on atypical attachments highlight the need to understand the component processes that underlie attachment. The research on atypical attachments presented in this *Monograph* suggests that attachment patterns are shaped by a variety of at least partly independent biological, emotional, cognitive, behavioral, and representational processes, and the environment plays a crucial role in how they become coordinated in the regulation of interpersonal goals. Third, the study of atypical patterns of attachment helps clarify the role development plays in the formation of attachment patterns. One of the implicit but potentially most exciting questions of attachment research is how to tease apart the separate biological, experiential, psychological, and behavioral mechanisms involved in attachment and how to determine the nature of their interactive influences on one another and on the developing individual over time. In these three regards, integrating findings from the study of atypicality is necessary for defining a comprehensive model of attachment. The study of atypical patterns of attachment and the study of attachment in atypical samples offer great promise for improving the validity of attachment theory.

In the following section, we examine how the study of atypical patterns of attachment requires a focus on a portion of attachment theory that has received scant conceptual and empirical attention, namely, the biological basis for attachment. Bowlby (1969/1982) held that attachments operate at two levels: a biological level that provides what he believed to be a species-general propensity to form attachments, and a psychological or representational level where individual differences were maintained or altered. Thus, attachment researchers have to examine the biological processes that underlie the propensity for attachment and the psychological processes that regulate individual differences. Although research on Ainsworth's original three patterns of attachment has contributed significantly toward understanding the development of representational models of attachment, research on atypical attachment provides information concerning the species-general processes that account for why attachments form. It also provides information on how biological, psychological, and behavioral processes are independent *and* connected. The concepts of "experience-expectant" and "experience-dependent" mechanisms of development (Gottlieb, 1991; Greenough, Black, & Wallace, 1987) offer a broad framework in which to map out the variety of biological and social factors in atypical attachment.

Attachment as "Experience-Expectant" Development

Attachment has been conceptualized as an experience-expectant phenomenon (Collins & Depue, 1992; Schore, 1996). From this perspective, the propensity to form attachments would be considered to be largely "hard-wired" in human neurobiology, and thereby, universally experienced by all members of the species. This is concordant with Bowlby's view that

174

attachment serves a universal purpose in ensuring human survival, and also implies how the development of attachment is biologically overdetermined. Experience-expectant mechanisms are believed to be robust in the face of a very wide range of potential developmental environments and therefore may be thought of as "experiential canalization" (Gottlieb, 1991; Greenough et al., 1987). From this neurodevelopmental perspective, the biological substrate necessary for attachment to develop would contain tremendous redundancy, and, thus, plasticity in case of all but devastating biological or environmental damage, deprivation, or abnormality. Only minimal, and thus highly probable, environmental input is required to set into motion the basic processes of attachment development. An analogous process is that of language development. The human brain appears prewired to develop language in the early years of life. Sufficient redundancy is built in so that in the event of loss of or damage to the regions normally dedicated to language functions, other parts of the brain take over the development of language with little or no loss of function, provided the event occurs early in development (Pirozzolo & Papanicolaou, 1986). Furthermore, the development of some language occurs in the presence of minimal linguistic stimulation. Only extreme deprivation results in serious interference with language development. Similarly, a child would be expected to develop some form of attachment given even minimal neurological capacity and minimal triggering input from a caregiver.

The underlying biological and psychological processes that maintain attachment comprise a highly flexible, but increasingly integrated, system. This biological system, in turn, coordinates and regulates the systems involved in the organization and manifestation of attachment behavior (e.g., attention to and perception of internal and external stimuli relevant to attachment). Because multiple biological systems take part in this regulatory function, damage to one component does not result in an overall failure to form attachments. For a variety of medical reasons, however, damage to one or more biological components may occur. When an underlying biological system is altered, atypical attachment patterns are likely to be the result. The Atkinson et al. study (this volume) highlights the influence of biological systems upon the morphology of attachment. Young children with Down syndrome exhibit a number of attachment-relevant differences in affective functioning, including more "noise" during affective signaling, muted distress reactions, less affective signaling, and so on (Atkinson et al., this volume; Ganiban, Wagner, & Cicchetti, 1990). These differences may alter the parental behaviors that are elicited and thus, over time, the shape of the attachment relationship. Behavioral manifestations of attachment also may be obscured by biological constraints. For instance, impairments can affect the deployment and coordination of attachment behavior. In cases of cerebral palsy and other central nervous system motor disorders, children will be likely to exhibit behaviors that characterize atypical patterns of attachment (Pipp-Siegel et al., this volume). These behaviors, however, are a result of damage to systems that underlie movement. As a result, behavior in the Strange Situation may look atypical, but only as an artifact of a medical disorder. The remaining attachment system appears different morphologically, but has the potential to function securely despite the motor difficulties (Barnett et al., in press; see also van IJzendoorn et al., 1992).

Although experience-expectant mechanisms suggest resilience and plasticity in the face of environmental challenges, they also suggest that extreme experiences can alter the underlying biological processes of attachment. Thus attachments could be both a cause and result of individual differences in neurochemistry. We believe that atypicality of attachment develops from disruption in the experience-expectant systems underlying attachment either through innate differences in the underlying biological systems, unusual experiences with caregivers (e.g., trauma or neglect), or a combination of both.

Observations of children reared in institutions and children who have experienced severe forms of human deprivation, war, separation, loss, and isolation were some of the initial data Bowlby and others considered in the development of attachment theory. Extreme conditions such as severe parental neglect, deprivation of basic human contact in orphanages, and repeated traumatic separations in early childhood because of parental loss or maltreatment still exist. Examination of children with these extreme forms of attachment trauma, using the methods developed by attachment researchers in the last 30 years, will prove informative. Currently, children adopted from Romanian orphanages are receiving empirical attention (e.g., Chisholm, 1998; Goldberg, 1997). Their early experiences of deprivation might be severe enough to have an impact on the neuropsychological systems regulating attachment relationships.

In cases of extreme deprivation, the nervous system is qualitatively altered, as has been found in some other species (Greenough et al., 1987). The absence of a consistently available primary caregiver may result in failure of the environment to stimulate the growth and maintenance of the neurological pathways regulating attachments. Goldberg (1997) examined the Strange Situations of 56 2- to 6-year-olds adopted from Romania. The sample included 19 children who had "prolonged experiences of deprivation"; the remainder were adopted after briefer experiences of deprivation restricted to the "first few months" of life. What is striking about her findings is that none of the adopted children demonstrated an avoidant attachment. Instead they were about evenly divided among the secure, dependent, and controlling/other categories of one preschool classification system (Cassidy & Marvin, in collaboration with the MacArthur Working Group on

Attachment, 1991). Chisholm (1998) also assessed attachment in a sample of 43 children adopted from Romanian orphanages (age range 4½–9½ years, adopted for at least 2 years) using a single separation procedure in the home (and a different preschool classification system; Crittenden, 1990–1995). She did not replicate Goldberg's finding that no adopted children were classified as avoidant, but consistently found a pattern of more extreme and atypical insecure attachments (e.g., Compulsive Caregiving, "A/C," and Insecure Other) in children who had spent at least their first 8 months in an orphanage. Goldberg (1997) offered four potential psychological explanations for the absence of Type A attachments in her sample. A fifth is that the early deprivation experiences changed the brain systems underlying attachment, resulting later in development in atypical classifications due to mixed strategies, more extreme attachment patterns, and/or difficulty in maintaining a consolidated avoidant stance.

Support for a biological explanation comes from the fact that psychophysiological markers (e.g., salivary cortisol and heart rate) have been found only in the cases of atypical patterns of attachment (Hertsgaard, Gunner, Erickson, & Nachmias, 1995; Spangler & Grossmann, 1993). These studies suggest that the hypothalamic-pituitary-adrenal-axis (HTPA) of children with Type D attachments may be more reactive than those of children with other patterns of attachment. The HTPA system is more generally involved in regulation to extreme forms of stress, and chronic activation of this system qualitatively changes the manner in which the system responds. Caregivers appear to be a natural buffer for HTPA arousal, and it is unclear how the arousal system is affected when the caregiver's behavior itself is anxiety-provoking (as Lyons-Ruth, Bronfman, & Parsons, this volume, found). One possibility is that the infant may momentarily habituate to or ignore one set of stimuli or the other, and thus the caregiver becomes alternately a stressor or a buffer. The infant may respond to the particular aspect of caregiving behavior that predominates or is most emotionally salient at any given moment, resulting in what appear to be inconsistent responses over time. Under these conditions, the attachment system may become overwhelmed and fail, at least momentarily, to organize affect and behavior in the face of conflicting input (see Crittenden, 1992a, for a description of possible functions of "disorganized" behavior).

Attachment as "Experience-Dependent" Development

A central tenet of attachment theory has been that the morphology of patterns of attachment (as opposed to the existence of attachment) is dependent on experience. Adopting an experience-expectant/experience-dependent model suggests that attachment patterns are also influenced

177

by underlying systems. These systems may create the capacity to form representations of attachment and to integrate representations with behavior. Once this capacity is present, attachment may be considered to be in the experience-dependent phase (cf. Crittenden, this volume). Continuing with the analogy of language acquisition, the type of language acquired by children depends upon the one to which they are exposed. Attachment researchers have concerned themselves primarily with children who are neurologically intact and, therefore, presumably have realized their capacity for attachment. The concern has been with the content of the attachment representation that guides the behavioral pattern or type of attachment adopted, rather than with the species-general mechanisms of attachment. The study of atypical samples of children with a variety of biological vulnerabilities suggests the importance of understanding the necessary underpinnings needed for attachments to emerge in typical varieties.

One possible conceptual framework that would account for variations in internal (child) and external (environmental) organizational capacity is illustrated in Figure 6. Knowledge about sources of atypicality should provide clues about the types of atypical patterns. Figure 6 presents a two-by-two table that includes three possible types of atypical patterns. One dimension represents the caregiving contribution. Caregiving that correlates with and may

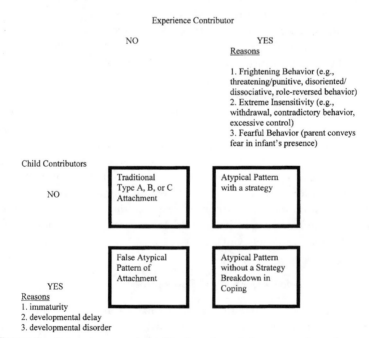

FIGURE 6.   Determinants and classification of atypical patterns of attachment

contribute to the development of an atypical pattern includes confusing and fear-inducing behaviors, such as the parent being extremely unresponsive or affectively contradictory, threatening/punitive, disoriented/dissociative, role-reversing, and/or communicating fearful states within themselves (i.e., disorganization of the external environment, which would then fail to support the timely development of internal organization; Barnett et al., this volume; Lyons-Ruth et al., this volume; Schuengel, Bakermans-Kranenburg, & van IJzendoorn, 1999).

The second dimension is the child's capacity to take in and organize input from the environment and regulate external behavior accordingly. A child with difficulty regulating internal affective states, communicating state needs to caregivers, exhibiting behavior that elicits positive involvement from caregivers, or making use of regulating input from others will have trouble organizing an effective attachment strategy. Similarly, a child who is highly reactive to external input may screen out necessary input in an effort to avoid being overwhelmed. Both may experience either a chronically over-whelmed, neurologically and affectively disorganized state or the effects of social deprivation because of a tendency to remain "shut down" to input.

In the first quadrant are children who do *not* have organic problems that make it difficult for them to internalize and/or execute a coherent attach-ment strategy and who do *not* have caregivers interfering with a coherent anticipation of their—either conditional (resulting in Types A and C attach-ments) or generally unconditional (Type B)—availability and style of inter-action. These are hypothesized to be children who develop A, B, or C attachment patterns.

In the second quadrant are children of sufficient mental age who do *not* have any developmental problems in forming a coherent representation of experience. They have caregivers, however, who are extremely insensitive to their cues and needs and behave inappropriately and unpredictably, and/or in a fearful or fear-inducing manner. Children in this quadrant show atypical patterns of attachment that have an identifiable strategy. This includes the in-fant "A/C" (Crittenden, 1988) and "D" attachments (Main & Solomon, 1990) that can readily be "force classified" (i.e., the indices of disorganization are in discrete behaviors such as stilling and backing into the caregiver, not in ex-pected sequences or patterns of behavior such as separation distress followed by strong avoidance at reunion). In the preschool period, this would include the Compulsive Compliant ("A4") and Compulsive Caregiving ("A3"), Coer-cive Helpless ("C4") and Coercive Aggressive ("C3"), and "A/C" (Crittenden, 1990–1995), and the Controlling-Caregiving, Controlling- Punitive, and Con-trolling-General attachment classifications (Cassidy & Marvin, in collabora-tion with MacArthur Working Group on Attachment, 1992).

In the third quadrant are children who do *not* have the developmen-tal maturity to internalize, integrate, or execute a coherent strategy, but nonetheless do *not* live in an environment conducive to atypical attachments. These children are likely to display attachment patterns that mimic the Type D pattern, but represent false disorganization. These are children who may have developmental delays such as mental retardation, neuromotor problems, or developmental disorders such as autism, but experience general sensitivity/responsiveness in their care. They are considered false disorganized in the sense that these behaviors are not a function of the attachment relationship. These children probably represent a *subset* of "unclassifiable" cases (Vaughn et al., 1994). As Atkinson et al. and Pipp-Siegel et al. (both this volume) discuss, it may sometimes be difficult to distinguish biological deficits leading to inability to form secure attachment from those leading only to inability to produce the behaviors by which researchers evaluate secure attachment. In impaired children, different behavioral cues may have to be used in the assessment. Barnett and his colleagues (in press) conducted a comparison of children with neurologically based birth defects and children with birth defects having no neurological involvement. They found that, using Pipp-Siegel et al's. (this volume) system, they were able to distinguish signs of Type D attachment that were due to neurological impairment from those that were based in the caregiver-child relationship. Neurologically impaired children initially had higher rates of D attachment than comparison children, but when the "neurological D signs" were controlled for, the incidence of D attachment did not differ between the two groups. These data support the argument that atypicality in attachment behavior may not always reflect an atypical relationship organization.

In the fourth quadrant are children who, we hypothesize, lack the developmental competence to form a coherent pattern of attachment *and* have caregivers who engage in atypically negative parenting practices. The greater the child's developmental jeopardy, the less extreme caregiving probably needs to be to result in an atypical attachment. Likewise, the more extreme the caregiving, the less problematic the child's development needs to be to result in an atypical attachment, demonstrating the connections to quadrants 2 (only caregiving casualty) and 3 (only child developmental disabilities). The interaction effect Atkinson and his colleagues (this volume) reported between infant mental development score and maternal sensitivity on attachment security versus unclassifiability in young children with Down syndrome supports the notion of combined influence. Infants in quadrant 4 are expected to display those Type D patterns of attachment (Main & Solomon, 1990) characterized by incongruous behavioral sequences (e.g., strong avoidance following separation distress, distress and resistance following an undistressed separation, the dramatic drop in avoidance across reunions that typifies the "Unstable A" classification) and causing difficulty among raters in choosing an appropriate forced classification. The majority of infants deemed "unclassifiable" in Atkinson et al.'s (this volume) and Vaughn et al.'s (1994) studies of children with Down syndrome may belong in this quadrant. Crittenden's (1990–1995) rare "D" classification for preschoolers who do not appear to behave strategically in relation to their caregiver would belong in this quadrant, and a significant portion of infants and children deemed "unclassifiable" may belong here as well. These are children who exhibit fear in reaction to their caregiver, but also distress in response to their caregiver's departure. They exhibit a breakdown in coping across episodes of the Strange Situation, often with symptoms of traumatic arousal.

It should be noted that, although this proposed scheme treats atypical attachments as distinct subtypes, inherent in the model are quantitative dimensions of degree of organic impairment, degree of child/caregiver compatibility, and degree of system organization. One of the central questions facing researchers is whether to conceptualize attachment, and in particular atypical attachment, as a categorical construct, in which individuals are rated as belonging to one class or type rather than another, or as a dimensional construct, in which degree or amount of, say, security or atypicality is the variable of interest. It may well be that, for the present, it should be treated as both (see Vondra et al., this volume). The categorical model has the virtue of simplicity and parsimony. Although parsimony is a goal in theory-building, however, the theory also must explain the phenomenon adequately. Physicists have debated whether light "behaves" more like a particle or a wave. It happens that both conceptualizations are necessary to describe and explain the phenomenon completely. Analogously, it may be necessary to conceptualize individual differences in attachment both as a category and as a dimensional construct as long as each has its merits in research and theory.

This conceptualization also makes it clear that atypical attachment is multiply determined and that there are multiple pathways by which it can occur. Child factors that may lead to an atypical attachment pattern include an organically based inability to regulate autonomic arousal and any resulting inability to be comforted, motoric delays that make it impossible to execute an organized strategy to gain the presence of the caregiver; and a developmentally based cognitive inability to form stable, integrated representations of the caregiver. Parent factors potentially contributing to atypicality include fearful, confusing, and/or frightening behavior that is communicated to the child, rendering it difficult for the child to manage internal arousal and organize adaptive behavior patterns at the same time. Such internalized fear also increases the likelihood of inaccurate or insufficient representation of the environment, and loss of representations to conscious awareness. This would further decrease the likelihood of obtaining environment support when it is available. Other parental factors include unpredictable, very harsh, or threatening behavior, making it impossible or dangerous to form an organized strategy to keep the caregiver nearby, as well as disengagement of cognition, behavior and affect in the caregiver, possibly due to mental illness or trauma. Not only would this be likely to result in inconsistent and contradictory behavior in the caregiver, but also it would model for the child a lack of integration of cognition, affect, and behavior. As noted previously, such a lack of integration may well be a defining feature of some forms of atypical attachment. Parents who frequently scare their infants may interfere with the latter's ability to coordinate information across affective, cognitive, and representational systems. Such findings have implications for prediction of later susceptibility to anxiety, hostility, dissociation, depression, violence, and other forms of affective and behavioral dysregulation (see Crittenden, this volume; Lyons-Ruth & Jacobvitz, in press).

Development and Attachment

An experience-expectant/experience-dependent model assumes that the influence of experience on behavior changes in degree and kind with development. Early in the first year of life, children's capacity to engage their caregivers is limited. Crying and calming are early states that hopefully guide caregivers to provide predictable, responsive, sensitive care; that is, infant physiological reactivity provides parameters for parent responses. By the second half of the 1st year, there is behavioral evidence that children are oriented toward particular caregivers with whom they have a history. One study using infrared cameras found that 4-month-olds' temperature regulation patterns were specific to attachment figures in contrast to strangers (Mizukami, Kobayashi, Ishii, & Iwata, 1990). Perhaps physiological parameters such as temperature regulation are classically conditioned in response to caregivers (see Crittenden, this volume; Pipp & Harmon, 1987). At a later point in development, mental representations of caregivers become more complex by integrating several states and experiences with the caregivers together into a richer psychological representation.

In the early weeks of life, the infant's needs for basic physiological state regulation may have a strong effect on canalizing the caregiver's response. In subsequent months, more subtle differences in responsiveness and sensitivity by caregivers may become increasingly significant to the infant. Later, symbolic and linguistic information influence attachment. Attachment-relevant events, thoughts, emotions, and physiological states eventually become represented in scripted or narrative forms, as reflected in children's pretend role play, family drawings, stories, and so on (Fury, Carlson, & Sroufe, 1997; Main, Kaplan, & Cassidy, 1985). Through these developmental changes, the types of experiences influencing attachment change with development. In the earliest months of development, the infant may be buffered from experience having much influence on the development of an attachment so that only gross differences in care have an impact on the underlying systems. When very early experience is extreme enough to have an impact, however, it will have a substantial influence because it is affecting the basic underlying neural mechanisms. Beginning around the 3rd through 6th months, subtle differences in caregiving have increasing influence because the psychological systems affected by those differences have developed. By the preschool period, new refinements in psychological sophistication give the child an increasingly powerful role in shaping attachment experiences.

One of the implications of this formulation is that, at least theoretically, the ability of a particular caregiver to provide the type of experiences needed by a particular child may change over the course of development. Therefore, there should be multiple opportunities across development for a secure attachment to develop or, possibly, be undone. A caregiver who was unable to provide sensitive care in regulating early physiological arousal states in infancy might be able to respond more adaptively to a child's affective expression later in development, or vice versa. This assumes that the "working model" remains open and working (Crittenden, 1990).

Stability, Change, and Adaptation in Attachment

The question then becomes how to interpret the stability and change of attachment classification over the course of development. Attachment is predicated on the formation of a "goal-corrected relationship" (Cicchetti, Cummings, Greenberg, & Marvin, 1990) in which the goal of the child is to keep the caregiver "close enough." The fact that the caregiver's ability to respond to the child may change over time—perhaps particularly in cases of insecure relationships—suggests that while the goal remains stable, the adaptive functioning of each partner demands alterations in the child's strategy to accomplish the goal. A caregiver whose availability is unpredictable might tend to produce "C" (resistant) behavior in the child to accomplish the goal of maximizing the caregiver's response to the child. As the child grows older, if the caregiver's expectations are for increased child independence and the caregiver becomes impatient and rejecting, the most adaptive response for the child could be to switch to an "A" (avoidant) strategy. Crittenden (this volume) proposes that certain attachment classifications may be particularly adaptive and possibly normative at different points in development. For instance, "C" attachment may become functional for more children after toddlerhood when increased cognitive and motor skills and a wider social circle make a child appear deceptively capable of independence when the child is actually still quite vulnerable. "A" attachment may be more normative in infancy (i.e., functional for more infants), when minimal levels of care are highly probable anyway, and the cost of potential rejection is too high to risk. Attachment stability lies in the distal, overarching goal of keeping the caregiver resources available to the child. The more proximal subgoals presumably depend on both the child's developing capacities and changing input from the environment. An avoidant strategy that prevents rejection in an abusive or intrusive caregiver is functionally adaptive; an avoidant attachment with a caregiver who ignores or neglects an undemanding child would not be in service to the goal of attachment. Atypical attachment patterns need to be evaluated in terms of their adaptive function for the child. To the extent that such adaptive functions can be identified in terms of the resources provided by the caregiving system and the needs and functional limitations of the child, we may be better able to understand the relation of atypical patterns to other patterns of attachment. Such a functional analysis also would be helpful in refining and further validating existing typologies of atypical attachment.

The caregiving environment places constraints on the extent to which any single strategy will be effective over time. An unpredictable interpersonal environment may make rapid shifting between "A" and "C" strategies maximally adaptive in maintaining the balance of the relationship. A dangerous situation makes this ability to be flexible important for survival. When alternations of attachment strategy are adaptive but do not occur, it may be because the individual has constraints on the strategic options available to him or her due to damage to the biological substrates that underlie attachment functioning. Thus the extreme forms of deprivation represented, for example, in the Romanian orphanages (Goldberg, 1997) may result in dysregulation of separation distress, making deployment of an avoidant strategy (low distress during separation, avoidance upon reunion) very difficult, if not impossible. Under conditions of extreme deprivation, an avoidant strategy may be fatal; consequently children who rely on such a strategy may not survive to adoption (R. Clifton, personal communication, 1999). In cases in which the capacities of the child and the caregiving environment are at odds, it may not be possible for the infant to develop any single, consistent strategy that will be adaptive. Such cases may result in truly disorganized attachment that lacks any strategy, or lacks a strategy effective in maintaining access to protection for the child (see Crittenden, this volume). Implied in this argument is the idea that adaptation in the form of development of an attachment strategy involves a degree of "matching" between the child's specific needs and capacities and the resources available in the caregiving environment.

The Ecology of Atypical Patterns of Attachment

Increasingly, work on attachment has shifted beyond a focus exclusively on the infant-caregiver dyad to include the development and maintenance of the caregiving system as a related, but separate, process. In particular, George and Solomon (1996) argued that there is a high degree of concordance between the caregiver's representational working model of caregiving, and the child's attachment organization. Lyons-Ruth and Jacobvitz (in press) review and discuss the concordance data for children with disorganized attachments. Although links have certainly been established between unresolved loss or trauma scored in mothers' adult attachment interviews (van IJzendoorn, 1995), maternal frightening/confusing/frightened behavior (Jacobvitz, Hazen, & Riggs, 1997), and mother-infant disorganized attachment (Lyons-Ruth et al., this volume), considerable unpredictability remains (Schuengel et al., in press).

Barnett and his colleagues (this volume) suggest that a lack of fit, or serious disjunction, between the caregiver's interactive style and the child's may prompt an insecure attachment to become an atypical one. For example, it may be that, given an interpersonal press toward insecure attachment, the child's temperament influences whether that child becomes avoidant or ambivalent (Belsky & Rovine, 1987). As George and Solomon (1996) noted, however, there is a considerable degree to which the caregiving system may press for one or the other. If the child and caregiver press in the same direction, the result may be simply an A or a C attachment. If there is a mismatch, however (e.g., if a parent whose caregiving system cannot tolerate high levels of emotionality has a highly reactive child), the disjunction between the two systems may result in atypical attachment.

Furthermore, merely insensitive parenting may be more responsive to environmental conditions of stress and support as well as to change in the face of developmental demands than more pathological parenting that stems from organic or psychological incapacity within the parent and is less susceptible to alterations from environmental change. Vondra and her colleagues (this volume) found attachment disorganization was associated with a constellation of hostile personality traits and with family instability and negative life events but was not associated with reported social support. Research is needed to delineate whether and how stability in the caregiving system is reflected in stability of atypical attachment.

ASSESSMENT AND CONSTRUCT VALIDATION ISSUES

The data on atypical patterns of attachment raise a number of questions that challenge the theoretical and empirical underpinnings of the

185

classificatory approach to attachment research. For example, should infants demonstrating such patterns be viewed as having a common attachment strategy or lacking one? On the one hand, Atkinson and his colleagues (this volume) found robust statistical differences in maternal care and child mental development status associated not only with all unclassifiable attachments, but all insecure attachments among children with Down syndrome. On the other hand, Lyons-Ruth and her colleagues (this volume) reported a meaningful pattern of differences in maternal care for those disorganized attachments that received a secure versus insecure forced classification. Are atypical infant responses linked by particular emotions (e.g., fear), experiences (e.g., trauma), or patterns of parent-infant interaction (e.g., frightening/confusing/frightened behavior)? Uncertainty remains about which, if any, behaviors should disqualify children from classification in a traditional category, which, if any, features unify atypical patterns, and how such patterns should be grouped. If all combinations of infant emotional and behavioral responsiveness occur, then perhaps quantitative, as opposed to, or in addition to, qualitative approaches to analyzing coded attachment behaviors are warranted. Infant-caregiver relationships would not necessarily be classified into groups, but examined along multiple affective and behavioral dimensions. Current interactive ratings (Ainsworth et al., 1978) can confound affect (e.g., duration of distress) with behavior (e.g., contact maintenance). But one of the hallmarks of Main and Solomon's (1990) indices of disorganization is the *mismatch* of affect and behavior (distress and contact seeking with gaze avoidance, distress and movement away from mother).

The resolution of these questions will require the continued delineation of etiological pathways involved in the development of atypical attachment. One of the most basic questions is whether one atypical pattern exists or many. In this *Monograph*, data were presented on four different atypical attachment patterns (Types D, U, A/C, and UA). The chapters in this volume present empirical support that children who demonstrate patterns inconsistent with one of the three traditional patterns should be considered as a separate grouping. By grouping atypical patterns together, statistical predictions from parenting and family data were supported as well as trends toward continuity of relationship atypicality up to 1½ years. Not consistently addressed in this *Monograph* was the degree of overlap among the various atypical attachments and whether it makes theoretical and empirical sense to distinguish among one or multiple atypical patterns of attachment (but see Lyons-Ruth et al., Vondra et al., both this volume). Different designations for some comparable behavioral profiles are summarized in Table 30. Investigation across laboratories and samples of these different ways of codifying atypicality will lead to further refinement of knowledge about what

TABLE 30

ALTERNATIVE ATTACHMENT DESIGNATIONS FOR ATYPICAL BEHAVIORAL PROFILES

Child Age	Attachment Designation	Behavioral Profile
1–2 years	• A/C (Crittenden, 1985, 1988) *also designated as*: • D/Insecure (a subset, Lyons-Ruth et al., 1991) • D (a subset, Main & Solomon, 1990)	moderate to high proximity-seeking without positive affect; moderate to high avoidance; moderate to high resistance; accompanied by "maladaptive" or "stress" behaviors including oblique, backward approaches, face covering, huddling on the floor, etc.
	• Unstable A (Lyons-Ruth et al., 1986, 1987) *also designated as*: • D/Secure (a subset, Lyons-Ruth et al., 1991) • D (a subset, Main & Solomon, 1990)	high avoidance in first reunion; no or low avoidance in second reunion (a decline of 4+ points), often combined with high distress only in the second separation and mild to moderate resistance in the second reunion;[1] usually accompanied by other indices of disorganization: gaze avoidance during child-initiated contact, depressed affect, falling prone during reunion, etc.
	• Unclassifiable (Vaughn et al., 1994; Atkinson et al., this volume)	no identifiable attachment pattern; behaving as if "unattached" to mother: little distress at or even notice of separation, calmed by stranger, lack of special attention to/preference for mother; fewer than three indices of disorganization (Main & Solomon, 1990)
2–5 years	• D/Controlling (Cassidy, Marvin et al., 1991) • C3-Aggressive (Crittenden, 1992a)	whiny, angry, hurtful, and/or resistant behavior used coercively with caregiver, often mixed with appeasing, inviting behavior
	• C-Dependent/Passive (Cassidy, Marvin et al., 1991) • C4-Helpless (Crittenden, 1992a)	marked passivity/inhibition, avoidance of stranger, exaggerated helpless and dependent behavior used to elicit caregiver involvement
	• D/Caregiving (Cassidy, Marvin et al., 1991) • A3-Compulsively Caregiving (Crittenden, 1992a)	bright affect with gaze avoidance; entertaining behavior for caregiver often with high activity level but no sustained, focused exploration; often distressed after departure
	• A4-Compulsively Compliant (Crittenden, 1992a) *also designated as*: • Insecure Other (a subset, Cassidy, Marvin et al., 1991)	wariness and vigilance; covert attentive to caregiver's whereabouts and emotions; avoids drawing attention to self through quiet play; flat affect overall with distress in separations only when caregiver would not notice

• A/C (Crittenden, 1992a) *also designated as*: • Insecure Other (a subset, Cassidy, Marvin et al., 1991)	alternate use of both defended strategies (inhibition of negative affect, caregiving, and/or compliance) and coercive strategies (threatening, appeasing, aggressive, and/or helpless behavior) in response to changing caregiver behavior
• AD-Anxious Depressed (Crittenden, 1992a) *also designated as*: • D (a subset, Cassidy, Marvin et al., 1991)	attachment behavior used for self-comfort (e.g., avoidance at start of a departure breaking down into high distress or attempts to leave with caregiver); sadness/resignation; elements of defended (gaze avoidance) and coercive behaviors (appeasing, helpless behaviors) without either being used strategically to get caregiver involvement
• D-Disorganized (Crittenden, 1992a) *also designated as*: • D (a subset, Cassidy, Marvin et al., 1991)	attachment strategies are alternated or used only piecemeal, but the dyssynchronies are not in relation to changing caregiver behavior and are unsuccessful either in self-comfort or in making caregiver's behavior predictable

[1] The dramatic decline in avoidance and only modest increase in resistance usually means that these children are given a secure forced classification.

attachment patterns are and about the processes involved with them at the biological, psychological, behavioral, and social level.

A defining question is that of the presence or absence of discernible strategy in the atypical attachment strategy. Crittenden's (this volume) work on the A/C classification suggests that an underlying coherence may characterize this type of organization. Supporting this are preliminary data suggesting that the atypical preschool designations, A/C and Anxious Depressed (AD) Types may be uniquely associated with subsequent internalizing behavior problems (Teti et al., 1995; Vondra et al., in press). In contrast, Type D infant attachments have been characterized as initially disorganized and lacking in any coherence, although they may later show a coherent, organized, controlling pattern of behavior, presumably to compensate for a disorganized caregiving system (Main & Cassidy, 1988; Wartner, Grossmann, Fremmer-Bombik, & Suess, 1994). Both arguments warrant further theoretical and empirical attention. The data connecting specific atypical attachment patterns with particular interactive experiences (Lyons-Ruth et al., this volume) and with risk for specific types of psychopathology are intriguing, but need further replication and expansion. Severe limits on sample size for these analyses (see Vondra et al., this volume) and differences across investigators in coding and classifying atypical patterns both argue for more collaboration across laboratories.

FUTURE DIRECTIONS

Figure 6 presents one potential scheme for grouping the atypical patterns of attachment described in this volume. Table 30 summarizes some of the overlapping designations currently in use to describe atypical patterns. Both raise the question of how an attachment category should be described and validated. Three foci for future research on atypical attachment are phenomenology, etiology, and prediction of sequelae. This parallels the validation studies of the traditional A, B, and C categories, in which distinct patterns of Strange Situation behavior were reliably demonstrated to be related to and predicted by distinct types of parenting behavior and, in turn, were predictive of social and behavioral outcomes in later childhood. Thus, a first question is whether atypical attachment patterns are consistently similar in their morphology, or whether their commonality is limited to being non-A, B, and C or, perhaps more simply, to being more extremely nonsecure? Important work has already been done in developing well-defined classification criteria for Type D. More needs to be done defining and contrasting A/C, Unstable A, Unclassifiable, and different subsets of Type D attachments (e.g., secure versus insecure forced classifications, those associated with maternal frightened versus frightening behavior) during infancy. Similarly research is needed comparing and contrasting the two existing preschool scoring systems (Cassidy in collaboration with the MacArthur Working Group on Attachment, Marvin, 1991; Crittenden, 1990–1995), which "cut the attachment pie" differently. Careful empirical documentation of the overlap in behavioral characteristics of these patterns, briefly summarized in Table 30, will be a necessary first step for testing the existence and function of distinct morphological patterns.

Basic research on the etiology of atypical attachment patterns is well under way. The relation of atypical attachment to ecological context, patterns of caregiving, and biological risk factors has been discussed throughout this *Monograph*. The next challenge will be to gather data on large enough samples of atypical children at different ages to draw reliable pathways between attachment behavior and internal and external etiological factors, and to distinguish among etiologies. Sample size is also an issue in the assessment of morphological data. Atypical attachments are (and should be) uncommon in low-risk populations. For that reason, they have generally been grouped together rather than examined as separate subtypes, and it has been difficult to garner support for and replication of distinctive links to experience and functioning. Further refinement requires focusing inquiry on samples at higher risk and greater collaboration among researchers or between researchers and clinicians to create large enough samples of atypical cases for careful study. With large samples, powerful statistical tools for the empirical validation of attachment subtypes, such as cluster analysis, discriminant function analysis, and factor analysis, can help researchers sort through the welter of data available to reveal underlying structural patterns and, ultimately, provide theoretical clarification. These tools, however, require not only large sample sizes but also a high degree of standardization of measures.

Work on atypical attachment would be greatly facilitated, not only by the availability of larger at-risk samples for study, but by increased standardization across labs in coding tapes and analyzing data. Large samples, such as the one used in the NICHD Early Child Care Research Network (1997) study, could be used as a basis for developing normative data for standardized coding systems. Large samples could also be useful in updating and/or revising both typological criteria and behavioral rating scales used in measuring dimensions of interactive behavior and in assigning categories. This will be critically important for obtaining reliable, sound data upon which to base decisions about whether to conceptualize atypical attachment as a categorical or dimensional construct. The identification of behaviors that diverge from prototypes of Type A, B, and C categories suggests the need for clarifying the boundaries between categories and re-examining the behavioral patterns captured by the interactive rating scales. Data from tables in the Ainsworth et al. (1978) and other small, Strange Situation samples from 10 or 20 years ago continue to be used to investigate infant attachment behavior and patterns by investigators (e.g., Richters, Waters, & Vaughn, 1988). These data, which form the basis of quantitative approaches to the study of infant attachment, need to be updated. Revision of interactive behavior scales and development of a database on a large sample of at-risk infants' behavior in the Strange Situation could significantly improve the reliability, and therefore validity, of future attachment research.

There is a need to understand how parenting is, itself, affected by a child's developmental level and by individual differences in children, including biological factors. It might be possible to gain some knowledge of the mechanisms by which precursors of, and risk factors for, atypical attachment become operative in particular situations. Thompson (1997) pointed out that it is not sufficient to know whether or how strongly sensitivity is related to attachment security; we also should ask why and how that association is operative. Similarly, knowledge of the mechanisms by which various etiological pathways result in atypical attachment will deepen our understanding both of attachment and of socioemotional development in general, and will yield additional tools with which to construct appropriate intervention.

As noted earlier, more work is needed not only on the role of atypical attachments in the etiology of childhood psychological disorders and intergenerational transmission of risk factors, but also on the development of attachment as it relates to systems beyond the child-caregiver dyad. For instance, the time is ripe for research on cultural influences that go beyond comparisons with "normative" middle-class samples. An increasing body of

research demonstrates the usefulness of attachment constructs and measures in ethnic minority and disadvantaged populations, but potentially different patterns of linkage to caregiving (De Wolff & van Ijzendoorn, 1997)
and development (Vondra et al., in press). More research is needed on the
specific determinants of attachment patterns in different contexts, however,
and on the meaning and outcome of attachment organization across contexts. This is especially important in the case of atypical attachment, which
may serve entirely different ends in some groups than in others. To do such
work requires not only cultural sensitivity, but also an understanding of the
workings of groups and cultures in general. Developmental psychology
could profit from collaboration with anthropologists, sociologists, and clinicians in such endeavors.

The need and opportunities for collaborative work across disciplines is
already apparent in some of the conceptual work being developed on attachment and psychopathology. When the cross-fertilization of ideas is reflected
in interdisciplinary or collaborative research studies, great strides in developmental theory may result. Clearly, developmentalists stand to gain much
from strengthening the bridge that attachment offers between developmental and clinical psychology. Both disciplines also stand to gain from sharing
their expertise in constructing relationships between theory, empirical data,
and applied data.

There is a dynamic balance between observation and theory. Theories
(like representational models of attachment) have a powerful influence on
how and what is observed. They influence which observations are considered most and least relevant, even which are most and least accurate. They
give meaning to what is observed. The influence a theory has on observation is often outside of awareness and not appropriately acknowledged. A
major advantage of cross-disciplinary collaboration is that the theoretical
assumptions which guide how we perceive observations are more likely to
be examined. Similarly, sharing of observations generates the creation of
more flexible, broader and more powerful theory. Such theory-building
might include the development of a dynamic systems model of attachment.
In such a model, attachment could be examined in the context of cognitive,
affective, and neuromotor development. Its influence on these developmental issues also remains to be investigated.

SUMMARY AND CONCLUSION

The study of atypical patterns of attachment challenges and broadens
notions derived from the study of the three original patterns. Research on
atypical attachments suggest that the developmental integration of biological,
psychological, and behavioral responses is more profoundly dependent on

social-environmental influences than even research focusing on Type A, B, and C attachments suggests. This relation also may shed light on the origins not simply of behavior problems, but of the kinds of dissociations of affect, cognition, and behavior that seem to be a fundamental part of some forms of later emerging psychopathology. It seems clear that understanding the nature and developmental progression of these atypical patterns of attachment may provide a key to understanding how normal and abnormal development both interface and diverge over time. The availability of long-term follow-up data will help to resolve the question about dimensions of attachment or types of pattern, particularly if they are studied from the perspective of individual adaptation to experience, and take into account both temperamental variation as well as variation in relationship experiences.

REFERENCES

Aicardi, J. (1986). Myoclonic epilepsies of infancy and childhood. In S. Fahn, C. D. Marsden & M. H. Van Woert (Eds.), *Advances in Neurology*. New York: Raven Press.

Aicardi, J. (1992). Paroxysmal disorders other than epilepsy. In J. Aicardi (Ed.), *Diseases of the nervous system in childhood*. New York: Cambridge University Press.

Ainsworth, M. D. S. (1979). Infant-mother attachment. *American Psychologist*, **34**, 932–937.

Ainsworth, M. D. S. (1989). Attachments beyond infancy. *American Psychologist*, **44**, 709–716.

Ainsworth, M. D. S., Bell, S. M., & Stayton, D. J. (1971). Individual differences in strange situation behavior of one-year-olds. In H. R. Schaffer (Ed.), *The origins of human social relations*. London: Academic.

Ainsworth, M. D. S., Blehar, M. C., Waters, E., & Wall S. (1978). *Patterns of attachment: A psychological study of the strange situation*. Hillsdale, NJ: Erlbaum.

Ainsworth, M. D. S., & Bowlby, J. (1991). An ethological approach to personality development. *American Psychologist*, **46**, 333–341.

Ainsworth, M. D. S., & Eichberg, C. (1991). Effects on infant-mother attachment of mother's unresolved loss of an attachment figure, or other traumatic experience. In C. M. Parkes, J. Stevenson-Hinde & P. Marris (Eds.), *Attachment across the life cycle*. New York: Routledge.

Ainsworth, M. D. S., & Marvin, R. S. (1995). On the shaping of attachment theory and research: An interview with Mary D. S. Ainsworth (Fall, 1994). In E. Waters, B. E. Vaughn, G. Posada, & K. Kondo-Ikemura (Eds.), Caregiving, cultural, and cognitive perspectives on secure-base behavior and working models: New growing points of attachment theory and research. *Monographs of the Society for Research in Child Development*, **60**, 3–21.

Ainsworth, M. D. S., & Wittig, B. A. (1969). Attachment and the exploratory behavior of one-year-olds in a strange situation. In B.M. Foss (Ed.), *Determinants of infant behavior* (Vol. 4). London: Methuen.

American Psychiatric Association (1994). *Diagnostic and statistical manual of mental disorders* (4th ed.). Washington, DC: American Psychiatric Association.

Ammerman, R. T., Lubetsky, M. J., Hersen, M., & Van Hasselt, V. B. (1988). Maltreatment of children and adolescents with multiple handicaps: Five examples. *Journal of the Multiply Handicapped Person*, **1**, 129–139.

Angelini, L., Rumi, V., Lamperti, E., & Nardocci, N. (1988). Transient paroxysmal dystonia in infancy. *Neuropediatrics*, **19**, 171–174.

Armsden, G. C., & Greenberg, M. T. (1987). The inventory of parent and peer attachment: Individual differences and their relationship to psychological well-being in adolescence. *Journal of Youth and Adolescence*, **16**, 427–454.

Atkinson, L., Chisholm, V. C., Scott, B., Goldberg, S., Blackwell, J., Dickens, S., & Tam, F. (1995). Cognitive coping, affective stress, and maternal sensitivity: Mothers of children with Down syndrome. *Developmental Psychology*, **31**(4), 668–676.

Barkley, R. A. (1997). *ADHD and the nature of self-control*. New York: Guilford Press.

Barnett, D. (1997). The effects of early intervention on maltreating parents and their children. In M. J. Guralnick (Ed.), *The effectiveness of early intervention: Directions for second generation research*. Baltimore, MD: Brookes.

Barnett, D., Hunt, K. H., Butler, C. M., McCaskill, J., Kaplan-Estrin, M., & Pipp-Siegel, S. (in press). Indices of attachment disorganization among toddlers with neurological problems. In J. Solomon and C. George (Eds.), *Attachment disorganization*. New York: Guilford.

Barnett, D., Kidwell, S. L., & Leung, K. H. (1998). Parenting and preschooler attachment among low-income urban African American families. *Child Development*, **69**, 1657–1671.

Barnett, D., & Ratner, H. H. (1997). Introduction: The organization and integration of cognition and emotion in development. *Journal of Experimental Child Psychology*, **67**, 303–316.

Bartholomew, K., & Horowitz, L. M. (1991). Attachment styles among young adults: A test of the four-category model. *Journal of Personality and Social Psychology*, **61**, 226–244.

Bates, J. E. (1980). The concept of difficult temperament. *Merrill-Palmer Quarterly*, **26**, 299–319.

Bates, J. E., Freeland, C. A., & Lounsbury, M. L. (1979). Measurement of infant difficultness. *Child Development*, **50**, 794–803.

Bayley, N. (1969). *Bayley Scales of Infant Development*. San Antonio: Psychological Corporation.

Beck, A. T., & Beamesderfer, A. (1974). Assessment of depression: The Depression Inventory. In P. Pichot (Ed.), *Psychological measurement in psychopharmacology: Modern problems in pharmacopsychiatry* (Vol. 7). Basel, Switzerland: Kanger.

Belsky, J. (1984). The determinants of parenting: A process model. *Child Development*, **55**, 83–96.

Belsky, J., & Braungart, J. M. (1991). Are insecure-avoidant infants with extensive day-care experience less stressed by and more independent in the strange situation? *Child Development*, **62**, 567–571.

Belsky, J., Campbell, S. B., Cohn, J. F., & Moore, G. (1996). Instability of infant-parent attachment security. *Developmental Psychology*, **32**(5), 921–924.

Belsky, J., & Cassidy, J. (1994). Attachment theory and evidence. In M. Rutter & D. Hay (Eds.), *Development through life: A handbook for clinicians*. Oxford: Blackwell.

Belsky, J., Hsieh, K. H., & Crnic, K. (1996). Infant positive and negative emotionality: One dimension for two? *Developmental Psychology*, **32**, 289–298.

Belsky, J., & Isabella, R. A. (1988). Maternal, infant, and social-contextual determinants of attachment security. In J. Belsky & T. Nezworski (Eds.), *Clinical implications of attachment*. Hillsdale, NJ: Erlbaum.

Belsky, J., & Nezworski, T. (1988). Clinical implications of attachment. In J. Belsky & T. Nezworski (Eds.), *Clinical implications of attachment*. Hillsdale, NJ: Erlbaum.

Belsky, J., & Rovine, M. J. (1987). Temperament and attachment security in the Strange Situation: An empirical rapprochement. *Child Development*, **55**, 718–728.

Belsky, J., Rovine, M. J., & Taylor, D. G. (1984). The Pennsylvania Infant and Family Development Project: III. The origins of individual differences in infant-mother attachment. *Child Development*, **55**, 718–728.

Berger, J., & Cunningham, C. C. (1986). Aspects of early social smiling by infants with Down's syndrome. *Child: Care, Health and Development*, **12**, 13–24.

Berry, P., Gunn, P., & Andrews, R. (1980). Behavior of Down syndrome infants in a strange situation. *American Journal of Mental Deficiency*, **85**, 213–218.

Bischof, N. (1975). A systems approach towards the functional connections of fear and attachment. *Child Development*, **46**, 801–817.

Blehar, M. C., Lieberman, A. F., & Ainsworth, M. D. S. (1977). Early face-to-face interaction and its relation to later infant-mother attachment. *Child Development*, **48**, 182–194.

Blishen, B. R., Carroll, W. K., & Moore, C. (1987). The 1981 socioeconomic index for occupations in Canada. *Canadian Review of Sociology and Anthropology*, **24**, 465–488.

Bowlby, J. (1969/1982). *Attachment and loss, Vol.I: Attachment*. New York: Basic Books.

Bowlby, J. (1973). *Attachment and loss, Vol.II: Separation*. New York: Basic Books.

Bowlby, J. (1980). *Attachment and loss, Vol.III: Loss*. New York: Basic Books.

Bowlby, J. (1988). *A secure base: Parent-child attachment and healthy human development*. New York: Basic Books.

Braungart, J. M., & Stifter, C. A. (1991). Regulation of negative reactivity during the Strange Situation: Temperament and attachment in 12-month-old infants. *Infant Behavior and Development*, **14**, 349–364.

Bretherton, I. (1985). Attachment Theory: Retrospect and prospect. In I. Bretherton & E. Waters (Eds.), *Growing points of attachment theory and research. Monographs of the Society for Research in Child Development*, **50**, 3–35.

Bretherton, I., & Ainsworth, M. D. S. (1974). Responses of one-year-olds to a stranger in a strange situation. In M. Lewis & L. A. Rosenblum (Eds.), *The origins of fear*. New York: International Universities Press.

Bridges, F. A., & Cicchetti, D. (1982). Mothers' rating of the temperament characteristics of Down syndrome infants. *Developmental Psychology*, **18**, 238–244.

Bridges, L. J., Connell, J. P., & Belsky, J. (1988). Similarities and differences in infant-mother and infant-father interactions in the Strange Situation: A component process analysis. *Developmental Psychology*, **24**, 92–100.

Bronfman, E. (1993). *The relation between maternal behavior ratings and disorganized attachment status in eighteen month old at-risk infants*. Unpublished doctoral dissertation, Boston College, Boston, MA.

Bronfman, E., Parsons, E., & Lyons-Ruth, K. (1993). *Atypical Maternal Behavior Instrument for Assessment and Classification (AMBIENCE): Manual for coding disrupted affective communication*. Unpublished. Available from K. Lyons-Ruth, Department of Psychiatry, Cambridge Hospital, 1493 Cambridge St., Cambridge, MA 02139.

Brunnquell, D., Crichton, L., & Egeland, B. (1981). Maternal personality and attitude in disturbances of childrearing. *American Journal of Orthopsychiatry*, **51**, 680–691.

Caldwell, B., & Bradley, R. (1984). *Home Observation for Measurement of the Environment*. Little Rock: University of Arkansas.

Calkins, S. D., & Fox, N. A. (1992). The relations among infant temperament, security of attachment, and behavioral inhibition at 24 months. *Child Development*, **63**, 1456–1472.

Campbell, S. B. (1991). Longitudinal studies of active and aggressive preschoolers: Individual differences in early behavior and in outcome. In D. Cicchetti & S. L. Toth (Eds.), *Internalizing and Externalizing Expression of Dysfunction, Rochester Symposium on Developmental Psychopathology* (Vol. 2). Hillsdale, NJ: Erlbaum.

Capps, L., Sigman, M., & Mundy, P. (1994). Attachment security in children with autism. *Development and Psychopathology*, **6**, 249–261.

Carlson, E. A. (1998). A prospective, longitudinal study of attachment disorganization/disorientation. *Child Development*, **69**, 1107–1128.

Carlson, E. A., & Sroufe, L. A. (1995). Contributions of attachment theory to developmental psychopathology. In D. Cicchetti & D. Cohen (Eds.), *Developmental Psychopathology: Vol. I. Theory and methods*. New York: Wiley.

Carlson, V., Cicchetti, D., Barnett, D., & Braunwald, K. (1989a). Finding order in disorganization: Lessons from research on maltreated infants' attachments to their caregivers. In D. Cicchetti & V. Carlson (Eds.), *Child maltreatment: Theory and research on the causes and consequences of child abuse and neglect.* New York: Cambridge University Press.

Carlson, V., Cicchetti, D., Barnett, D., & Braunwald, K. (1989b). Disorganized/disoriented attachment relationships in maltreated infants. *Developmental Psychology,* **25,** 525–531.

Case, R. (1996). The role of psychological defenses in the representation and regulation of close personal relationships across the life span. In G. Noam & K. Fischer (Eds.), *Development and vulnerability in close relationships across the lifespan.* Mahwah, NJ: Erlbaum.

Cassidy, J. (1994). Emotion regulation: Influences of attachment relationships. In N. A. Fox (Ed.), The development of emotion regulation: Biological and behavioral considerations. *Monographs of the Society for Research in Child Development,* **59,** 228–249.

Cassidy, J., & Berlin, L. (1994). The Insecure/Ambivalent pattern of attachment: Theory and research. *Child Development,* **65,** 971–991.

Cassidy, J., & Kobak, R. (1988). Avoidance and its relationship to other defensive properties. In J. Belsky & T. Nezworksi (Eds.), *Clinical implications of attachment.* Hillsdale, NJ: Lawrence Erlbaum.

Cassidy, J., & Marvin, R., in collaboration with the MacArthur Working Group on Attachment. (1991). *Attachment organization in three-and four-year olds: Coding guidelines.* Unpublished manuscript, Pennsylvania State University and University of Virginia.

Cermak, S. (1985). Developmental dyspraxia. In E. Roy (Ed.), *Neuropsychological studies of apraxia and related disorders.* Amsterdam: Elsivier.

Chisholm, K. (1998). A three-year follow-up of attachment and indiscriminate friendliness in children adopted from Romanian orphanages. *Child Development,* **69,** 1092–1106.

Cicchetti, D., & Barnett, D. (1991). Attachment organization in maltreated preschoolers. *Development and Psychopathology,* **3,** 397–411.

Cicchetti, D., & Beeghly, M. (1990). An organizational approach to the study of Down syndrome: Contributions to an integrative theory of development. In D. Cicchetti & M. Beeghly (Eds.), *Children with Down syndrome: A developmental perspective.* Cambridge: Cambridge University Press.

Cicchetti, D., Beeghly, M., Carlson, V., & Toth, S. L. (1990). The emergence of self in atypical populations. In D. Cicchetti & M. Beeghley (Eds.), *The self in transition.* Chicago: University of Chicago Press.

Cicchetti, D., Cummings, E. M., Greenberg, M. T., & Marvin, R. S. (1990). An organizational perspective on attachment beyond infancy: Implications for theory, measurement and research. In M. T. Greenberg, D. Cicchetti, and E. M. Cummings (Eds.), *Attachment in the preschool years.* Chicago: University of Chicago Press.

Cicchetti, D., Ganiban, J., & Barnett, D. (1991). Contributions from the study of high-risk populations to understanding the development of emotion regulation. In J. Garber & K. A. Dodge (Eds.), *The development of emotion regulation and dysregulation.* New York: Cambridge University Press.

Cicchetti, D., & Greenberg, M. T. (Eds.). (1991). Attachment and developmental psychopathology [Special issue]. *Development and Psychopathology,* **3,** 347–527.

Cicchetti, D., & Manly, J. T. (1990). A personal perspective on conducting research with maltreating families: Problems and solutions. In G. H. Brody & I. E. Sigel (Eds.), *Methods of family research: Biographies of research projects: Vol. 2. Clinical populations.* Hillsdale, NJ: Erlbaum.

Cicchetti, D., & Rizley, R. (1981). Developmental perspectives on the etiology intergenerational transmission and sequelae of child maltreatment. In R. Rizley & D. Cicchetti (Eds.), *Developmental perspectives in child maltreatment: New directions of child development* (Vol. 11). San Francisco: Jossey-Bass.

Cicchetti, D., & Serafica, F. C. (1981). Interplay among behavioral systems: Illustrations from the study of attachment affiliation and wariness in young children with Down's syndrome. *Developmental Psychology,* **17,** 36–49.

Cicchetti, D., & Sroufe, L. A. (1976). The relationship between affective and cognitive development in Down's syndrome infants. *Child Development,* **47,** 920–929.

Cohen, J. (1988). *Statistical power analysis for the behavioral sciences.* New York: Academic Press.

Collins, P. F., & Depue, R. A. (1992). A neurobehavioral systems approach to developmental psychopathology: Implications for disorders of affect. In D. Cicchetti and S. Toth (Eds.), *The Rochester Symposium on Developmental Psychopathology, Vol. 4. Developmental perspectives on depression.* Rochester, NY: University of Rochester Press.

Connell, D. B. (1976). *Individual differences in attachment: An investigation into stability, implications, and relationships to structure of early language development.* Unpublished doctoral dissertation, Syracuse University, Syracuse, New York.

Crittenden, P. M. (1981). Abusing, neglecting, problematic, and adequate dyads: Differentiating by patterns of interaction. *Merrill-Palmer Quarterly,* **27,** 201–218.

Crittenden, P. M. (1985). Maltreated infants: Vulnerability and resilience. *Journal of Child Psychology and Psychiatry,* **26,** 85–96.

Crittenden, P. M. (1988). Relationships at risk. In J. Belsky & T. Nezworski (Eds.), *Clinical implications of attachment.* Hillsdale, NJ: Erlbaum.

Crittenden, P. M. (1990). Internal representational models of attachment relationships. *Infant Mental Health Journal,* **11,** 259–277.

Crittenden, P. M. (1990–1995). *Preschool Assessment of Attachment: Coding Manual.* Unpublished manuscript, Family Relations Institute, Miami, FL. Available from the author.

Crittenden, P. M. (1992a). Quality of attachment in the preschool years. *Development and Psychopathology,* **4,** 209–241.

Crittenden, P. M. (1992b). Children's strategies for coping with adverse home environments. *International Journal of Child Abuse and Neglect,* **16,** 329–343.

Crittenden, P. M. (1994). Peering into the black box: An exploratory treatise on the development of self in young children. In D. Cicchetti & S. Toth (Eds.), *Rochester Symposium on Developmental Psychopathology, Vol. 5. The self and its disorders.* Rochester, NY: University of Rochester Press.

Crittenden, P. M. (1995). Attachment and psychopathology. In S. Goldberg, R. Muir, & J. Kerr (Eds.), *Attachment theory: Social, developmental, and clinical perspectives.* Hillsdale, NJ: The Analytic Press.

Crittenden, P. M. (1997a). Toward an integrative theory of trauma: A dynamic-maturational approach. In D. Cicchetti and S. Toth (Eds.), *The Rochester Symposium on Developmental Psychopathology, Vol. 10. Risk, trauma, and mental processes.* Rochester, NY: University of Rochester Press.

Crittenden, P. M. (1997b). Truth, error, omission, distortion, and deception: The application of attachment theory to the assessment and treatment of psychological disorder. In S. M. C. Dollinger and L. F. DiLalla (Eds.), *Assessment and intervention across the lifespan.* Hillsdale, NJ: Erlbaum.

Crittenden, P. M. (in press-a). A dynamic-maturational approach to continuity and change in pattern of attachment. In P. M. Crittenden and A. H. Claussen (Eds.), *The organization of attachment relationships: Maturation, culture, and context,* New York: Cambridge University Press.

Crittenden, P. M. (in press-b). A dynamic-maturational exploration of the meaning of security and adaptation: Empirical, cultural, and theoretical considerations. In P. M. Crittenden and A. H. Claussen (Eds.), *The organization of attachment relationships: Maturation, culture, and context,* New York: Cambridge University Press.

Crittenden, P. M., & Ainsworth, M. D. S. (1989). Child maltreatment and attachment theory. In D. Cicchetti & V. Carlson (Eds.), *Child maltreatment: Theory and research on the causes and consequences of child abuse and neglect.* New York: Cambridge University Press.

Crittenden, P. M., & DiLalla, D. (1988). Compulsive compliance: The development of an inhibitory coping strategy in infancy. *Journal of Abnormal Child Psychology,* **16,** 585–599.

Crockenberg, S. (1981). Infant irritability, mother responsiveness, and social support influences on the security of infant-mother attachment. *Child Development,* **52,** 857–869.

Crossley, N. (1996). *Intersubjectivity: The fabric of social being.* London: Sage.

Crown, D. L., Feldstein, S., Jasnow, M. D., Beebe, B., & Jaffe, J. (1992). Down's syndrome and infant gaze. *Acta Paedopsychiatrica,* **55,** 51–55.

Cummings, J. S., Pellegrini, D. S., Notarius, C. I., & Cummings, E. M. (1989). Children's responses to angry adult behavior as a function of marital distress and history of interparent hostility. *Child Development,* **60,** 1035–1043.

Cytryn, L. (1975). Studies of behavior in children with Down's syndrome. In E. J. Anthony (Ed.), *Explorations in child psychiatry.* New York: Plenum.

Damasio, A. R. (1994). *Descartes' error: Emotion, reason, and the human brain.* New York: Avon Books.

DeKlyen, M., Speltz, M., & Greenberg, M. (1995, March). *Predictors of clinical referral and continuity of externalizing symptoms among oppositional preschool boys.* Presented at the biennial meeting of the Society for Research in Child Development, Indianapolis, IN.

DeMulder, E., & Radke-Yarrow, M. (1991). Attachment with affectively ill and well mothers: Concurrent behavioral correlates. *Development and Psychopathology,* **3,** 227–242.

De Wolff, M. S., & van IJzendoorn, M. (1997). Sensitivity and attachment: A meta-analysis on parental antecedents of infant attachment. *Child Development,* **68,** 571–591.

Donovan, W. L., & Leavitt, L. A. (1985). Physiologic assessment of mother-infant attachment. *Journal of the American Academy of Child Psychiatry,* **24,** 65–70.

Drake, M. E., Jackson, R. D., & Miller, C. A. (1987). Paroxysmal choreoathetosis after head injury. *Journal of Neurology, Neurosurgery and Psychiatry,* **49,** 837–838.

Drell, M. J., Siegel, C. H., & Gaensbauer, T. J. (1993). Post-traumatic stress disorder. In C. H. Zeanah (Ed.), *Handbook of infant mental health.* New York: Guilford Press.

Easterbrooks, M. A., Lyons-Ruth, K., Biesecker, G., & Carper, A. (1996, April). *Infancy predictors of emotional availability in middle childhood: The role of attachment and maternal depression.* Paper presented at the International Conference on Infant Studies, Providence, RI.

Egeland, B., & Erickson, M. F. (1987). Psychologically unavailable caregiving. In M. R. Brassard, R. Germain, & S. N. Hart (Eds.), *Psychological maltreatment of children and youth.* New York: Pergamon Press.

Egeland, B., & Farber, E. (1984). Infant-mother attachment: Factors related to its development and changes over time. *Child Development,* **55,** 753–771.

Egeland, B., & Sroufe, L. A. (1981a). Attachment and early maltreatment. *Child Development,* **52,** 44–52.

Egeland, B., & Sroufe, L. A. (1981b). Developmental sequelae of maltreatment in infancy. In R. Rizley & D. Cicchetti (Eds.), Developmental perspectives on child maltreatment. *New Directions for Child Development.* San Francisco: Jossey-Bass.

Eibl-Eibesfeldt, I. (1979). Human ethology: Concepts and implications for the sciences of man. *Behavioral and Brain Sciences,* **2,** 1–57.

Elder, G., Caspi, A., & Downey, G. (1986). Problem behavior and family relationships: Life course and intergenerational themes. In A. Sorenson, F. Weinert, & L. Sherrod (Eds.), *Human development: Interdisciplinary perspectives.* Hillsdale, NJ: Erlbaum.

Emde, R. N., & Brown, C. (1978). Adaptation to the birth of a Down's syndrome infant: Grieving and maternal attachment. *Journal of the American Academy of Child Psychiatry*, **17**, 299–323.

Emde, R. N., Katz, E. L., & Thorpe, J. K. (1978). Emotional expression in infancy: II. Early deviations in Down's syndrome. In M. Lewis & L. A. Rosenblum (Eds.), *The development of affect*. New York: Plenum.

Emery, R. E., & O'Leary, K. D. (1982). Children's perceptions of marital discord and behavior problems of boys and girls. *Journal of Abnormal Child Psychology*, **10**, 11–24.

Engfer, A. (1986). Antecedents of perceived behavior problems in infancy. In G. Kohnstamm (Ed.), *Temperament discussed*. Berwyn, PA: Swets North America.

Erickson, M. F., Sroufe, L. A., & Egeland, B. (1985). The relationship between quality of attachment and behavior problems in preschool in a high risk sample. In I. Bretherton & E. Waters (Eds.), *Growing points in attachment theory and research. Monographs of the Society for Research in Child Development*, **50**(1–2, Serial No. 209).

Fagot, B., & Pears, K. (1996). From infancy to seven years: Continuities and change. *Development and Psychopathology*, **8**, 325–344.

Fish, M., Stifter, C. A., & Belsky, J. (1991). Conditions of continuity and discontinuity in infant negative emotionality: Newborn to five months. *Child Development*, **62**, 1525–1537.

Fogel, A. (1993). *Developing through relationships: Origins of communication, self, and culture*. Chicago: University of Chicago Press.

Fonagy, P., Steele, M., Steele, H., Moran, G., & Higgitt, A. (1991). The capacity for understanding mental states: The reflective self in parent and child and its significance for security of attachment. *Infant Mental Health Journal*, **12**, 201–218.

Fox, N. A., Kimmerly, N. L., & Schafer, W. D. (1991). Attachment to mother/attachment to father: A meta-analysis. *Child Development*, **62**, 210–225.

Frodi, A., Grolnick, W., & Bridges, L. (1985). Maternal correlates of stability and change in infant-mother attachment. *Infant Mental Health Journal*, **6**, 60–67.

Frodi, A., & Thompson, R. (1985). Infants' affective responses in the Strange Situation: Effects of prematurity and of quality of attachment. *Child Development*, **56**, 1280–1290.

Fury, G., Carlson, E. A., & Sroufe, L. A. (1997). Children's representations of attachment relationships in family drawings. *Child Development*, **68**, 1154–1164.

Ganiban, J., Barnett, D., & Cicchetti, D. (in press). Negative reactivity and attachment: Down syndrome's contribution to the attachment-temperament debate. *Development and Psychopathology*.

Ganiban, J., Wagner, S., & Cicchetti, D. (1990). Temperament and Down syndrome. In D. Cicchetti & M. Beeghly (Eds.), *Children with Down syndrome: A developmental perspective*. Cambridge: Cambridge University Press.

George, C., & Solomon, J. (1993, March). *Internal working models of caregiving*. Paper presented at the Biennial Meeting of the Society for Research in Child Development, New Orleans, LA.

George, C., & Solomon, J. (1996). Representational models of relationships: Links between caregiving and attachment. *Infant Mental Health Journal*, **17**, 198–216.

Giovannoni, J., & Becerra, R. M. (1979). *Defining child abuse*. New York: Free Press.

Goldberg, S. (1988). Risk-factors in infant-mother attachment. *Canadian Journal of Psychology*, **42**, 173–188.

Goldberg, S. (1997). Attachment and childhood behavior problems in normal, at-risk, and clinical samples. In L. Atkinson & K. J. Zucker (Eds.), *Attachment and psychopathology*. New York: Guilford.

Goldberg, S., Perotta, M., Minde, K., & Corter, C. (1986). Maternal behavior and attachment in low birthweight twins and singletons. *Child Development*, **57**, 34–46.

Goldberg, S., Washington, J., Myhal, N., Janus, M., Simmons, R. J., MacCluskey, I., & Fowler, R. S. (1998). *Stability and change in attachment from infancy to preschool.* Manuscript under review, Hospital for Sick Children, Toronto, Ontario.

Goldsmith, H. H., & Alansky, J. (1987). Maternal and infant temperamental predictors of attachment: A meta-analytic review. *Journal of Consulting and Clinical Psychology,* **55,** 805–816.

Gordon, N. (1993). Startle disease in hyperekplexia. *Developmental Medicine and Child Neurology,* **35,** 1015.

Gottlieb, G. (1991). Experiential canalization of behavioral development: Theory. *Developmental Psychology,* **27,** 4–13.

Gottman, J., Markman, H., & Notarius, C. (1977). The topography of marital conflict: A sequential analysis of verbal and nonverbal behavior. *Journal of Marriage and the Family,* **39,** 461–477.

Greenberg, M. T., Speltz, M. L., DeKlyen, M., & Endriga, M. C. (1991). Attachment security in preschoolers with and without externalizing problems: A replication. *Development and Psychopathology,* **3,** 413–430.

Greenough, W. T., Black, J. E., & Wallace, C. S. (1987). Experience and brain development. *Child Development,* **58,** 539–560.

Grossmann, K., & Grossmann, K. E. (1991a). Newborn behavior, the quality of early parenting and later toddler-parent relationships in a group of German infants. In J. K. Nugent, B. M. Lester, & T. B. Brazelton (Eds.), *The cultural context of infancy, Vol. II.* Norwood, NJ: Ablex.

Grossmann, K. E., & Grossmann, K. (1991b). Attachment quality as an organizer of emotional and behavioral responses in a longitudinal perspective. In C. Parkes, J. Stevenson-Hinde, & P. Marris (Eds.), *Attachment across the life cycle.* London: Tavistock/Routledge.

Grossmann, K., Grossmann, K. E., Spangler, G., Suess, G., & Unzner, L. (1985). Maternal sensitivity and newborns' orientation responses as related to quality of attachment in northern Germany. In I. Bretherton & E. Waters (Eds.), *Growing points in attachment theory and research. Monographs of the Society for Research in Child Development,* **50**(1–2, Serial No. 209).

Gunn, P., Berry, P., & Andrews, R. J. (1982). Looking behavior of Down syndrome infants. *American Journal of Mental Deficiency,* **87,** 344–347.

Gunner, M. R., Mangelsdorf, S., Larson, M., & Hertsgaard, L. (1989). Attachment, temperament, and adrenocortical activity in infancy: A study of psychoendocrine regulation. *Developmental Psychology,* **25,** 355–363.

Hann, D. M., Castino, R. J., Jarosinski, J., & Britton, H. (1991, April). *Relating mother- toddler negotiation patterns to infant attachment and maternal depression with an adolescent mother sample.* Paper presented at the biennial meeting of the Society for Research in Child Development, Seattle, WA.

Harding, C. G. (1984). Acting with intention: A framework for examining the development of the intention to communicate. In L. Feagans, D. Garvey, & R. M. Golinkoff (Eds.), *The origins and growth of communication.* Norwood, NJ: Ablex.

Hazan, C., & Shaver, P. (1987). Romantic love conceptualized as an attachment process. *Journal of Personality and Social Psychology,* **52,** 511–524.

Hershorn, M., & Rosenbaum, A. (1983). *A closer look at the unintended victims.* Unpublished manuscript, Syracuse University.

Hertsgaard, L., Gunnar, M., Erickson, M. F., & Nachmias, M. (1995). Adrenocortical responses to the Strange Situation in infants with Disorganized/Disoriented attachment relationships. *Child Development,* **66,** 1100–1106.

Hesse, E. (1996). Discourse, memory, and the Adult Attachment Interview: A note with emphasis on the emerging Cannot Classify category. *Infant Mental Health Journal*, **17**, 4–11.

Hommerding, K. D., Shaw, D. S., & Vondra, J. I. (1993). *Stability and change in infant-mother attachment.* Unpublished manuscript, University of Pittsburgh, Department of Psychology.

Howes, C., & Hamilton, C. E. (1992). Children's relationships with caregivers: Mothers and child care teachers. *Child Development*, **63**, 859–866.

Isabella, R. A. (1993). Origins of attachment: Maternal interactive behavior across the first year. *Child Development*, **64**, 605–621.

Isabella, R. A., Belsky, J., & von Eye, A. (1989). Origins of infant-mother attachment: An examination of interactional synchrony during the infant's first year. *Developmental Psychology*, **25**, 12–21.

Izard, C. E., Porges, S. W., Simons, R. F., Haynes, O. M., Hyde, C., Parisi, M., & Cohen, B. (1991). Infant cardiac activity: Developmental changes and relations with attachment. *Developmental Psychology*, **27**, 432–439.

Jackson, D. H. (1989). *Personality Research Form Manual.* New York: Research Psychologists Press.

Jackson, D. H., & Morf, M. (1973). An empirical evaluation of factor reliability. *Multivariate Behavioral Research*, **8**, 439–459.

Jacobvitz, D., Hazen, N., & Riggs, S. (1997, April). *Disorganized mental processes in mothers, frightening/frightened caregiving, and disoriented/disorganized behavior in infancy.* Paper presented at the Biennial Meeting of the Society for Research in Child Development, Washington, DC.

Jones, E. E. (Ed.) (1996). Special section: Attachment and psychopathology, Part 1. *Journal of Consulting and Clinical Psychology*, **64**, 5–73.

Jones, E. E., Main, M., & del Carmen, R. (1996). Special section: Attachment and psychopathology, Part II. *Journal of Consulting and Clinical Psychology*, **64**, 237–294.

Jones, O. J. M. (1979). A comparative study of mother child communication with Down's syndrome and normal infants. In D. Schaffer & J. Dunn (Eds.), *The first year of life: Psychological and medical implications of early experience.* New York: Wiley.

Koester, L. S. (1995). Face-to-face interactions between hearing mothers and their deaf or hearing infants. *Infant Behavior and Development*, **18**, 145–153.

Kolb, L. C. (1987). A neuropsychological hypothesis explaining post-traumatic stress disorders. *American Journal of Psychiatry*, **144**, 989–995.

Kurland, R., & Shoulson, I. (1983). Familial paroxysmal dystonic choreoathetosis and response to alternate day oxazepam therapy. *Annals of Neurology*, **13**, 456–457.

Lamb, M. E., Thompson, R. A., Gardner, W., & Charnov, E. L. (1985). *Infant-mother attachment: The origins and developmental significance of individual differences in Strange Situation behavior.* Hillsdale, NJ: Erlbaum.

Lance, J. W. (1977). Familial paroxysmal dystonic choreoathetosis and its differentiation from related syndromes. *Annals of Neurology*, **2**, 285–293.

Langois, J. H., Ritter, J. M., Casey, R. J., & Sawin, D. B. (1995). Infant attractiveness predicts maternal behaviors and attitudes. *Developmental Psychology*, **31**, 464–472.

Lees, A. J. (1985). Tics and related disorders. *Clinical Neurology and Neurosurgery Monographs*, 7, 1–6.

Lewis, M., & Feiring, C. (1989). Infant, mother, and mother-infant interaction behavior and subsequent attachment. *Child Development*, **60**, 831–837.

Locke, H. J., & Wallace, K. M. (1959). Short marital adjustment and prediction tests: Their reliability and validity. *Marriage and Family Living*, **21**, 251–255.

Londerville, S., & Main, M. (1981). Security of attachment, compliance, and maternal training methods in the second year of life. *Developmental Psychology*, **17**, 289–299.

Lynch, M. M., & Cicchetti, D. (1991). Patterns of relatedness in maltreated and nonmaltreated children: Connections among multiple representational models. *Development and Psychopathology*, **3**, 207–226.

Lyons-Ruth, K. (1992). Maternal depressive symptoms, disorganized infant-mother attachment relationships and hostile-aggressive behavior in the preschool classroom: A prospective longitudinal view from infancy to age five. In D. Cicchetti & S. Toth (Eds.), *The
Rochester Symposium on Developmental Psychopathology, Vol. 4. A developmental approach to
affective disorders*. Rochester, NY: University of Rochester Press.

Lyons-Ruth, K. (1996). Attachment relationships among children with aggressive behavior
problems: The role of disorganized early attachment patterns. *Journal of Consulting and
Clinical Psychology*, **64**, 64–73.

Lyons-Ruth, K., Alpern, L., & Repacholi, B. (1993). Disorganized infant attachment classification and maternal psychosocial problems as predictors of hostile-aggressive behavior in the preschool classroom. *Child Development*, **64**, 572–585.

Lyons-Ruth, K., & Block, D. (1996). The disturbed caregiving system: Relations among
childhood trauma, maternal caregiving, and infant affect and attachment. *Infant
Mental Health Journal*, **17**, 257–275.

Lyons-Ruth, K., Bronfman, E., & Atwood, G. (in press). A relational diathesis model
of hostile-helpless states of mind: Expressions in mother-infant interaction. In J. Solomon & C. George (Eds.), *Attachment disorganization*. New York: Guilford.

Lyons-Ruth, K., Connell, D., Grunebaum, H., & Botein, S. (1990). Infants at social risk:
Maternal depression and family support services as mediators of infant development
and security of attachment. *Child Development*, **61**, 85–98.

Lyons-Ruth, K., Connell, D., & Zoll, D. (1989). Patterns of maternal behavior among infants
at risk for abuse: Relations with infant attachment behavior and infant development at
12 months of age. In D. Cicchetti & V. Carlson (Eds.), *Child maltreatment: Theory and
research on the causes and consequences of child abuse and neglect*. New York: Cambridge
University Press.

Lyons-Ruth, K., Connell, D., Zoll, D., & Stahl, J. (1987). Infants at social risk: Relationships
among infant maltreatment maternal behavior and infant attachment behavior. *Developmental Psychology*, **23**, 223–232.

Lyons-Ruth, K., Easterbrooks, A., & Cibelli, C. (1997). Infant attachment strategies, infant
mental lag, and maternal depressive symptoms: Predictors of internalizing and
externalizing problems at age 7. *Developmental Psychology*, **33**, 681–692.

Lyons-Ruth, K., & Jacobvitz, D. (in press). Attachment disorganization: Unresolved loss,
relational violence, and lapses in behavioral and attentional strategies. In J. Cassidy &
P. Shaver (Eds.), *Handbook of attachment theory and research*. New York: Guilford Press.

Lyons-Ruth, K., Repacholi, B., McLeod, S., & Silva, E. (1991). Disorganized attachment
behavior in infancy: Short-term stability maternal and infant correlates and risk-
related subtypes. *Development and Psychopathology*, **4**, 377–396.

Lyons-Ruth, K., Zoll, D., Connell, D., & Grunebaum, H. (1986). The depressed mother and
her one-year-old infant: Environment, interaction, attachment, and infant development. In E. Tronick & T. Field (Eds.), *Maternal depression and infant disturbance*. San
Francisco: Jossey-Bass.

Lyons-Ruth, K., Zoll, D., Connell, D., & Grunebaum, H. (1989). Family deviance and family
disruption in childhood: Associations with maternal behavior and infant maltreatment during the first two years of life. *Development and Psychopathology*, **1**, 219–236.

MacCullum, R. C., & Mar, C. M. (1995). Distinguishing between moderator and quadratic
effects in multiple regression. *Psychological Bulletin*, **118**, 405–421.

Main, M. (1981). Avoidance in the service of attachment: A working paper. In K. Immelmann, G. Barlow, L. Petrinovich, & M. Main (Eds.), *Behavioral development: The Bielefeld Interdisciplinary Project*. New York: Cambridge University Press.

Main, M., & Cassidy, J. (1988). Categories of response to reunion with the parent at age six: Predictability from infant attachment classifications and stable across a one-month period. *Developmental Psychology*, **24,** 415–426.

Main, M., & Goldwyn, R. (in preparation). Adult attachment classification system. In M. Main (Ed.), *A topology of human attachment organization: Assessed in discourse, drawing, and interviews*. Cambridge: Cambridge University Press.

Main, M., & Hesse, E. (1990). Parents' unresolved traumatic experiences are related to infant disorganized attachment status: Is frightened and/or frightening parental behavior the linking mechanism? In M. Greenberg, D. Cicchetti, & E. M. Cummings (Eds.), *Attachment in the preschool years: Theory, research, and intervention*. Chicago: University of Chicago Press.

Main, M., & Hesse, E. (1992). *Frightening, frightened, dissociated, or disorganized behavior on the part of the parent: A coding system for parent-infant interactions* (4th ed.). Unpublished manuscript, University of California, Berkeley.

Main, M., Kaplan, N., & Cassidy, J. (1985). Security in infancy childhood and adulthood: A move to the level of representation. In I. Bretherton & E. Waters (Eds.), *Growing points of attachment theory and research. Monographs of the Society for Research in Child Development*, **50**(1–2, Serial No. 209), 66–104.

Main, M., & Solomon, J. (1986). Discovery of a disorganized disoriented attachment pattern. In T. B. Brazelton & M. W. Yogman (Eds.), *Affective development in infancy*. Norwood, NJ: Ablex.

Main, M., & Solomon, J. (1990). Procedures for identifying infants as disorganized/ disoriented during the Ainsworth Strange Situation. In M. Greenberg, D. Cicchetti, & E. M. Cummings (Eds.), *Attachment in the preschool years: Theory, research, and intervention*. Chicago: University of Chicago Press.

Main, M., Tomasini, L., & Tolan, W. (1979). Differences among mothers of infants judged to differ in security of attachment. *Developmental Psychology*, **15,** 472–473.

Main, M., & Weston, D. (1981). The quality of the toddler's relationship to mother and father. *Child Development*, **52,** 932–940.

Mangelsdorf, S. C., Gunnar, M., Kestenbaum, R., Lang, S., & Andreas, D. (1990). Infant proneness-to-distress temperament, maternal personality, and mother-infant attachment: Associations and goodness of fit. *Child Development*, **61,** 820–831.

Mangelsdorf, S. C., Plunkett, J. W., Dedrick, C. F., Berlin, M., Meisels, S. J., McHale, J. L., & Dichtellmiller, M. (1996). Attachment security in very low birth weight infants. *Developmental Psychology*, **32**(5), 914–920.

Martin, J. (1981). A longitudinal study of the consequences of early mother-infant interaction: A microanalytic approach. Monographs of the Society for Research in Child Development, **46**(3, Serial No. 190).

Marvin, R. S. (1977). An ethological-cognitive model for the attenuation of mother-child attachment behavior. In T. M. Alloway, L. Kramer, & P. Pliner (Eds.), *Advances in the study of communication and affect (Vol. 3): The development of social attachments*. New York: Plenum.

Maslin-Cole, C. A., & Spieker, S. J. (1990). Attachment as a basis for independent motivation: A view from risk and non-risk samples. In M. T. Greenberg, D. Cicchetti, & E. M. Cummings (Eds.), *Attachment in the preschool years: Theory, research, and intervention*. Chicago: University of Chicago Press.

Maslow, A. H. (1970). *Motivation and personality* (2nd ed.). New York: Harper & Row.

Matheny, A. (1986). Stability and change of infant temperament: Contributions from the infant, mother, and family environment. In G. Kohnstamm (Ed.), *Temperament discussed*. Berwyn, PA: Swets North America.

McClelland, D. C. (1987). *Human motivation*. New York: Cambridge University Press.

McClelland, G. G., & Judd, C. M. (1993). Statistical difficulties of detecting interactions and moderator effects. *Psychological Bulletin*, **114**, 376–390.

Meadow-Orlans, K. P., & Steinberg, A. G. (1993). Effects of infant hearing loss and maternal support on mother-infant interactions at 18 months. *Journal of Applied Developmental Psychology*, **14**, 407–426.

Menkes, J. H. (1995). *Textbook of child neurology*. Baltimore: Williams and Wilkins.

Miller, N. (1986). Developmental dyspraxia. In N. Miller (Ed.), *Dyspraxia*. Rockville, MD: Aspen Publishers.

Mizukami, K., Kobayashi, N., Ishii, T., & Iwata, H. (1990). First selective attachment begins in early infancy: A study using telethermography. *Infant Behavior and Development*, **13**(3) 257–272.

Moran, G., Pederson, D., Pettit, P., & Krupka, A. (1992). Maternal sensitivity and infant mother attachment in a developmentally delayed sample. *Infant Behavior and Development*, **15**, 427–442.

Moss, E., Parent, S., Gosselin, C., Rousseau, D., & St. Laurent, D. (1996). Attachment and teacher-reported behavior problems during the preschool and early school-age period. *Development and Psychopathology*, **8**, 511–526.

Moss, E., Rousseau, D., Parent, S., St. Laurent, D., & Saintong, J. (1998). Correlates of attachment at school age: Maternal reported behavior problems during the preschool and early school-age period. *Development and Psychopathology*, **8**, 511–526.

National Center for Health Statistics. (1988). *1988 National Maternal and Infant Health Survey* (OCLC No. 17941791). Hyattsville, MD: Author.

NICHD Early Child Care Research Network (1997). The effects of infant child care on infant-mother attachment security: Results of the NICHD Study of Early Child Care. *Child Development*, **68**, 860–879.

O'Connor, M. J., Sigman, M., & Brill, N. (1987). Disorganization of attachment in relation to maternal alcohol consumption. *Journal of Consulting and Clinical Psychology*, **55**, 831–836.

O'Connor, M. J., Sigman, M., & Kasari, C. (1992). Attachment behavior of infants exposed prenatally to alcohol: Mediating effects of infant affect and mother-infant interaction. *Development and Psychopathology*, **4**, 243–256.

Oppenheim, D., Sagi, A., & Lamb, M. (1988). Infant-adult attachments on the kibbutz and their relation to socioemotional development 4 years later. *Developmental Psychology*, **24**, 427–433.

Owen, M. T., Easterbrooks, M. A., Chase-Lansdale, L., & Goldberg, W. A. (1984). The relation between maternal employment status and the stability of attachments to mother and to father. *Child Development*, **55**, 1894–1901.

Paneth, N., & Kiely, J. (1984). The frequency of cerebral palsy: A review of population based studies in industrialized nations since 1950. In F. Stanley & E. Alberman (Eds.), *The epidemiology of the cerebral palsies*. Oxford: Blackwell Ltd.

Parsons, E. (1991). *Maternal behavior and disorganized attachment: relational sequelae of traumatic experience*. Unpublished doctoral dissertation, Massachusetts School of Professional Psychology, Dedham, MA.

Patterson, G. R. (1982). *A social learning approach to family intervention. III. Coercive family process*. Eugene, OR: Castalia.

Pederson, D. R., Moran, G., Sitko, C., Campbell, K., Ghesquire, K., & Acton, H. (1990). Maternal sensitivity and the security of infant-mother attachment: A Q-sort study. *Child Development*, **61**, 1974–1983.

Pipp, S., & Harmon, R. J. (1987). Attachment as regulation: A commentary. *Child Development*, **58**, 648–652.

Pirozzolo, F. J., & Papanicolaou, A. C. (1986). Plasticity and recovery of function in the central nervous system. In J. E. Obrzut and G. W. Hynd (Eds.), *Child neuropsychology* (Vol. 1): *Theory and research*. New York: Academic Press.

Preisler, G. N. (1990). Early patterns of interaction between blind infants and their sighted mothers. *Child Care, Health, and Development*, **17**, 65–90.

Radke-Yarrow, M., Cummings, E. M., Kuczynski, L., & Chapman, M. (1985). Patterns of attachment in two-and three-year-olds in normal families and families with parental depression. *Child Development*, **56**, 884–893.

Radke-Yarrow, M., McCann, K., DeMulder, E., Belmont, B., Martinez, P., & Richardson, D. T. (1995). Attachment in the context of high-risk conditions. *Development and Psychopathology*, **7**, 247–265.

Rauh, H., Ziegenhain, U., Müller, B., & Wijnroks, L. (in press). Stability and change in mother-infant attachment in the second year of life: Relations to parenting quality and varying degrees of daycare experience. In P. Crittenden (Ed.), *The organization of attachment relationships: Maturation, context, and culture*. London: Cambridge University Press.

Richters, J. E., Waters, E., & Vaughn, B. E. (1988). Empirical classification of infant-mother relationships from interactive behavior and crying during reunion. *Child Development*, **59**, 512–522.

Robinshaw, H. M., & Evans, R. (1995). Caregivers' sensitivity to the communicative and linguistic needs of their deaf infants. *Early Child Development and Care*, **109**, 23–41.

Rodning, C., Beckwith, L., & Howard, J. (1989). Characteristics of attachment organization and play organization in prenatally drug-exposed toddlers. *Development and Psychopathology*, **1**, 277–289.

Rodning, C., Beckwith, L., & Howard, J. (1991). Quality of attachment and home environments in children prenatally exposed to PCP and cocaine. *Development and Psychopathology*, **3**, 351–366.

Rogers, S. J., Ozonoff, S., & Maslin-Cole, C. (1991). A comparative study of attachment behavior in young children with autism or other psychiatric disorders. *Journal of the American Academy of Child and Adolescent Psychiatry*, **30**, 483–488.

Rosenbaum, A., & O'Leary, K. D. (1981). Marital violence: Characteristics of abusive couples. *Journal of Consulting and Clinical Psychology*, **49**, 63–71.

Rothbart, M. K., & Hanson, M. J. (1983). A caregiver report comparison of temperamental characteristics of Down syndrome and normal infants. *Developmental Psychology*, **19**, 766–769.

Sameroff, A., & Chandler, M. (1975). Reproductive risk and the continuum of caretaking casualty. In F. Horowitz (Ed.), *Review of child development research* (Vol. 4). Chicago: University of Chicago Press.

Sander, J. E., Layzer, R. B., & Goldsobel, A. B. (1980). Congenital stiff man syndrome. *Annals of Neurology*, **8**, 544–547.

Sarason, I., Johnson, J., & Siegel, J. (1978). Assessing the impact of life changes: Development of the Life Experiences Survey. *Journal of Consulting and Clinical Psychology*, **45**, 932–946.

Sattler, J. M. (1988). *Assessment of children's intelligence and special abilities* (3rd ed.). San Diego: Jerome M. Sattler.

Schneider-Rosen, K., Braunwald, K., Carlson, V. & Cicchetti, D. (1985). Current perspectives in attachment theory: Illustrations from the study of maltreated infants. In

I. Bretherton & E. Waters (Eds.), Growing points in attachment theory and research. *Monographs of the Society for Research in Child Development*, **50,** 194–210.

Schneider-Rosen, K., & Rothbaum, F. (1993). Quality of parental caregiving and security of attachment. *Developmental Psychology*, **29,** 358–367.

Schore, A. N. (1996). The experience-dependent maturation of a regulatory system in the orbital prefrontal cortex and the origin of developmental psychopathology. *Development and Psychopathology*, **8**(1), 59–88.

Schuengel, C., Bakermans-Kranenburg, M. J., & van IJzendoorn, M. H. (1999). Attachment and loss: Frightening maternal behavior linking unresolved loss and disorganized infant attachment. *Journal of Consulting and Clinical Psychology*, **67,** 54–63.

Seifer, R., Schiller, M., Sameroff, A. J., Resnick, S., & Riordan, K. (1996). Attachment, maternal sensitivity, and infant temperament during the first year of life. *Developmental Psychology*, **32,** 12–25.

Serafica, F. C., & Cicchetti, D. (1976). Down's syndrome children in a strange situation: Attachment and exploration behaviors. *Merrill Palmer Quarterly*, **22,** 137–150.

Shaw, D. S., Keenan, K., Owens, E., Winslow, E., Hood, N., & Garcia, M. (1995, April). *Developmental precursors of externalizing behavior among two samples of low-income families: Ages 1 to 5.* Paper presented at the Biennial Meeting of the Society for Research in Child Development, Indianapolis, IN.

Shaw, D. S., Owens, E. B., Vondra, J. I., Keenan, K., & Winslow, E. B. (1996). Early risk factors and pathways in the development of early, disruptive behavior problems. *Development and Psychopathology*, **8,** 679–699.

Shiller, V. M., Izard, C. E., & Hembree, E. A. (1986). Patterns of emotion expression during separation in the Strange-Situation procedure. *Developmental Psychology*, **22,** 378–382.

Smith, P. B., & Pederson, D. R. (1988). Maternal sensitivity and patterns of infant-mother attachment. *Child Development*, **59,** 1097–1101.

Solomon, J., George, C., & DeJong, A. (1995). Children classified as controlling at age six: Evidence of disorganized representational strategies and aggression at home and at school. *Development and Psychopathology*, **7,** 447–463.

Solomon, J., George, C. & Ivins, B. (1987, April). *Mother-child interaction in the home and security of attachment at age 6.* Paper presented at the Biennial Meeting of the Society for Research in Child Development, Baltimore, MD.

Sorce, J. F., & Emde, R. N. (1982). The meaning of infant emotional expressions: Regularities in caregiving responses in normal and Down's syndrome infants. *Journal of Child Psychology and Psychiatry*, **23,** 145–158.

Sorce, J. F., Emde, R. N., & Frank, M. (1982). Maternal referencing in normal and Down's syndrome infants: A longitudinal analysis. In R. N. Emde & R. J. Jarmon (Eds.), *The development of attachment and affiliative systems.* New York: Plenum.

Spangler, G., & Grossmann, K. E. (1993). Biobehavioral organization in securely and insecurely attached infants. *Child Development*, **64,** 1439–1450.

Sparrow, S. S., Balla, D. A., & Cicchetti, D. V. (1984). *Vineland Adaptive Behavior Scales interview edition survey form manual.* Circle Pines, MN: American Guidance Service.

Speltz, M. L., Greenberg, M. T., & DeKlyen, M. (1990). Attachment in preschoolers with disruptive behavior: A comparison of clinic referred and non-problem children. *Development and Psychopathology*, **2,** 31–46.

Spieker, S. J., & Booth, C. (1988). Maternal antecedents of attachment quality. In J. Belsky & T. Nezworski (Eds.), *Clinical implications of attachment.* Hillsdale, NJ: Erlbaum.

Spielberger, C. D. (1991). *State-Trait Anger Expression Inventory.* Odessa, FL: Psychological Assessment Resources, Inc.

Sroufe, L. A. (1979). The coherence of individual development: Early care, attachment, and subsequent developmental issues. *American Psychologist*, **34,** 834–841.

Sroufe, L. A. (1983). Infant-caregiver attachment and patterns of adaptation in preschool: The roots of maladaptation and competence. In M. Perlmutter (Ed.), *Minnesota Symposium in Child Psychology, No. 16*. Minneapolis: University of Minnesota Press.

Sroufe, L. A. (1985). Attachment classification from the perspective of infant-caregiver relationships and infant temperament. *Child Development, 56*, 1–14.

Sroufe, L. A. (1990). An organizational perspective on the self. In D. Cicchetti & M. Beeghly (Eds.), *The self in transition: Infancy to childhood*. Chicago: University of Chicago Press.

Sroufe, L. A., Carlson, E., & Shulman, S. (1993). The development of individuals in relationships: From infancy through adolescence. In D. C. Funder, R. Parke, C. Tomlinson-Keesey, & K. Widaman (Eds.), *Studying lives through time: Approaches to personality and development*. Washington, DC: American Psychological Association.

Sroufe, L. A., Egeland, B., & Kreutzer, T. (1990). The fate of early experience following developmental change: Longitudinal approaches to individual adaptation in childhood. *Child Development, 61*, 1363–1373.

Sroufe, L. A., Jacobvitz, D., Mangelsdorf, S., DeAngelo, E., & Ward, M. J. (1985). Generational boundary dissolution between mothers and their preschool children: A relational systems approach. *Child Development, 56*, 317–325.

Sroufe, L. A., & Waters, E. (1977). Attachment as an organizational construct. *Child Development, 48*, 1184–1199.

Stanley, J. C., & Wang, M. D. (1969). Restrictions on the possible values of r_{12} given r_{13} and r_{23}. *Educational and Psychological Measurement, 29*, 579–591.

Stevenson-Hinde, J., & Shouldice, A. (1990). Fear and attachment in 2.5 year olds. *British Journal of Developmental Psychology, 8*, 319–333.

Stevenson-Hinde, J., & Shouldice, A. (1995). Maternal interactions and self-reports related to attachment classification at 4.5 years. *Child Development, 66*, 583–596.

Stoel-Gammon, C. (1990, September). Effects on language development. *American Speech Language Hearing Association*, 42–44.

Stone, N. W., & Chesney, B. H. (1978). Attachment behaviors in handicapped infants. *Mental Retardation, 16*, 8–12.

Stumpf, H., Wieck, T., & Jackson, D. H. (1976). Personality Research Form (PRF). *Revidierte Uebersetzung*. Psychologisches Institut der Universetaet Bonn.

Sutcliffe, J. (1969). Sandifer's Syndrome. *Progress in Pediatric Neurology, 2*, 190–197.

Teti, D. M., Gelfand, D. M., Messinger, D. S., & Isabella, R. (1995). Maternal depression and the quality of early attachment: An examination of infants, preschoolers, and their mothers. *Developmental Psychology, 31*, 364–376.

Teti, D. M., Sakin, J. W., Kucera, E., Corns, K. M., & Eiden, R. D. (1996). And baby makes four: Predictors of attachment security among preschool-age firstborn during the transition to siblinghood. *Child Development, 67*, 579–596.

Thompson, R. A. (1997). Sensitivity and security: New questions to ponder. *Child Development, 68*, 595–597.

Thompson, R. A., Cicchetti, D., Lamb, M. E., & Malkin, C. (1985). Emotional responses of Down syndrome and normal infants in the Strange Situation: The organization of affective behavior in infants. *Developmental Psychology, 21*, 828–841.

Thompson, R. A., & Lamb, M. E. (1984). Assessing qualitative dimensions of emotional responsiveness in infants: Separation reactions in the Strange Situation. *Infant Behavior and Development, 7*, 423–445.

Thompson, R. A., Lamb, M. E., & Estes, D. (1982). Stability of infant-mother attachment and its relationship to changing life circumstances in an unselected middle-class sample. *Child Development, 53*, 144–148.

Tomkins, S. S. (1991). *Affect, imagery, consciousness, Vol. III: The negative affects: Anger and fear*. New York: Springer.

Tooby, J., & Cosmides, L. (1990). On the universality of human nature and the uniqueness of the individual: The role of genetics and adaptation. *Journal of Personality*, **58**, 17–67.

Tracy, J. A., Ghose, S. S., Strecher, T., McFall, R. M., & Steinmetz, J. E. (1999). Classical conditioning in a non-clinical obsessive-compulsive population. *Psychological Science*, **10**, 9–13.

Tracy, R., & Ainsworth, M. (1981). Maternal affectionate behavior and infant-mother attachment patterns. *Child Development*, **52**, 1341–1343.

Valenzuela, M. (1990). Attachment in chronically underweight children. *Child Development*, **61**, 1984–1996.

van den Boom, D. C. (1989). Neonatal irritability and the development of attachment. In G. Kohnstamm, J. Bates, & M. K. Rothbart (Eds.), *Temperament in childhood*. New York: Wiley.

van den Boom, D. C. (1994). The influence of temperament and mothering on attachment and exploration: An experimental manipulation of sensitive responsiveness among lower-class mothers with irritable infants. *Child Development*, **65**, 1457–1477.

van den Boom, D. C., & Hoeksma, J. B. (1994). The effect of infant irritability on mother-child interaction: A growth curve analysis. *Developmental Psychology*, **30**, 581–590.

van der Kolk, B. A. (1987). The separation cry and the trauma response: Developmental issues in the psychobiology of attachment and separation. In B. A. van der Kolk (Ed.), *Psychological trauma*. Washington, DC: American Psychiatric Press.

van der Kolk, B. A. (1988). The trauma spectrum: The interaction of biological and social events in the genesis of the trauma response. *Journal of Traumatic Stress*, **1**, 273–290.

van IJzendoorn, M. H. (1995). Adult attachment representations, parental responsiveness, and infant attachment: A meta analysis on the predictive validity of the Adult Attachment Interview. *Psychological Bulletin*, **117**, 387–403.

van IJzendoorn, M. H., Goldberg, S., Kroonenberg, P. M., & Frenkel, O. J. (1992). The relative effects of maternal and child problems on the quality of attachment: A meta-analysis of attachment in clinical samples. *Child Development*, **63**, 840–858.

van IJzendoorn, M. H., Juffer, F., & Duyvesteyn, M. G. C. (1995). Breaking the intergenerational cycle of insecure attachment: A review of the effects of attachment-based interventions on maternal sensitivity and infant security. *Journal of Child and Adolescent Psychology and Psychiatry*, **36**, 225–248.

van IJzendoorn, M. H., & Kroonenberg, P. M. (1988). Cross-cultural patterns of attachment: A meta-analysis of the Strange Situation. *Child Development*, **59**, 147–156.

van IJzendoorn, M. H., Schuengel, C., & Bakermans-Kranenburg, M. H. (1999). Disorganized attachment in early childhood. Meta-analysis of precursors, concomitants and sequelae. *Development and Psychopathology*, **11**, 225–249.

van IJzendoorn, M. H., Vereijken, M. J. L., & Riksen-Walraven, M. J. M. A. (in press). Is the Attachment Q-Sort a valid measure of attachment security in young children? In B. E. Vaughn & E. Waters (Eds.), *Patterns of secure base behavior: Q-sort perspectives on attachment and caregiving*. Hillsdale, NJ: Erlbaum.

Vaughn, B. E., Goldberg, S., Atkinson, L., Marcovitch, S., MacGregor, D., & Seifer, R. (1994). Quality of toddler-mother attachment in children with Down syndrome: Limits to interpretation of Strange Situation behavior. *Child Development*, **65**, 95–108.

Vaughn, B. E., Lefever, G., Seifer, R., & Barglow, P. (1989). Attachment behavior, attachment security, and temperament during infancy. *Child Development*, **60**, 728–737.

Vaughn, B. E., & Waters, E. (1990). Attachment behavior at home and in the laboratory: Q-set observations and Strange Situation classifications of one-year-olds. *Child Development*, **61**, 1965–1973.

Vaughn, B. E., Waters, E., Egeland, B., & Sroufe, L. A. (1979). Individual differences in infant-mother attachment at twelve and eighteen months: Stability and change in families under stress. *Child Development*, **50**, 971–975.

Vondra, J. I., & Belsky, J. (1993). Developmental origins of parenting: Personality and relationship factors. In T. Luster & L. Okagaki (Eds.), *Parenting: An ecological perspective.* Hillsdale, NJ: Lawrence Erlbaum.

Vondra, J. I., Shaw, D. S., & Kevenides, M. C. (1995). Predicting infant attachment classifications from multiple contemporaneous measures of maternal care. *Infant Behavior and Development*, **18**, 415–425.

Vondra, J. I., Shaw, D. S., Swearingen, L., Cohen, M., & Owens, E. B. (In press). Attachment stability and emotional and behavioral regulation from infancy to preschool age. *Development and Psychopathology.*

Wartner, U. G., Grossmann, K., Fremmer-Bombik, E., & Suess, G. (1994). Attachment patterns at age six in South Germany: Predictability from infancy and implications for preschool behavior. *Child Development*, **65**, 1014–1027.

Waters, E. (1978). The reliability and stability of individual differences in infant-mother attachment. *Child Development*, **49**, 483–494.

Waters, E., & Deane, K. E. (1985). Defining and assessing individual differences in attachment relationships: Q-methodology and the organization of behavior in infancy and early childhood. In I. Bretherton & E. Waters (Eds.), *Growing points of attachment theory and research. Monographs of the Society for Research in Child Development*, **50**(1–2, Serial No. 209), 41–65.

Waters, E., Kondo-Ikemura, K., Posada, G., & Richters, J. E. (1995). Learning to love: Mechanisms and milestones. In M. Gunner & L. A. Sroufe (Eds.), *Self processes and development. The Minnesota Symposia on Child Development.* Hillsdale, NJ: Lawrence Erlbaum.

Waters, E., & Sroufe, L. A. (1983). A road careened into the woods: Comments on Dr. Morrison's commentary. *Developmental Review*, **3**, 108–114.

Waters, E., Vaughn, B., Posada, G., & Kondo-Ikemura, (1995). Constructs, cultures, and caregiving: New growing points of attachment theory and research. *Monographs for the Society for Research in Child Development*, **60**(Nos. 2–3).

Waters, E., Wippman, J., & Sroufe, L. A. (1979). Attachment, positive affect, and competence in the peer group: Two studies in construct validation. *Child Development*, **50**, 821–829.

Weinberger, D. R. (1993). A connectionist approach to the prefrontal cortex. *Journal of Neuropsychiatry and Clinical Neuroscience*, **5**, 241–253.

Yoder, P. J., & Feagans, L. (1988). Mothers' attributions of communication to prelinguistic behavior of developmentally delayed and mentally retarded infants. *American Journal on Mental Retardation*, **93**, 36–43.

ACKNOWLEDGMENTS

We would like to express our sincere appreciation for the thoughtful, diligent, and painstaking efforts of the series editor, Rachel Clifton, who encouraged and rewarded our perseverence. We would also like to thank our reviewers, who devoted great time and effort to providing helpful feedback on not one, but two, drafts of this *Monograph*. Finally, we would like to recognize the invaluable contributions of Dante Cicchetti, whose vision, confidence, and mentoring helped provide some of the personal foundations for this collaborative endeavor.

CHAPTER I

Barnett and Vondra

Requests for reprints should be mailed to the first author at Wayne State University, Department of Psychology, 71 West Warren Avenue, Detroit, MI 48202

CHAPTER II

Pipp-Siegel, Siegel, and Dean

The first two authors were partially supported by the Center for Adaptive Pathways while writing this chapter. Warm thanks to Douglas Barnett, Rachel Clifton, Carol George, Sally Rogers, Joan Vondra, and all anonymous reviewers for extremely helpful comments on this manuscript.

CHAPTER III

Atkinson, Chisholm, Scott, Goldberg, Vaughn, Blackwell, Dickens, and Tam

This research was supported by funds from the Ontario Ministry of Community and Social Services Research Programme administered through the Ontario Mental Health Foundation, and by funds from the Laidlaw Foundation and Surrey Place Centre. We are most grateful to participant families for their ongoing involvement in this project. Alison Niccols offered insights in the early stages of this study. Mary Main and Lynn Oldershaw were generous in their comments on an earlier draft of this chapter. Tom Bowman, Ellen Boychyn, Ann Cooper, and Sue Mosten offered administrative assistance, which is greatly appreciated. Thanks are also extended to Lori Poulton and Jackie Bush for technical assistance, and to Murray Hutchins for equipment loan.

CHAPTER IV

Lyons-Ruth, Bronfman, and Parsons

Reprints are available from K. Lyons-Ruth, Department of Psychiatry, Cambridge Hospital, 1493 Cambridge St., Cambridge, MA 02139.

CHAPTER V

Barnett, Ganiban, and Cicchetti

The research reported herein was supported by grants from the National Center on Child Abuse and Neglect, the National Institute of Mental Health, and the Spunk Fund, Inc. to Dante Cicchetti. We gratefully acknowledge Christine Butler, Judy Bigelow, Karen Braunwald, Vicki Carlson, Melissa Clements, Carol Kottmeier, Mary Main, Jill Meade, Cathy Palazzolo, and Karen Schneider-Rosen for their assistance in the collection or coding of the data.

CHAPTER VI

Vondra, Hommerding, and Shaw

Funding for this investigation was provided by the Buhl Foundation and by the Office of Child Development, Department of Psychology in Education, Department of Psychology, and Western Psychiatric Institute and Clinic of the University of Pittsburg. Requests for reprints should be mailed to the first author at University of Pittsburgh, Department of Psychology in Education, 5C01 Forbes Quadrangle, Pittsburgh, PA 15260.

CHAPTER VII

Crittenden

Address for correspondence: 9481 SW 147 St., Miami, FL 33176.

CHAPTER VIII

Barnett, Butler, and Vondra

Authorship of this chapter was supported by grants from the National Institute of Mental Health and the March of Dimes Birth Defects Foundation. Requests for reprints should be mailed to the first author at the Department of Psychology, Wayne State University, 71 W. Warren Avenue, Detroit, MI 48202.

COMMENTARY

ATYPICAL ATTACHMENT IN ATYPICAL CIRCUMSTANCES

Everett Waters and Judith A. Crowell

One of Freud's earliest insights was that a successful theory should comprehend both normal and clinical phenomena within the same framework. This is generally accepted today, even by theorists and researchers with little interest in psychoanalysis. Indeed, it is one of the cornerstones of the emerging field of developmental psychopathology. Studies of children who experienced major separations and losses played a prominent role in the development of attachment theory, and the search for effective clinical applications remains one of its primary goals. Nonetheless, as the study of attachment developed from its clinical origins to an empirical science, it focused increasingly on individual differences within the "normal" range of developmental outcomes and this largely within "normal" rearing environments. This *Monograph* is a timely reminder that there is much to be gained and much important work that can only be done by bringing atypical attachment behavior and attachment in high-risk environments closer to center stage in attachment theory and research.

Unfortunately, new directions always entail risks. Perhaps greatest is the risk of trying to assimilate or explain too much, losing focus, and attachment theory becoming little more than the theory that "all good (and all bad) things go together." Fortunately, these risks are easily avoided by (a) keeping in mind the logic of Bowlby's attachment theory, (b) giving naturalistic observation of secure base behavior across time and contexts a central role in research design and assessment, and (c) submitting key postulates to severe tests that, if not passed, would require real changes in the theory.

The Logic of Attachment Theory

One of Bowlby's primary goals in developing modern attachment theory was to preserve the kernels of truth in Freud's best insights about close relationships. These insights included the notion that infant-mother and adult-adult close relationships are similar in kind and that early relationship experience influences later development. In order to preserve these and related insights, he replaced Freud's image of a needy, dependent infant motivated by drive reduction with one of a sophisticated, competence-motivated infant using its primary caregiver as a secure base from which to explore and, when necessary, as a haven of safety and a source of comfort. In doing so, Bowlby added original insights about the importance of ordinary (as opposed to emergency) experience and real (as opposed to fantasy) experience during development. He also insured attachment theory a place in the mainstream of modern scientific psychology by focusing on information and representation rather than the dynamics of mental energy as the key explanatory constructs for understanding attachment behavior and development (viz. Waters, Kondo-Ikemura, Posada, & Richters, 1995).

The first step in Bowlby's reanalysis was to reconceptualize the child's tie to its mother as a secure base relationship. From this starting point, Bowlby drew on control-systems theory to explain the infant's keen awareness of its environment and the apparently purposeful organization of its exploratory and proximity seeking behavior over time and situations. He realized, however, that replacing Freud's cathectic bonds with neurally based control-systems would amount to little more than replacing one kind of magic with another unless he could explain the origin and nature of behavioral control-systems. For this, he turned to evolutionary theory, arguing from many examples that such control-systems reflect species-specific biases in learning abilities and that these can be shaped by evolution. Thus, the child's tie to its mother reflects the operating characteristics of an underlying control system that collates information about the infant's state, the state of the environment, past and current access to the caregiver in a pattern Bowlby referred to as the secure base phenomenon. The evolution of attachment reflects not the evolution of specific behaviors but of a control system that integrates them into a useful behavioral system.

The attachment control system is constructed during development through interaction between biases in our learning abilities and experience with caregivers and environments. These biases in our learning abilities are part of our primate heritage and are available to every human infant. Because each individual's secure base control system is constructed through experience, not prewired, early relationship experience plays an important role in setting its operating characteristics. Both the caregiver and the child contribute to this experience. The caregiver through sensitivity to signals, cooperation with ongoing behavior, physical and psychological availability, and assigning high priority to the secure base role; the infant through its signaling, the organization it imposes on the interaction, and its responsiveness to the caregiver's efforts. As Barnett, Butler, and Vondra (this volume) point out, children at developmental risk offer a wide range of opportunities for examining child contributions to attachment development.

The Secure Base Phenomenon

Ainsworth undertook her studies of attachment behavior in Uganda and Baltimore in search of descriptive insights into the origins and organization of infant secure base behavior. In the course of these observations, she noticed a wide range of individual differences in infants' ability to use their primary caregiver as a secure base from which to explore and, when needed, as a haven of safety. These patterns of attachment proved to be important tools for research on the role of early experience and the significance of attachment relationships for later development. Of course, naturalistic observation of behavior across time and contexts is difficult, expensive, and difficult to quantify. Fortunately, the ability of healthy, middle-class home-reared infants to use mother as a secure base in naturalistic settings can be economically diagnosed from distinctive signs during reunion episodes in the Strange Situation (Ainsworth, Blehar, Waters, & Wall, 1978; Vaughn & Waters, 1990). This mapping is important because secure and insecure attachment are defined by secure base use in naturalistic settings, not Strange Situation behavior. If behavior in the Strange Situation is not related to secure base behavior at home in some populations, we can always follow Ainsworth's example and directly assess secure base use in the home.

Atypical Attachment Among Children at Developmental Risk

The chapters in this *Monograph* describe and explore atypical attachment behavior in populations of children at some developmental risk due to their psychosocial environment or inherent characteristics. Investigating attachment behavior in special populations can help define the operating characteristics of the attachment control system and the extent to which its organization can adapt to constraints imposed by atypical development and difficult environments. These are important issue for advancing attachment theory and developing options for prevention and intervention.

Patterns and Attachment. As this *Monograph* illustrates (see also Solomon & George, 1999), the discovery of "disorganized" or "atypical" attachment patterns in the Strange Situation (Main & Solomon, 1986) is proving an important stimulus to new research on the nature of attachment patterns seen in the Strange Situation. This can only benefit attachment theory. At the same time, there is a risk of focusing on behavior in the Strange Situation at the expense of secure base behavior in naturalistic settings. The Strange Situation is a test situation. It predicts to important real world criteria. But just as cognitive psychology cannot build a detailed theory of intellectual development on analyses of IQ test items, we cannot build a detailed understanding of secure base relationships from Strange Situation behavior alone. Thus, we view much of the research in this *Monograph* as useful descriptive explorations, opportunities to develop hypotheses, and opportunities to become familiar with new populations. Our hope is that both the theoretical and empirical directions initiated here will soon be carried into naturalistic settings.

For several reasons, this will prove a useful exercise. First, key behaviors such as avoidance, resistance, and many indications of atypical attachment may prove rather specific to the challenges inherent in the Strange Situation. We label infants who turn away when mothers returns in the Strange Situation "avoidant," often forgetting how dependent this response is on the context of reunion. Unlike shyness and sociability, these are not pervasive behavioral styles in nontest situations, and the home behavior they point to can look very different. For example, avoidance in the Strange Situation is associated with low rates of crying and proximity seeking in the laboratory but with increased crying and (by toddlerhood) dependency at home (Sroufe & Pancake, 1983).

Second, as Pipp-Siegel, Siegel, and Dean (this volume) and Barnett, Butler, and Vondra (this volume) point out, behavior in the Strange Situation has many determinants. The discriminant validity of avoidance and resistance during reunion episodes is well established. Less so are the behavioral indicators of disorganized or atypical attachment. Research on infants and children with neurological and developmental problems and recent traumatic experiences can play an important role in distinguishing attachment disorganization from other sources of behavioral and affective disorganization and generalized coping styles. Of course, learning that a specific *atypical* behavior is not due to problems in the secure base control system does not make it unimportant or uninteresting. Problems in affective and behavioral regulation have important implications for child-parent interaction. If they make it difficult for the caregiver to respond sensitively or cooperate with ongoing behavior, they have obvious implications for the child's attachment security. Thus, the direction of effects and the possibility of mediated effects is an important consideration in research on atypical behavior in children at risk and clinical populations. Fortunately, these difficulties can be overcome by careful research design and close attention to relations between behavior in the Strange Situation and at home.

216

Child Contributions and the Attachment Control System. Traditional research on child contributions has focused on the possibility that Strange Situation classifications reflect primarily traitlike differences in behavioral or affective response styles rather than the child's confidence in a particular caregiver's availability and responsiveness. The best empirical evidence supports the secure base interpretation (e.g. Sroufe, 1985; Barnett, Ganiban, & Cicchetti, this volume). Atkinson and colleagues (this volume), focus on how a child's abilities or disabilities influence its secure base interactions and may require adjustments or alterations in the organization of their attachment behavior. This approach is long overdue and promises important new insights into the secure base phenomenon.

Continuity of Care and Attachment Stability. As pointed out by Waters, Kondo-Ikemura, Posada, and Richters (1991), one of the most significant oversights in attachment theory and research is the lack of attention to transformations and coherence in the way caregivers provide secure base support from infancy through adolescence. This is an important issue because stability in the quality of care can contribute to correlations between infant security and later developmental outcomes. That is, caregivers who provides sensitive, cooperative care early also may make important contributions to a wide range of later developmental outcomes. Hopefully, the paper by Vondra, Hommerding, and Shaw (this volume) will serve as a model for research on continuity of care. In addition to emphasizing the importance and influence of caregiver input across time, they illustrate the useful strategy of relating it to change in attachment classifications in longitudinal designs. They also point out the advantages of implementing this strategy in at-risk populations.

The Frightened and Frightening Caregiver Hypothesis. One of the most surprising hypotheses in recent attachment study is that disorganized behavior in the Strange Situation reflects not merely insensitive, intrusive, or inaccessible caregiving but a specific pattern of frightened or frightening behavior (Main & Hesse, 1990). Several papers in this *Monograph* (e.g., Vondra, Hommerding, & Shaw; Barnett, Ganiban, & Cicchetti) provide useful support for this hypothesis. They also make clear that such patterns present in a variety of ways and can be multiply-determined. For example, Lyons-Ruth, Bronfman and Parsons (this volume) suggest that it may prove important to maintain a distinction between children with frightening mothers and those who have experienced fearfulness in their mothers. This is consistent with differences in the developmental consequences of abuse or witnessing violence versus loss. The generality of the link between frightened and frightening care and disorganized attachment behavior is also discussed in the volume edited by Solomon and George (1999). Determining

217

whether this is truly an explanation or merely an association created by other variables will require close theoretical and empirical analysis (Waters & Valenzuela, 1999). Whatever the outcome, this can only benefit attachment theory.

Stability and Change. Stability and change have long been important issues in attachment theory and research. In part this reflects Bowlby's emphasis on the importance of early experience for later development. It also reflects the fact that, throughout the 1970s, conventional wisdom held that individual differences were neither coherent, stable, nor clinically significant. Ultimately, successes in two areas, attachment and temperament, helped sustain the individual differences perspective in developmental psychology until it returned to the mainstream of scientific psychology.

Several of the chapters in this *Monograph* examine the stability of attachment patterns in at-risk populations such as children with Down syndrome (Atkinson, this volume), children who have been maltreated (Barnett, this volume), or children from low-income families (Vondra, this volume). Two of these studies, by Atkinson and colleagues and Vondra, Hommerding, and Shaw, found attachment patterns were somewhat less stable in their at-risk samples, consistent with previous work with such populations (Egeland & Farber, 1984; Schneider-Rosen, 1985; Vaughn, Egeland, Sroufe, & Waters, 1979). The third study, by Barnett, Ganiban, and Cicchetti, compared a maltreating group with a comparison group and found comparable stability in the two. Overall, these studies found that disorganized attachment behavior associated with abuse or maltreatment (a consistently high-risk caregiving environment) is similar in stability to the secure classification in low-risk samples. The extent to which patterns of stability reflect the development of enduring strategies or response styles versus consistent (high or low) levels of stress in the environment deserves close attention in future research.

Is Disorganized Attachment Really Disorganized? Both support for exploration in ordinary circumstances and serving as a haven of safety in emergencies are essential to the logic of Bowlby's attachment theory and the definition of the secure base phenomenon. Protection from danger is only part of the picture and perhaps not the greater part (Waters, Kondo-Ikemura, Posada, & Richter, 1991). The supportive function of attachment in ordinary circumstances is central to its role in the development of competence. It also is important to understanding the functions of attachment in adult-adult close relationships and parenting. In our view, Crittenden's (this volume) emphasis on attachment in emergency situations unnecessarily restricts her analysis of attachment behavior in the face of insensitive and coercive care. Nonetheless, she raises several interesting points about the interpretation of "disorganized" behavior, particularly about using this label for behavior that is closely attuned to the context and may at times serve a useful function. The term "atypical" somewhat avoids this problem but it has little descriptive value. Hopefully, close observation of such behavior in laboratory and naturalistic settings will soon provide descriptive insights that will help us better understand the organization of disorganized attachment behavior.

Atypical Attachment and Psychopathology. Attachment theory always has had theoretical links to the development of psychopathology (Bowlby, 1973, 1980). Insecure attachment is associated with decreased social competence and seems to be a risk factor for the development of some types of psychopathology. In the study of atypical, at-risk children, there is a greater blurring of the distinction between attachment and psychopathology, and the attachment relationship can be seen an etiological agent as opposed to a risk factor. Children at risk are most likely to need intervention, and investigation of the issues outlined above can provide support for the development of attachment-based therapies and interventions.

Conclusion

The studies reported in this *Monograph* address issues regarding the functioning of the child as a factor in the expression of secure base behavior, the role of the caregiving environment and specific maternal behaviors, and the issue of stability. Along with the chapters in the volume edited by Solomon and George (1999), they are a useful starting point for new directions in attachment theory and research. Our hope is that those who follow their lead also will follow their example, resisting the temptation to apply attachment measures in every at-risk population and instead focusing on opportunities to formulate testable empirical hypotheses. This is the best way to advance attachment theory and research and provide real service to children and families at risk.

References

Ainsworth, M., Blehar, M., Waters, E., & Wall, S. (1978). *Patterns of attachment.* Hillsdale, NJ: Erlbaum.

Bowlby, J. (1973). *Attachment and loss (Vol. 2): Separation: Anxiety and anger.* London: Hogarth Press.

Bowlby, J. (1980). *Attachment and loss (Vol. 3): Loss, sadness and depression.* London: Hogarth Press.

Egeland, B., & Farber, A. (1984). Infant-mother attachment: Factors related to its development and changes over time. *Child Development,* **55,** 753–771.

Main, M., & Hesse, E. (1990). Parents' unresolved traumatic experiences are related to infant disorganized attachment status: Is frightened/frightening parental behavior the linking mechanism? In M. Greenberg, D. Cicchetti, & M. Cummings (Eds.), *Attachment in the preschool years*. Chicago: University of Chicago Press.

Main, M., & Solomon, J. (1986). Discovery of a new, insecure-disorganized/disoriented attachment pattern. In T. B. Brazelton & M. Yogman (Eds.), *Affective development in infancy*. Norwood, NJ: Ablex.

Schneider-Rosen, K., Braunwald, K., Carlson, V., & Cicchetti, D. (1985). Current perspectives in attachment theory: Illustrations from the study of maltreated infants. In I. Bretherton & E. Waters (Eds.), *Growing points in attachment theory and research. Monographs of the Society for Research in Child Development*, **50** (1–2, Serial No. 209), 194–210.

Solomon, J., & George, C. (Eds.). (1999). *Attachment disorganization*. New York: Guilford Press.

Sroufe, L. A. (1985). Attachment classification from the perspective of infant-caregiver relationships and infant temperament. *Child Development*, **56,** 1–14.

Sroufe, L. A., Fox, N., & Pancake, V. (1983). Attachment and dependency in developmental perspective. *Child Development*, **54,** 1615–1627.

Vaughn, B. E., Egeland, B., Sroufe, L.A., & Waters, E. (1979). Individual differences in infant-mother attachment at twelve and eighteen months: Stability and change in families under stress. *Child Development*, **50,** 971–975.

Vaughn, B. E., & Waters, E. (1990). Attachment behavior at home and in the laboratory: Q-sort observations and strange situation classifications of one-year-olds. *Child Development*, **61,** 1965–1973.

Waters, E., Kondo-Ikemura, K., Posada, G., & Richters, J. (1991). Learning to love: Mechanisms and milestones. In M. Gunner and Alan Sroufe (Eds.), *Minnesota Symposia on Child Psychology (Vol. 23): Self Processes and Development*. Hillsdale, NJ: Erlbaum.

Waters, E., & Valenzuela, M. (1999). Explaining disorganized attachment: Clues from research on mild-to-moderately undernourished children in Chile. In J. Solomon & C. George (Eds.), *Attachment disorganization*. New York: Guilford Press.

Author Notes

This paper was supported in part by grant no. MH44935 from the National Institute of Mental Health to the authors. Address correspondence regarding this commentary to the authors at the Department of Psychology, State University of New York, Stony Brook, NY 11794-2500.

Leslie Atkinson (Ph.D., 1986, York University) is Deputy Head of the Centre for Addiction and Mental Health clinical programs in Child and Adolescent Psychiatry in Toronto, Ontario. He is also an associate professor of psychiatry, psychology, and education at the University of Toronto. His research interests have been in the area of psychometrics, with a particular focus on "cleaning" estimated scores. More recently, he has conducted research on attachment.

Douglas Barnett (Ph.D., 1993, University of Rochester) is Associate Professor of Psychology at Wayne State University in Detroit. His research interests include parenting and interventions that promote the development of healthy attachments and sense of self among children at high risk for socioemotional and scholastic problems.

Janis Blackwell (B.A., 1988, University of Toronto) is currently a teacher with the North York School Board, Ontario, Canada.

Elisa T. Bronfman (Ph.D., 1993, Boston College) is an Instructor in Psychology at Harvard Medical School and a Staff Psychologist in the Department of Psychiatry at Children's Hospital, Boston. Her research interests include the effects of medical illnesses on children, parent-child interaction patterns associated with disorganized attachments, and the effects of trauma on children and adults.

Christine M. Butler (M.A., 1996, Wayne State University) is a doctoral student in the Department of Psychology at Wayne State University in Detroit. Her research interests include the role of attachment in the primary prevention of socioemotional disorders in high-risk children.

Vivienne Chisholm (Ph.D., 1985, University of Edinburgh) is a Lecturer in Psychology at Queen Margaret College in Edinburgh, Scotland. Her research activities have concerned the adjustment of children with biological disorders and peer relations in early childhood.

Dante Cicchetti (Ph.D., 1977, University of Minnesota) is a Professor of Psychology, Psychiatry, and Pediatrics at the University of Rochester, where he also is Director of the Mt. Hope Family Center. He is the founding editor of *Development and Psychopathology* and the *Rochester Symposium on Developmental Psychopathology*. Cicchetti's major interests lie in the formulation and testing of an integrative theoretical perspective that examines the interplay between normal and atypical development. His research foci include: the biological and psychological developmental sequelae of childhood and adult trauma; the effects of parental psychopathology on psychological and biological development; the implementation of preventive interventions as tests of developmental theory; the impact of social experiences on brain development and plasticity; and the identification of pathways to resilient outcomes.

Patricia M. Crittenden (Ph.D., 1983, University of Virginia) has been a faculty member at the University of Miami and a visiting faculty member at the University of Virginia, San Diego State University, New South Wales Institute of Psychiatry, and the University of Helsinki. Her interests include child maltreatment and attachment and cross-cultural aspects of parent-child adaptation. Her most recent work focuses on a dynamic-maturational approach to the development of psychopathology across the lifespan.

Judith A. Crowell (M.D., 1978, University of Vermont) is Associate Professor of Child Psychiatry and Director of Clinical Training in Child Psychiatry at the State University of New York at Stony Brook Health Sciences Center. Her primary research interests are in stability and change in attachment across the lifespan, working models, and secure base behavior in current adult-adult close relationships. She is co-investigator with Everett Waters on a 10-year longitudinal study of the development of attachment working models in marriage.

Janet Dean (M.S.W., 1980, University of Denver) is Clinical Director of the Community Infant Program, Mental Health Center of Boulder County, Colorado. Her clinical and research interests are in infant/parent psychotherapy.

Susan Dickens (M.A., 1992, York University) is currently a Research Scientist with the Centre for Addiction and Mental Health, Toronto, Canada.

Jody Ganiban (Ph.D.,1993, University of Rochester) is Assistant Professor of Psychology at the George Washington University, Washington, DC. Her research interests include emotion regulation processes and developmental psychopathology.

Susan Goldberg (Ph.D., 1975, University of Massachusetts–Amherst) is a Research Scientist at the Hospital for Sick Children in Toronto and Professor of Psychiatry and Psychology at the University of Toronto. She has conducted numerous studies of attachment in atypical populations including infants born prematurely, those with developmental delays, congenital heart disease, and CF as well as children adopted after prolonged institutional care.

Katherine Dowdell Hommerding (M.S., 1994, University of Pittsburgh) is interested in stability and change in infant attachment and their ecological and experiential correlates.

Karlen Lyons-Ruth (Ph.D., 1974, Harvard University) is an Associate Professor of Psychology in the Department of Psychiatry at Harvard Medical School. Her research interests center on identifying developmental pathways from infancy to adolescence among socially at-risk children, as well as developing preventive intervention strategies to alter those early trajectories.

Elizabeth Parsons (Psy.D., 1991, Massachusetts School of Professional Psychology) is an Instructor in Psychology at Harvard Medical School and Associate Director of Training at the Victims of Violence Program, Cambridge Hospital. Her research interests focus on identifying parenting contributions to the intergenerational transmission of trauma and developing therapeutic group treatment services capable of altering the process of intergenerational transmission.

Sandra Pipp-Siegel (Ph.D., 1978, University of Denver) is an Assistant Research Professor of Speech, Language and Hearing Sciences at the University of Colorado, Boulder and Assistant Clinical Professor at the University of Colorado Health Sciences Center. Her research examines the relation between attachment and self-development in clinical and nonclinical populations and the social-emotional development in deaf/hard-of-hearing infants.

Brian S. Scott (Ph.D. [Zoology] 1967, University of Toronto; Ph.D. [Psychology] 1988, University of Windsor) is currently in private practice in Malaysia. His research interests include neurological and psychosocial aspects of developmental disability.

Daniel S. Shaw (Ph.D., 1988, University of Virginia) is an Associate Professor of Psychology and Psychiatry at the University of Pittsburgh. His research interests focus on the developmental antecedents of externalizing and internalizing behavior problems in children.

Clifford H. Siegel (M.D., 1976, Baylor College of Medicine) is an Assistant Clinical Professor and Co-Director of the Infant Psychiatry Clinic at the University of Colorado Heath Sciences Center as well as in private practice. His research focuses on mood disorders in children.

Frances Tam (M.Sc., University of Toronto, 1995) is a biostatistician at Pharmacia and Upjohn, Toronto, Canada.

Brian E. Vaughn (Ph.D., 1979, University of Minnesota) is Human Sciences Professor of Human Development and Family Studies at Auburn University. His research interests include the antecedents and consequences of early child-parent attachments and relations between attachment, social support networks of children, and peer social competence. He is co-author (with Kelly K. Bost) of *Social Competence and Social Support Networks of Preschool Children Attending Head Start*.

Joan I. Vondra (Ph.D., 1986, Pennsylvania State University) is an Associate Professor of Psychology in Education at the University of Pittsburgh. Her research interests are in the development of competence among children at social and demographic risk for later school problems and failure.

Everett Waters (Ph.D., 1977, Institute of Child Development, University of Minnesota) is Professor of Psychology and Head of the Program in Social and Health Psychology at the State University of New York. He is the co-author with Mary Ainsworth and colleagues of *Patterns of Attachment* (1978), and co-editor of two previous SRCD Monographs, *Growing Points of Attachment Theory and Research* (1985), and *Caregiving, Cultural, and Cognitive Perspectives on Secure Base Behavior and Working Models* (1995). His interests include observational methods for assessing attachment behavior beyond infancy and the impact of early experience on secure base behavior in close adult-adult relationships and parenting.

STATEMENT OF EDITORIAL POLICY

The *Monographs* series is intended as an outlet for major reports of developmental research that generate authoritative new findings and use these to foster a fresh and/or better-integrated perspective on some conceptually significant issue or controversy. Submissions from programmatic research projects are particularly welcome; these may consist of individually or group-authored reports of findings from some single large-scale investigation or of a sequence of experiments centering on some particular question. Multiauthored sets of independent studies that center on the same underlying question can also be appropriate; a critical requirement in such instances is that the various authors address common issues and that the contribution arising from the set as a whole be both unique and substantial. In essence, irrespective of how it may be framed, any work that contributes significant data and/or extends developmental thinking will be taken under editorial consideration.

Submissions should contain a minimum of 80 manuscript pages (including tables and references); the upper limit of 150–175 pages is much more flexible (please submit four copies; a copy of every submission and associated correspondence is deposited eventually in the archives of the SRCD). Neither membership in the Society for Research in Child Development nor affiliation with the academic discipline of psychology is relevant; the significance of the work in extending developmental theory and in contributing new empirical information is by far the most crucial consideration. Because the aim of the series is not only to advance knowledge on specialized topics but also to enhance cross-fertilization among disciplines or subfields, it is important that the links between the specific issues under study and larger questions relating to developmental processes emerge as clearly to the general reader as to specialists on the given topic.

The corresponding author for any manuscript must, in the submission letter, warrant that all coauthors are in agreement with the content of the manuscript. The corresponding author also is responsible for informing all coauthors, in a timely manner, of manuscript submission, editorial decisions, reviews received, and any revisions recommended. Before publication, the corresponding author also must warrant in the submission letter that the study has been conducted according to the ethical guidelines of the Society for Research in Child Development.

Potential authors who may be unsure whether the manuscript they are planning would make an appropriate submission are invited to draft an outline of what they propose and send it to the Editor for assessment. This mechanism, as well as a more detailed desctiption of all editorial policies, evaluation processes, and format requirements, is given in the "Guidelines for the Preparation of *Monographs* Submissions," which can be obtained by contacting the Editor-Elect, Willis Overton, Department of Psychology, 567 Weiss Hall, Temple University, Philadelphia, PA 19122 [e-mail: overton@vm.temple.edu].